D1578885

ANCIENT TRACKS

WALKING THROUGH HISTORIC BRITAIN

Des Hannigan

PHOTOGRAPHS BY
Simon McBride

PAVILION

First published in Great Britain in 1994 by
PAVILION BOOKS LIMITED
26 Upper Ground, London SE1 9PD

Text copyright © Des Hannigan 1994
Photographs copyright © Simon McBride 1994

Designed by Andrew Barron & Collis Clements Associates
Maps drawn by Don Sargeant

The moral right of the author has been asserted

A CIP catalogue record for this book is available from
the British Library

ISBN 1 85793 095 9

Typeset by Litho Link Ltd, Welshpool, Powys, Wales
Printed and bound in Spain by Cayfosa, Barcelona

10 9 8 7 6 5 4 3 2 1

This book may be ordered by post direct from the publisher.
Please contact the Marketing Department.
But try your bookshop first.

The routes of the walks described in this book are believed to follow public
footpaths, rights of way or permitted paths that existed at the time of the book
going to press. No responsibility can be taken by the author or publisher for any
accidents that may befall walkers, or for any action that may be taken against
users of the book.

*Frontispiece: The sweeping
lines of the Lakeland Fells.*

Contents

ACKNOWLEDGEMENTS

Des Hannigan wishes to acknowledge the kindness of numerous people who inspired him with their intimate knowledge of local places, and helped him to see more than just the track ahead. Special thanks for help and hospitality to David, Sally, Jenny and Tom Hillebrandt; Nick and Sandra Crowhurst; Barry Hitchcox and Gail Cheeseman; Sam, Sian and Gwenver Salmon; Sheila Tyler and Adrian Childs; Molly and Merrhis Tyler-Childs; Len and Stella Wilson; and Ian and Jackie Brien.

Public and private libraries throughout the country were always helpful in dealing with queries and in supplying books and documents. The staff at Penzance Public Library were especially helpful and efficient.

The highest praise is due for the relevant work done by many private landowners, local authorities, English Heritage, the National Park Authorities, the National Trust, the National Trust for Scotland, the Scottish Rights of Way Society, the Ramblers' Association, the National Open Spaces Society, and other conservation organizations, in maintaining and conserving public paths, rights of way, permitted paths, and the general fabric of the countryside.

Finally, a very special thank you to Anita Ronke and Alex Pitt for supplying peace and quiet in Cornwall. And gratitude above all to my family for patience, encouragement and loving support.

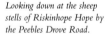

Looking down at the sheep stells of Riskinhope Hope by the Peebles Drove Road.

INTRODUCTION

The author setting out on the Glen Callater section of Jock's Road, Grampian.

This is a book about history underfoot. The seventeen walks described follow tracks and paths that are crowded with the ghosts of prehistoric hunters and early colonists, Roman soldiers, cattle drovers, saints, pilgrims, merchants, packmen, thieves, rebels and refugees – a bustling procession of colourful men and women who made their way determinedly through often savage country, for business rather than pleasure. Behind them, like a snail's trace, they left their mark on the landscape.

Today, we do most of our travelling along ribboned tarmac, oblivious of the countryside to either side. Even when we choose the 'scenic' route, we pass by at speeds that blur the landscape into a two-dimensional view. A map of modern Britain shows a complex network of surfaced roads. It is like a grid clamped down on the countryside, emphasizing the shrinking patches of farmland and wilderness; a painting done by numbers, of a map that grows denser each year round the urban sprawls.

The process has been inevitable. Technology has subdued the landscape, and today we move sizeable hills, if not yet mountains, to accommodate our roads. Yet the lines of ancient tracks and paths survive, and though they are often fragmented, or are overlaid in places by modern roads, many can still be followed on foot for great distances through landscapes that have resisted our worst efforts at exploitation. These ancient ways were flexible, and had a naturalness in the manner in which they followed the lie of the land. They were sunk into the landscape rather than imposed upon it, and today their character is often little different from what it was during their use as working routes.

I have tried to make this more than a step-by-step walking guide because I believe that some knowledge of the history of old tracks and paths enhances the pleasure of walking along them. Ancient ways were functional. We are fortunate that we can continue to use them for recreation, especially when they pass through beautiful countryside.

The historical background to each route is given in the main text, and this is followed by a general impression of what it is like to travel the route today, and what it may have been like in the past. These descriptions are followed by a section that gives practical information and detailed route directions, first for a main walk and then for a shorter circular walk.

All the routes described in the book follow rights of way, sections of official long-distance routes, or permitted routes within National Parks or within National Trust property.

THE LOCH MAREE POST ROAD
Poolewe
Gairloch
Kinlochewe
Inverness

THE THIEVES' ROAD
Aberdeen
Braemar
JOCK'S ROAD
Dalwhinnie
Fort William
Kirriemuir
THE BALQUHIDDER ROAD
Perth
Dundee
Callander

Glasgow
Edinburgh

Peebles
THE PEEBLES DROVE ROAD
Selkirk

Penrith
HIGH STREET
Ambleside
Guisborough
Whitby
THE MONKS' TROD

Hull

Manchester
Penistone
JAGGERS' GATE
Hayfield

Bangor
Bethesda
Blaenau Ffestiniog
THE SLATE ROAD

Holm next the Sea
THE PEDDARS WAY
King's Lynn
Norwich
Birmingham
Thetford

OFFA'S DYKE
Monmouth
Chepstow
THE RIDGEWAY
Oxford
Cardiff
London
Bristol
Swindon
Goring

Parracombe
Maidstone
Canterbury
Wheddon Cross
Salisbury
Charing
THE EXMOOR RIDGEWAY
ACKLING DYKE
Dover
THE PILGRIMS' WAY

Padstow
Exeter
Blandford Forum
Tavistock
THE SAINTS' WAY
Buckfastleigh
Fowey
THE CROSS ROAD

INFORMATION AND ADVICE

Many of the lowland walks and most of the circular walks described can be undertaken by averagely fit walkers. Most lowland long-distance walks have convenient escape routes. Clothing and equipment should be for country walking relative to the time of year.

The long-distance walks through hill and mountain country are best undertaken by very fit parties of at least two people. Inexperienced mountain walkers should be accompanied on such walks by experienced companions. Long-distance walks in hill and mountain country under winter conditions should only be undertaken by very experienced and well-equipped parties.

Preparations

Precise details of the planned route, with date and estimated time of return, allowing for reasonable delays, should be left with a responsible person. Walking speed in mountain areas is approximately two miles/just over three kilometres per hour. This is steady progress. A lower estimate should be made in bad weather and for very steep terrain. Confirmation of safe return must be made *as soon as possible* to avoid a potentially wasteful call-out of emergency services. Abandonment of the walk should also be confirmed.

Always carry an Ordnance Survey map, a compass, a whistle and head torches. Skilled use of map and compass is essential for walking in hills and mountains, where poor visibility is common.

Weather conditions, especially in hill and mountain areas, can change quickly, and often for the worse, at any time of year. Local weather forecasts should be obtained before setting out. Such forecasts are available at Tourist Information Centres (TICs) and National Park Centres. Weather reports for most mountain areas can be obtained on special call lines.

Carry a first aid kit. At least one member of the party should have first aid experience.

Equipment

The most damaging effect of bad weather, especially in hill and mountain areas, is from wind-chill; more so, if a person is wet through. Warm, waterproof and windproof clothing, including overtrousers, should be worn, or carried, even in fine weather, as well as spare clothing. Use only the most reliable weatherproof garments. Specialist winter clothing and equipment is essential for winter walking in hill and mountain country. Warm and weatherproof headgear protects against heat loss.

Proper footwear is essential, especially in wild country. Boots with good ankle support and cleated soles are advised, and they should be waterproof. New boots should be well broken in before attempting the long-distance walks described in this book. Full-length gaiters are an advantage in wet and muddy areas.

Emergency bivouac equipment should be carried in hill and mountain areas. Large ventilated polythene 'bivvy-bags' are excellent for reducing wind-chill in an emergency. More substantial equipment is required for overnight bivouacking.

Maps

Sketch maps accompany the route descriptions in the book. They are intended as a quick and useful reference to the line of a route (shown by a broken line and numbered points within squares) and its main features, as well as to the circular walks (shown by a dotted line and numbered points within circles). For precise route-finding, walkers are advised to use the Ordnance Survey Landranger series (1:50 000) for the relevant area. For many mountain areas, the Ordnance Survey Outdoor Leisure series (1:25 000) gives greater detail. Distances are given in miles and kilometres.

Travel

Many walkers may wish to organize their own car transport from the end of long-distance walks. Public transport is often available, but walkers need to get their timing right. Keeping a rendezvous with the last bus out of a remote area can be nightmarish, and may turn the last bit of a walk into an exhausting gallop. Local bus services are reliable in general, but it is wise to check timetables and venues when planning a walk, and remember that timetables change from summer to winter services. Advice can be had from local Tourist Information Centres. In some places, local rail connections can be used.

Accommodation

On lowland routes, there is usually a good choice of accommodation along the way. This ranges from hotels, guest houses and bed and breakfast establishments, to youth hostels and camp sites. In mountain areas, similar, though sometimes limited, accommodation is usually available at towns and villages at either end of the route.

Conservation

Erosion is as relevant to our recreational use of ancient tracks and paths as it was when such routes were used for a purpose. Numerous reports from the sixteenth century onwards lament the 'stranding' of cartways and packhorse routes, and the chaos of broken and eroded ground caused by neglect and poor maintenance. But in one way this reflected the landscape's dominance. People had to struggle to pass through it, even with wagons and packhorse trains.

Nowadays, the pressure of walkers' feet, of horses' hooves, and of the wheels of mountain bikes and off-road vehicles is becoming critical in many overly popular areas. The dilemma is obvious, especially for the writer of a book like this one. Yet to travel on

Previous pages:
Looking north from
High Street to Hayeswater.

foot through beautiful landscapes along established ways is a positive and enriching experience that should not be curtailed. To follow such routes with the minimum of physical intrusion and with perhaps an active and vigilant concern for conservation and protection is the best way forward.

General Advice

Always exercise care and concentration when crossing bare rock, grass or mud, during wet conditions. Stream and river crossings must be made with good judgement especially after heavy rain.

Hot dry weather may cause dehydration during long-distance walks. Sufficient liquid for drinking should be carried as well as food, and emergency rations. Guard against potential sunburn or sunstroke.

Culicoides impunctatus, the 'biting midge', is a major pest in the Scottish Highlands, especially during the period from June to October, and particularly during late afternoon and evening. There are numerous 'anti-midge' products on the market. The basic antidote is thick skin and gritted teeth. Don't swim at dusk.

In areas where shooting may be in progress, it is wise to check details beforehand. Tourist Information Centres in such areas usually have current details of shooting schedules. Rights of way remain open to walkers during shooting seasons.

The Country Code

FOLLOW THE COUNTRY CODE
Enjoy the countryside and respect its life and work
Guard against all risk of fire
Fasten all gates
Keep your dogs under close control
Keep to public paths across farmland
Use gates and stiles to cross fences, hedges and walls
Leave livestock, crops and machinery alone
Take your litter home
Help to keep all water clean
Protect wildlife, plants and trees
Take special care on country roads
Make no unnecessary noise.

THE LOCH MAREE POST ROAD
North-West Highlands

Poolewe to Kinlochewe 20 miles/32 kms

'Our only letter carrier was . . . little Duncan, a bit of kilted india-rubber, who, with a sheepskin knapsack on his back to keep his despatches dry, left the west on Monday, got the sixty miles done on Wednesday, and returning on Thursday, delivered up his mail to my father on the Saturday.'

Dr John Mackenzie, *Odd and End Stories*, 1803–1860

This challenging walk follows part of a route taken by nineteenth-century post runners through one of Britain's finest mountain areas. The route has been used for hundreds of years by all types of travellers. It is a true wilderness way that invites respect.

In the North-West Highlands today, smart-looking post buses carry the mail along well-maintained roads. They cover the twenty miles/thirty-two kilometres along the west shore of Loch Maree between Poolewe and Kinlochewe in less than half an hour. Yet two hundred years ago remarkable men supplied a mail-carrying service, on foot, between Poolewe and Dingwall, sixty miles/ eighty-two kilometres, to the east. Their route led along the east side of Loch Maree, on a track that had been long established as the main line of communication between Inverness, Poolewe and the Isle of Lewis.

There was also a road of sorts on the west side of Loch Maree where the modern road now runs. But it was little used and was generally impassable until the improvements of the mid eighteenth century made it the main route to the west. The geography of these routes was significant. Loch Maree, inland from the coast, extends for twelve miles/twenty kilometres along a north-west to south-east line. It has always acted as a natural barrier to penetration from the uncertain south into the northern mountains and into the coastal settlements around Poolewe. For the people of the Western Isles and the north-west Highlands, Inverness was the centre of the world, and a main route to Inverness, along the east shore of Loch Maree, was the natural line to follow.

For many years before the time of the post runners the route served busy communities along the lochside. From the beginning of the seventeenth cenury there were iron-smelting works sited at intervals along Loch Maree's eastern shore. They were known as 'bloomeries' and they were the leading centres of iron production in Scotland at the time. Place names like Furnace and A Cheardach Ruadh, the 'Red Smiddy', bear witness to an industry that drew on local bog iron as well as imported ore. Today, the treeless upper slopes of the great mountains are the result of a ruthless harvesting of ancient woodland to fuel the smelting works. So all-consuming was the work, that the Red Smiddy furnace alone used 300 acres/120 hectares of trees each year; and Red Smiddy operated for sixty years.

Ironworks became established in such a remote area because the Elizabethan Parliament had restricted the cutting of timber in English iron-smelting areas such as Cumbria. There were no such restrictions in Scotland, and entrepreneurs quickly moved in, bringing Cumbrian ironworkers with them. But the initial plunder of Loch Maree's woodland soon led to an Act of the Scottish Parliament, prohibiting the making of iron, 'with wood or timber under pain of confiscation of the whole iron'. Even James VI was shocked by the extent of timber cutting and by the 'utter waisting and consumeing of the sadis woodis . . .'

But James sought to bridle a powerful vassal in the person of the Loch Maree ironmaster Sir George Hay, Earl of Drummond. Hay had 'acquired' the forest of Letterewe by exchanging his stewardship of the Isle of Lewis with Mackenzie of Kintail for part of the Letterewe forest. This was a time of domestic imperialism when great swathes of land were dealt out like playing cards amongst a select hierarchy. It was also a time of ruthless political and economic influence. Within months of Parliament's bid to save the forests of Letterewe, Sir George Hay succeeded in rescinding the edict, and by 1612 James had given Hay a monopoly of glass and iron manufacture in Scotland for a thirty-one year period. There was no sparing of the tree when commerce ruled.

Today, relics of the iron industry survive on Loch Mareeside, at the Red Smiddy and Letterewe, and at Fasagh near Kinlochewe. In the surviving woodland, east of Letterewe, the bones of old settlements nestle amidst the undergrowth at Innis Ghlas, Coppachy and Regoilachy where several families once lived. The people moved out at the end of the seventeenth century when the mountain iron industry declined. There seems little doubt that the route along the eastern shore was used regularly during the iron-working period, although waterborne transport was also available.

On the Post Road along the shores of Loch Kernsary, with Beinn Airigh Charr in the distance.

Throughout the eighteenth century, routes on the east side of Loch Maree remained the main links between Poolewe and the east coast of the country. There was an initial choice of routes between Kernsary and Letterewe. One way led inland from Kernsary up the valley of the Fionn Loch and then through the Strathan Buidhe to Letterewe. This route was used by cattle drovers making for the October market at Muir of Ord near Inverness. The older route from Kernsary ran along the lochside through Ardlair to Letterewe, but it was unsuited to heavy traffic. Midway, the line was blocked for three miles by the wooded cliffs of Creag Tharbh, the Bull Rock, where travellers probably detoured inland.

Yet, by 1837, this lochside route was being surveyed with a view to laying a surfaced road along its course. On paper, the cliffs of Creag Tharbh posed no problem to the surveyor, who planned a steep detour inland. There was nothing new about such enterprise. An earlier survey in 1793 had proposed laying a surfaced road, sixteen feet/five metres wide, along the inland route through the Fionn Loch valley. It is hard to appreciate how much of the wild country that we cherish today was once targeted for road-building. The Victorian ambition of subduing the wilderness was especially righteous.

The great lands of Loch Maree were owned by the Mackenzie family throughout the nineteenth century, and it is to the formidable Sir Osgood Hanbury Mackenzie of Inverewe that we owe much of the detail of the area's history. Sir Osgood created the famous Inverewe Gardens, where the sheltered north shore of Poolewe Bay supports splendid ornamental shrubberies nurtured by the moist warmth of the Gulf Stream Drift. The gardens are now in the care of the National Trust for Scotland.

Osgood Mackenzie was a man of great intelligence and humanity. But he had the Victorian confidence that blunted other sensibilities. His era was that of the Highland estate as shooting gallery. His stewardship of his land was admirable, as was his treatment of local people. Yet in his book, *One Hundred Years in the Highlands*, Sir Osgood reflects graphically the unquestioning and ruthless attitude of Victorian 'sportsmen', which helped to reduce the teeming fauna of the Scottish Highlands in the name of game preservation. During the nineteenth century especially, any wild creature that was assumed to be a threat to game birds and to deer, salmon and trout, was ruthlessly destroyed as 'vermin'. White-tailed and golden eagles, osprey, pine marten, wildcat, badger and otter, as much as hoodie crows, were all slaughtered with bullet, or trap, or poison. 'Strychnine is a wonderfully handy drug,' comments Sir Osgood briskly when recording the poisoning of two white ermines.

The huge tally of shot game birds was every bit as murderous as the toll of destroyed 'vermin'. And while grouse, ptarmigan and blackcock account for most of the bags, anything on the wing was considered fair game, including swans, mergansers, black-throated divers, rock doves and all seabirds. In one chilling aside that reflects the attitude of the time, Sir Osgood condemns early attempts at protecting eagles, and states, 'We have had far too many eagles in our country of late, and when one can see seven in the air at once it is about time to thin them out.'

It is Osgood Mackenzie and his uncle, Dr John Mackenzie, who have left us a record of the Loch Maree post runners. Letters may have been carried to and from the west during the late eighteenth century, but the first mention of a foot post comes in Dr Mackenzie's writings of the early years of the nineteenth century. For many years the Mackenzie family moved each spring from their winter quarters at Contin, near Dingwall, to the family home of Flowerdale at Gairloch. At some time during this period a weekly postal service, which also served the mail to and from the Isle of Lewis, seems to have been established.

One runner was employed at first. This was 'Little Duncan' of india-rubber fame. The runner left Poolewe on a Monday morning, soon after the Lewis boat arrived. There were sixty hard mountain miles/eighty-two kilometres ahead, and he would cover them in three days, to reach Dingwall on the Wednesday. There he collected the mail from Inverness and headed back west, to arrive at Poolewe by Saturday. The service operated during the summer months only, and eventually two runners delivered the post twice a week.

The route of the post runners led from Kernsary, through Ardlair to Letterewe, and thence to Kinlochewe and on through Glen Docherty. Where the Bull Rock of Creag Tharbh projects into the loch, like the hoary neck of a Highland bull, the runners would have carved out the easiest way round the three miles/five kilometres of cliff. It was still a tough route. The last of the post runners was John Mackenzie, known as *Iain Mor am Posda*, Big John the Post. He was a powerful giant of a man, who once had to carry on his back, 'through the rock', a London postal overseer who had fainted at the prospect of the Creag Tharbh cliffs.

Others had similar tales. The Ettrick Poet, James Hogg, made his own tour of the Highlands in 1803. Hogg travelled irascibly at times, but always with fervour. He has left a vivid record of being forced to cross Bull Rock when a storm-lashed attempt at reaching Poolewe by boat left him and his companions stranded on the loch-side. Hogg was accompanied by two Highlanders and a Miss Jane Downie, the daughter of a minister. Miss Downie seems to have

The Bull Rock (Creag Tharbh). The nineteenth-century post runners traversed these cliffs. The route is now impassable.

made the crossing of the cliffs with some style. But this was 1802 and gentlemen poets were not to be outdone. As they clawed their way along narrow ledges above sheer drops, and against a tearing wind, Hogg records that he was 'in the greatest distress on account of the lady'. But the aptly named Miss Jane seemed in complete control amidst such Tarzan territory. 'It was . . . a scene worthy of these regions, to see a lady of most delicate form and elegantly dressed in such a situation,' breathed the poet. Hogg was very concerned about Miss Downie's clothing which was being 'partly torn and otherwise abused' by the wind. His own clung to him in a fine old lather. What more could a poet ask for? Yet no verse emerged from this lively experience. Robert Burns would have capitalized on such events with relish.

Today there is no path across Creag Tharbh and the way can only be followed with great difficulty. Some rock-climbing ability is needed on quite dangerous ground, and route-finding can be a nightmare of wrong turnings. The better option is to forget poets and post runners for a while, and instead, follow the inland track from Kernsary through the heart-stopping splendour of the Fionn Loch valley. The Ettrick Poet later enjoyed a less stressful visit to the Fionn Loch, but without Miss Downie, who was probably sailing single-handed to the Hebrides.

The first section of our walk follows the line of the post road from Poolewe through a jungle of scrubby gorse and then more pleasantly along the shores of Loch Kernsary. There is a point reached some distance before the loch when the great mountains come dramatically into view. To the south lie the sculpted peaks of Torridon; Beinn Eighe, the mighty Liathach, and Beinn Alligin. Ice has scooped and trimmed the layered sandstone of these mountains into sphinx-like shapes and has dressed the ridges of Beinn Eighe with white quartz like drifted snow. In the near distance the wooded face of Craig Tollie looms above Loch Maree's western shore. Ahead, the mountains above Ardlair lead the eye towards the great cirque of lonely peaks at the head of the Fionn Loch.

The view is lost for a time at the loch's end where the path leads under shady oak trees and birches to Kernsary. Here the post runners headed south towards Ardlair and the Bull Rock. But our route leads east through sweetly smelling pinewoods and out across the peaty ground below the buttresses of Spidean Moirich, Martha's Peak. Ahead, the valley of the Fionn Loch is ringed by a fretted wall of mountains. The northern side of the valley is dominated by Beinn a' Chaisgein Mor and its outliers. To the north of here a magnificent wilderness runs for ten miles/sixteen kilometres across the lonely valley of Shenavall and the mighty ridge of An Teallach.

At the head of the valley the Fionn Loch narrows to a channel bridged by a causeway, then opens into the smaller Dubh Loch. The two names are prosaic enough: *Fionn* for white or fair, *Dubh* for black. They are well suited. The Fionn Loch valley spreads wide-mouthed towards the sea. The Dubh Loch lies under beetling cliffs that are shot through with bands of pale pegmatite. To the left of these cliffs is the bulking shoulder of A' Mhaighdean, The Maiden, an exquisite mountain at the heartland of the wilderness. In its highest corrie is the Fuar Loch Mor, deep, translucent, and icy cold, even on the hottest summer's day. The Maiden is all ice, capped with light grey gneiss, yet crowded on its northern side by the warm red sandstone of Ruadh Stac Mor. To the right of Creag an Dubh Loch is the pass that leads to Lochan Fada; right again is the sharply defined edge of Beinn Lair with the dome of Meall Mheinnidh in the foreground.

It is towards the last that our route leads. The floor of the Fionn Loch valley is a tumbling sea of blanket bog seamed with pools and wandering streams. It can be very wet underfoot in this doused landscape. But the ground is well drained where our path winds past glacial moraines and ruined shielings to bear south into the pass of the Strathan Buidhe.

At the head of the pass, the ridge of Beinn Eighe shows to the south. Eastward lies Slioch, The Spear, with its trident-like buttresses of sandstone. From here a good track winds down

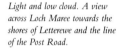

Light and low cloud. A view across Loch Maree towards the shores of Letterewe and the line of the Post Road.

towards Letterewe across battling streams and past a deep gorge where fragile blooms of wild strawberry and primrose lie bedded on the mossy banks.

Letterewe is a remarkable settlement. Its English name has the simple meaning of 'slope by the water'. Loch Maree was originally named Loch Ewe, hence the root names of settlements along its length as far as Kinlochewe. The Letterewe estate was owned by the Mackenzie family until the late eighteenth century, and Letterewe House dates from that time. The settlement was a busy place in its day. There was a school here for the children of estate workers. The old watch house on the shore has oriole windows and a glazed niche behind which a light was kept to guide boats across the loch from the western shore when most traffic to and fro was by water. Small steamers sailed between Kinlochewe and Poolewe during the late nineteenth century, and stopped at Letterewe quay to offload goods and passengers.

The natives here were a lively lot. And so were the midges, Scotland's irritating micro-gnats that cloud the air in late summer and make life unbearable with their pin-prick nibbling. There is an apocryphal story about Letterewe midges and a Presbyterian minister called John Morrison. The minister was appointed to Gairloch parish in 1711 at a time when many Highlanders of all classes held to the Episcopalian faith as they held to their language and to their customs. The Revd Morrison had a hard time of it. He tried to preach at Kinlochewe, but he and his servants were locked up for several days in a stinking cow shed with the approval of the Mackenzie laird. The Revd John survived this outrage, but fell in with wonderfully monstrous treatment at Letterewe where the inhabitants stripped him naked and tied him to a birch tree. It was fecund autumn. The midges were teeming, and biting like bees. The demented minister suffered far into the midge-munching dusk until a Letterewe woman took pity and released him. It hardly bears thinking about.

Today, Letterewe is less busy or biting a place, although the midge is still an occupational hazard. The mood of peaceful isolation demands respect from those who pass by along the walled lane that leads east to the bridge over the Abhainn an Fuirneis. The name Furnace marks this eastern edge of Letterewe as the site of one of the old iron foundries begun by Sir George Hay in 1607. Beyond the bridge the right of way leads onto higher ground and to the firm path that runs east towards Kinlochewe.

From here, for nine miles/fourteen kilometres the route follows the path of the post runners along the southern slopes of the mighty Slioch. To the south of Loch Maree the Torridon hills bulk large. Their great presence contains the loch within its narrow bed.

In the far distance the blurred outlines of Kinlochewe measure out the distance. It is a long road, but it leads through a mosaic of heather and gorse and shady birch woods, dips suddenly into narrow ravines, where primroses grow, and passes above the broken walls of the old houses and field walls that lie shrouded with grass and ferns. The view south across the pale loch from above the ruins at Coppachy is of the green mouth of Glen Grudie with the distant peaks of Sail Mhor and Beinn Dearg dark blue in the distance.

Above the jutting promontory of Rubh' a' Ghiubhais the path climbs from the woods towards the rocky rib of Slioch's shoulder. It leads on through the boulder-strewn pass of Clais na Leac, the hollow of the flagstones, and then swings inland across the grassy cradle of Smiorasair with its headwall cascade of streams. There was a settlement here; unquestionably a true shieling at this ideal summer grazing. Beyond Smiorasair the path crosses rocky slopes, then descends steeply to the mouth of Gleann Bianasdail and the bridge over the Abhainn an Fhasaigh.

The flat green delta at the river's mouth is called Fasagh and was the site of an ironworks in the seventeenth century. Sir George Hay brought ironworkers here from Fife and the lowlands, and some from Cumbria. None spoke gaelic and all were dubbed 'Sasganaich', or 'Saxon' English. A short distance north of the river's mouth is a small pool close to the shore. Beside it is Cladh nan Sasunnach, the burial place of the English. Tradition claims that it was here that the ironworkers were buried, although the Gairloch writer John H. Dixon suggests that the twenty-four rough graves in evidence are much older than the seventeenth century, and that the ironworkers were buried on the 'sacred' Isle Maree further down the loch.

The three miles/nearly five kilometres of track from Fasagh to Kinlochewe lie along the easy ground of the river flats. For the post runners Kinlochewe would have meant a night's rest before the next day's hard slog up Glen Docherty and on towards Dingwall thirty-six miles/fifty-eight kilometres away. Not all the post runners coped with the strains of the job. One young runner was found dead, apparently of a heart attack, on the lonely track above Glen Docherty.

But by the middle of the nineteenth century the post runners were no longer needed. Improvements were made to the old military road along Loch Maree's western shore and wheeled traffic took over delivery of all goods, while steamships plied on Loch Maree. When that time came, Big John the Post, the last of the runners, emigrated to Australia. The way through the rock of Creag Tharbh fell back into wilderness, and men lost the skill and the need of moving rapidly on foot through the great hills.

THE LOCH MAREE POST ROAD
Information

Distance 20 miles/32 kms

Maps OS Landranger 19 (Gairloch & Ullapool); OS Outdoor Leisure 8 (The Cuillin & Torridon Hills)

Nature of Walk The route described from Kernsary to Letterewe follows the northern track via the Strathan Buidhe. *The historical route from Kernsary along the shores of Loch Maree via Ardlair is not recommended. There is no clear path and sections of the route are difficult and may be dangerous.*

The paths and tracks along the route described are generally excellent. This is a good, tough expedition through magnificent country. Fit and experienced walkers should be able to complete the route in a day. Clothing and equipment (including emergency bivouac gear) should be suitable for mountain conditions. *Weather conditions can be severe at any time of the year, but especially so outside the summer season. The route is not advised in bad snow conditions.*

The Letterewe Estate, through which this walk passes, is of great environmental significance and sensitivity. The estate's owner, in conjunction with representatives of leading outdoor organizations, has drawn up an accord comprising a set of principles, the aim of which is to enhance public awareness of wild land needs and to provide a guide to the proper use of such wild land. The fundamental principle of the accord is a recognition that all who enter Letterewe 'must cherish and safeguard the area's wildlife and its outstanding beauty'. Visitors to the area are encouraged to visit in small, rather than large, groups.

The route described here passes through estates where selective culling of deer for good management is carried out, the key period being from mid-August to mid-November, though precise details may vary from estate to estate. Before going into the hills, visitors are strongly advised to contact the TIC at Gairloch for initial guidance on stalking schedules. The estates can also be contacted for advice about stalking, or for advice on planned visits at any time of the year.

Accommodation At Poolewe, Kinlochewe and Gairloch. Youth hostel at Gairloch; camp site at Poolewe and Gairloch.

Transport Poolewe can be reached by bus from Inverness and from the rail station at Achnasheen. Service bus and post bus connections run between Kinlochewe and Poolewe daily, except Sundays. Timetables from the TIC at Gairloch.

Evening light on Loch Kernsary.

Further Information Tourist Information Centre, Gairloch, tel. (0445) 2130.

Start Poolewe

1 From the bridge over the River Ewe on the A832, walk north-east along the road for about ⅓ mile/0.5 kms to reach a long, white-walled building at Srondubh. Go through a metal gate on the left of this building (sign: 'No Bikes'). Follow the rising track to where it leads along the north-east side of Loch Kernsary. Just beyond the end of the loch, and past a small building on the left, bear down right to cross a stream beneath a spreading oak tree. Continue up a grassy path to join the estate track by the gate at Kernsary at OS 893795. (3 miles/4.8 kms)

2 Go left along the track for about ¼ mile/0.4 kms, then turn off right by a deer fence and climb over a step-stile. Continue along the rough track for about ½ mile/0.8 kms to where it becomes grassier amidst conifers. *The following directions should be noted carefully.* Just before the track curves sharply left at OS 905739, look for an open break running down through the trees on the right. Follow a faint path down this break and cross another faint path to reach the pine-fringed banks of a stream. Turn left and follow a path alongside the stream, to reach a gate in a deer fence at the edge of the forest. Go over a step-stile onto open ground. (1¼ miles/2 kms)

3 Follow the path steadily uphill alongside the Allt na Creige through peaty ground that can be very wet in places. Continue past Loch an Doire Crionaich, crossing a small causeway at its western end. Continue to where the path curves south into the mouth of Strathan Buidhe at OS 943760. (3 miles/4.8 kms)

4 Continue on a good path up Strathan Buidhe and on over the col at the glen head. Follow the descending path to reach Letterewe above a keeper's cottage. Keep left above the lodge grounds until a lane is reached. (3 miles/4.8 kms)

5 Turn left along the lane for about ½ mile/0.8 kms. Where the lane veers left towards a house, keep straight ahead, leaving the lane, and go through a gate into a field. Continue with the field edge on your left, then follow a track down right alongside a river. Turn left across a bridge. *The following*

Looking towards the head of the Fionn Loch valley: 'a tumbling sea of blanket bog seamed with pools and wandering streams'.

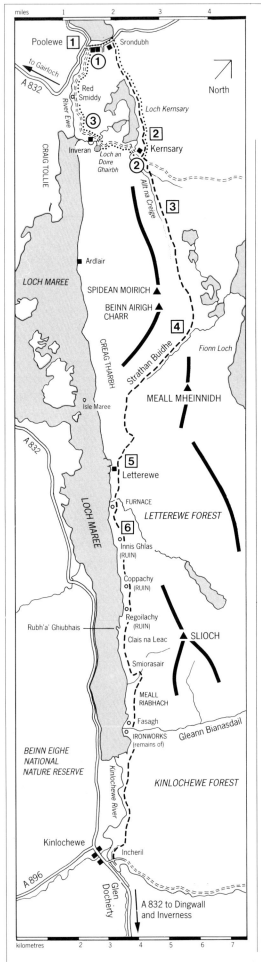

directions should be noted carefully. A few yards beyond the bridge at OS 959705, go sharply left just before an oak tree. Follow a path uphill through scrubby ground to reach a metal gate in a deer fence. Beyond the gate, bear up left over stony and marshy ground to reach a good path. Turn right along this path. (¾ mile/1.2 kms)

6 Follow the excellent path high above Loch Maree. Keep to the main path at all times to reach the mouth of Gleann Bianasdail at OS 012657, from where a good track leads to Incheril and thence to Kinlochewe. (9 miles/14.4 kms)

CIRCULAR WALK 6 miles/9.6 kms

This pleasant 3-hour walk follows the old post road from Poolewe as far as Kernsary then follows an estate road back to Poolewe. The latter part of the walk passes the site of a seventeenth-century ironworks.

Start Poolewe

1 As for (1) on the main walk as far as Kernsary.

2 At Kernsary, turn right through the gate and follow the broad track past the cottages. Cross a bridge and keep on the main track for about 1 mile/1.6 kms to reach another bridge and a gate. *Red deer may be seen grazing at certain times of the year in the grassy river meadows at Kernsary.*

3 Follow the track past the entrance to Inveran, where the track becomes a surfaced road leading back to Poolewe. *About ¾ mile/1.2 kms beyond Inveran, at a point where the River Ewe becomes shallow and stony, is the site of the ancient ironworks known as A Cheardach Ruadh, the Red Smiddy.*

The Thieves' Road
Central Highlands

Dalwhinnie to Fort William 43 miles/68.8 kms

*'They go out in parties
from ten to thirty men,
traverse large tracts of
mountains till they
arrive at the lowlands
where they design
to commit their
depredations, which
they choose to do in
places distant from the
glens which they
inhabit.'*

Major General George Wade,
*Report on the State of the
Highlands,* 1724

This is a long and demanding route through the great mountains that lie between Badenoch and Lochaber. The route was followed by cattle thieves and fighting men throughout the centuries. It leads past the great mountains of Ben Alder and Ben Nevis, crosses two remote passes, and skirts the northern edge of Rannoch Moor.

———————

The stealing of cattle, or 'reiving', was commonplace throughout Scotland from the earliest times. William the Lion, King of Scotland in the twelfth century, made it unlawful for anyone to buy cattle without obtaining certification that such cattle had been honestly bought in turn. There were probably Scots cattle thieves before the Flood.

Reiving was justified on the grounds that upland cattle were owned in common, because, like red deer, they fed on the common land of the hills. It was justified further by the argument that if a clan were starving to death, as often threatened in such a harsh country, a chieftain was duty bound to support his people by taking cattle from those who had a surplus. Reiving was seen also as a way of keeping the fighting men of the clan in good fettle. Its justification was testily summed up in a government report of 1746 that spoke of cattle-thieving by Highlanders as being, 'the principal source of all their barbarity, cruelty, cunning and revenge . . . which . . . trains them up to the use of arms, love of plunder, thirst for revenge'.

Highland cattle-thieving encourages sentimentality in modern observers, and characters such as Rob Roy MacGregor have lent a romantic gloss to what was essentially a criminal activity. There were many who made a trade out of thieving, and there was an underclass of ruffians who stole small numbers of beasts, as well as goods and chattels, for profit, killing and tormenting as they went.

The name 'cateran', from the Gaelic word *ceithern* meaning 'fighting man', was used to describe such raiders. In many cases, they were men who had been driven out by their own overlords. Trial records of 1591 speak of 'broken' men from the west, who entered Glen Clova in Angus by the Jock's Road pass and, 'invadit the inhabitants and murthourit and slew three or four innocent men and women and reft and took away ane grit pray of guidis'.

The authorities could do little to stop such plunder. The Highlands had long been considered out of bounds for officialdom. In the great hills the King's Writ carried no weight, and during the early sixteenth century it was said that officers of the law dared not pass through the Highlands, 'for fear of yair lyvis'. The Crown and Privy Council might listen to a complaint of theft and find the charge proven; they might even pronounce the guilty to be

On the track alongside Loch Ericht. 'The loch runs far to the west and, like a great river, it probes the heart of Rannoch twenty miles away.'

outlaws. But that was often as far as it went. The Privy Council could charge chieftains or landowners, under whose patronage the guilty caterans lived, to appear before the Crown to answer for them. Not surprisingly, none ever did.

After the Jacobite Rebellions of 1715 and 1745, reiving increased. Cattle were still the main source of quick money and many of the rebel Highlanders were destitute and desperate. There was also an element of bitterness in their preying on those Highland landowners and clans which had supported the Hanoverian cause or had stood aside and grown fat while others lost their birthrights. Cattle-stealing became a trade; stolen beasts were sold on, or 're-set', rather than used for feeding hungry people.

Long distances were covered by the reivers. In his report to the Crown in 1724, Wade described how the caterans drove stolen cattle through the night, hiding by day in high passes and corries, or in the dripping birch woods, in order to sell the beasts at fairs and markets, and to buyers, far from where they had been stolen.

The great wilderness areas to the west of Speyside and Badenoch were ideal breeding grounds for the generally lawless. Lochaber, on the western seaboard, was another country. Here, the loyalties and sympathies of the people rested with the Western Highlands and Islands. Between Badenoch and Lochaber lay the great waste of Rannoch Moor and the barrier of the Ben Alder mountains – a forty-mile/sixty-four-kilometre expanse of truly un-neighbourly terrain. A further sixty or so miles/ninety-six kilometres separated Speyside from the eastern glens.

There were few family or social ties between the western clans and the people of the east, and, although Jacobite unity spanned the nation in times of war, the general rule was everyone for themselves. Black acts could be carried out in Angus or Perthshire by 'the thievish sett' who travelled from the west along the various routes that shared the name the 'Thieves' Road. Pangs of conscience, if any, eased quickly as the heathery miles were passed on that same road home.

In the 1740s the annual loss from cattle-thieving throughout the Highlands and the Scottish Borders was estimated to be £37,000. A developing economy could not suffer such freelance enterprise for long, especially when legitimate cattle-dealing was increasing. Even notorious cattle thieves, such as Rob Roy MacGregor, were abandoning theft for honest droving. This expansion of the Highland economy coincided with the authorities acquiring the will and the means to impose law on life and behaviour in the region, and after 1745 the Hanoverian government began to feel more confident that the Stuart Cause had been fatally reversed. Rigorous and brutal 'pacification' of the north followed; the end of cattle-thieving was seen as being a major part of the process of modernization.

The authorities believed that the best way of stopping raids from the west was to guard a line that ran north from Blair Atholl through Glen Garry and Badenoch to the Upper Spey. This is the line of the modern A9 and of the Perth to Inverness railway. The mountain passes leading east from this line were the routes taken by the caterans when they emerged from the fastness of Ben Alder and Laggan and it was along these routes that stolen cattle were driven back to the west. By controlling such routes the authorities hoped to dissuade the caterans.

The English government manipulated the turmoil and contradictions of Highland society for its own ends. From the 1720s onwards, the chiefs of the central and southern Highlands were paid to raise special companies to stop cattle-thieving. These were the famous Black Watch, named for their occupation and for the dark tartan the government dressed them in. They were to become one of the finest regiments of the British Army. But at first they were set to police the wild hills and their wilder countrymen, and although it took another generation before large-scale reiving ended, the eighteenth century closed the book on a way of life – and sometimes death – that was celebrated even in song as being 'just the deeds of pretty men'. The Black Watch were based at such places as Dalwhinnie, from where our walk begins.

In the days of the caterans, the landscape round Dalwhinnie was little different to what it is now, beneath its modern overlay of railway, roads and buildings. There was no handsome distillery until the late 1890s, and no restraining dam to Loch Ericht. But the essence of the place was the same. This was the 'meeting place' on the *dal*, the flat land, so called because of its situation at the crossroads of hill routes from all quarters. Before the days of road and rail, this great space would have been bare but impressive, like a Tibetan plain secure amidst the mountains. Now, it is a mere passing place, sliced through by concrete and iron. It is unrelentingly bleak and featureless. Rounded hills sweep away in all directions. In winter the road over the nearby Drumochter Pass is often blocked with snow, its course picked out by a trail of trapped lorries and cars. If the rail track is cleared, only the slow, crawling movement of an occasional train enlivens the icy monotony of this Scottish Siberia. At any time Dalwhinnie invites escape into the magnificent mountains to either side.

The finest prospect is to the west, along Loch Erichtside. An estate track runs for five miles/eight kilometres to Ben Alder Lodge down the loch's western shore, and seems a trudge at times. But once the railway is crossed and the lodge gate passed, the view to the west is encouraging. The track is crowded by plantations and is fringed by large stands of broom, luminous with golden flowers. The loch runs far to the west, and like a great river it probes the heart of Rannoch twenty miles/thirty-two kilometres away. In the middle distance, Beinn Bheoil, the eastern spur of Ben Alder, bulks large, its cliffs often streaked with snow even in the warmest of summers.

Just before Ben Alder Lodge, our route bears right and uphill. The lodge stands nicely sheltered by trees. In front, meadows run down to the lochside. Beyond the main house are the stables and a scattering of buildings built of corrugated iron, the ubiquitous 'crinkly tin' that has become an acceptable element of Highland vernacular architecture. Rising above the buildings are the pine-covered slopes of Meall Dubh and Meall Beag. For another mile/two kilometres or so, the broad track runs on along the edge of the trees towards Loch Pattack.

This is famous deer country and Ben Alder is one of the great deer 'forests' of the Highlands. It marches with the other fine estates, of Ardverikie to the north and Corrour to the west, across thousands of acres/hectares of spectacular wilderness where great herds roam. Today, the red deer flourishes in even greater numbers than before, and such estates can have several thousand stags and hinds within their marches.

Bred for sport since Victorian times, the red deer has bred its own need for judicious culling, and the craft of the stalker is as richly endowed with skilled experts today as it ever was.

Before the stalking season begins in August, the walker has a good chance of seeing sizeable herds of mixed beasts beside the track, where it runs above the lodge, the stags uneasy perhaps, but not yet runnable. Outside the shooting season, deer are often fed with maize on such low ground, where they become accustomed to human presence. As late summer approaches, the stags especially begin to move out, the furry 'velvet' covering on their newly grown horns flying in tatters as it decays. Soon the hills echo to the hollow crack of the rifle, each shot carefully planned. By October, the marvellous deep-throated 'belling' of the rutting stags overpowers all other sounds.

Red deer are remarkable creatures. They are elegant, and even lovely, each one a prehistoric relic on legs, the last of the big beasts of Britain's wild areas. They were hunted with deer hounds throughout the medieval period, but the weight of numbers and the vastness of their wilderness home ensured survival. Victorian deer-hunting was popularized by an early 'sportsman', William Scrope, who wrote a book about his activities. The book, illustrated by Edwin and Charles Landseer, caught the fancy of the new breed of wealthy Victorian industrialists who aspired to landownership. The result was a new boom for impoverished Highland lairds. The ubiquitous sheep had displaced people a century before. Now the sheep themselves were displaced and the red deer allowed to flourish. Hunting estates became the norm; pretension spawned the Scots Baronial style of architecture, part schloss, part château.

Hunting with hounds and corraling deer herds for indiscriminate slaughter were the methods still followed by the early Victorians. But improvements in firearms led to the more skilled stalking of individual beasts and to an ethos of good management. Traditionally, much of a stalker's time was spent culling animals that were old or infirm.

The management of wild deer, today especially, is a far more complex business than popular perception makes of it, and during the stalking season walkers should seek advice about shooting activities.

The deer road from the lodge takes us into the heart of the Ben Alder range. Height is gained steadily to where the track levels out above the green river flats through which the waters of the Allt a' Chaoil-reidhe drain to Loch Pattack. In clear weather, the view west is magnificent. Ben Alder dominates, its massive bulk made graceful by the curving fall of the corries on its eastern face. The mountain is 3,757 feet/1,148 m high. Its vast summit plateau is carpeted with tufted hair grass, and patchworked with deep snowfields throughout the year.

The Black Pass, the Bealach Dubh, up which the path makes its way, strikes a perfect balance between the main bulk of the mountain and the sharp prow of Sgor Iutharn to its north. On the wings of this centrepiece, green slopes of lesser hills fall gracefully to the vast grassy bed of the river flats where a handful of white-skinned ponies often graze. These are the broad-backed Highland 'garrons', the work horses of the deer forest, the carriers of stag carcasses from the barely accessible high ground.

The way west leads past Culra bothy. The building is now an open shelter, but was used originally by ghillies and had stabling for ponies. Beyond the bothy, the path runs south-west on a steady rise towards the summit of the Bealach Dubh. It draws the walker into the heart of the wilderness, between the massive flanking shoulder of Ben Alder and the long ridge of Sgor Iutharn that is known as the 'Lancet Edge'. Below the sharply-pointed summit of Sgor Iutharn there is a spectacular area of flood-devastated ground, where the swollen waters of Loch an Sgoir erupted from their rocky basin, during the early part of 1990, to smash through the hillside. Looking back, the river flats of the Chaoil-reidhe run like a green sea towards the precise geometry of the conifer plantations on the facing hills.

Amidst this lonely wilderness, Charles Edward Stuart, the Young Pretender, made his way during his frantic wanderings after Culloden. The Prince had sheltered on the southern slopes of Ben Alder at the famous Cluny's Cave (Prince Charlie's Cave), in the company of a splendid roll-call of Jacobite chieftains. These included the formidable Ewan 'Cluny' Macpherson and Cameron of Lochiel. It was through the Ben Alder mountains that the last of the Stuarts made his way to Loch nan Uamh between Moidart and Arisaig, where he boarded a boat that took him to France and a pathetic decline. In such wild country, Bonnie Prince Charlie perhaps enjoyed the only real freedom of his lost kingdom, as he crossed the brooding passes in the company of the last of the true Highlanders.

Most mountain passes are as grudging as the Stuart fortunes. You plod ever upwards and breast a final rise to find a mile or so of blanket bog ahead and no objective in view. But the Bealach Dubh rises to a hard-won, startling climax. Beyond the final rise, the whole of the valley of the Uisge Labhair opens up ahead, with Loch Ossian gleaming in the distance. The far hills of Mamore and Glencoe fill the western horizon, blue-black under a vast sky. It is a prospect to gladden the heart of royalty or reiver. The silver stream snakes its way down the glen through emerald patches of sweet grass, Loch Ossian seems only a step or two away, and the Lochaber hills are promising.

The reality is a long journey still. The western end of Loch Ossian is seven miles/eleven kilometres distant, and Fort William is eighteen miles/twenty-two kilometres away. But for now the route is downhill, and once the path on the north side of the Uisge Labhair is reached, the way to Corrour Lodge is a delightful tramp

Opposite: The great waterfall of An Steall Bhan, the 'White Spout', cascades from the slopes of An Gharbhanach above Glen Nevis.

alongside the boulder-strewn river, and the air sweet with the smell of heather and damp grass. At a junction with Strath Ossian, the Labhair pours its floods down a series of granite slabs and scooped basins in a wide-spreading fan of frothing water. In contrast, the head of Loch Ossian is a leafy enclave of broad-leaved trees and flowering shrubbery. Yellow broom and birches fringe the lochside, and dark banks of conifers march along the shoreline to the west. The lochside road is a level plod between the flanking conifers, but it leads into a spacious northern corner of the Moor of Rannoch by Corrour Station.

Rannoch is the desolate heart of the Highlands, 'an immense vacuity, with nothing in it to contemplate', according to the Revd John Lettice who toured Scotland in 1792. But he was from Sussex. Certainly, the great moor is like some vast lunar basin, an awesome landscape of blanket bog, of dark peat hags and weeping mires, rimmed with jagged peaks that fret the low horizon. This vast basin was gouged by glaciers, shattered by permafrost and deluged by water. The result is one of the most extensive areas of blanket bog in the Highlands.

Yet ways have been found through this wilderness. Telford planned a road across the moor in the early nineteenth century, but the project was never attempted. It was the railway that triumphed, and today it still trails its iron lines across the moor. The building of the line began in 1892. It was a remarkable engineering feat that involved long sections of track being 'floated' across the boggiest sections of the moor. Deep drainage channels were first cut, then layers of turf and brushwood were packed along the planned course. Soil and rubble were added, along with thousands of tons of ash and clinker brought north from the industrial lowlands and carried across the moor on a temporary track. The West Highland Line was opened in 1894.

Today, Corrour Station is still a famous rail halt, and the West Highland still offers one of the great rail journeys of Britain, even though the adventurous days of steam are long gone. Unlike a road, the railway is somehow unobtrusive within this wilderness, and the caterpillar-crawl of the occasional train seems an acceptable presence. Our route leads under the track to the north of Corrour, then winds round the head of Loch Treig through a fine vista of hills and tumbling streams before striking west along the banks of the Abhainn Rath towards Glen Nevis.

An alternative leg of the Thieves' Road led north from the doleful ruin of Creaguaineach at Loch Treig head. It is a fine stretch of walking that leads over the Lairig Leacach and onto Spean Bridge, and it was the route taken by Highlanders travelling to and from Kintail and Skye.

The way west runs high above the rattling waters of the Abhainn Rath, through a dark green landscape of birches and ferns to where the path descends to the river's edge by Staoineag bothy, remote on its high ground on the opposite bank of the river. Ahead lie the great ranges of the Mamores and the Aonachs. The path west is a good one, though muddy in wet conditions. It leads to the ruins of Luibeilt and to Meanach bothy, a rough building in a desolate place, with a soot-blackened, stony interior; a cateran's den if ever there was one.

At Luibeilt the river is crossed, with care, and a reedy track followed through the wide strath to Tom an Eite, the well-named Hill of the Watershed, where the streams fall to east and west. This is a drowned landscape at the best of times, a sump for the cloud-bursting hills to either side. In driving rain, it is bitter here; the damp cold of the mountains is whipped across your face, the quaking ground sucks at your feet. Cattle thieves and campaigners probably went barefoot, but snug in enfolding plaid and wide-brimmed bonnets, close-woven to throw off the drenching rain.

By Tom an Eite another river-crossing has to be made, again with great caution when the streams are full. Soon the homeward path to Glen Nevis is reached. To its north are the secretive Grey Corries of Killiechonate; to the south is the shapely peak of Binnein Mor, highest of the Mamores; and its smaller sister, Binnein Beag, doused with quartzite screes, rising gracefully above the glen.

Two miles/three kilometres of track leads alongside the Water of Nevis to where the great waterfall of An Steall Bhan, the 'White Spout', cascades for 350 feet/100 metres from the slopes of An Garbhanach. Steall is bested only by the Falls of Glomach in Kintail, and then by a mere twenty feet/six metres. When the clouds are down, the curling mist seems to wring itself out above the falls, thickened by a permanent haze of spume.

All this water has scoured out a magnificent gorge through the head of the glen, slicing across the interlocking bulwarks of Ben Nevis to the north and Sgurr a' Mhaim to the south. Nevis is known in one form as Beinn-nimh-uisg, the 'mountain of the biting cold water'. There is even a water-worn path down through the trees, above where the river roars through its rocky cauldrons. The gorge is within easy reach of the car park at the road head, and its tree-shrouded path is sown with tumbled rocks, exposed by water and the stumbling feet of thousands of sightseers. Where the rocky walls open out beneath Nevis's vast slopes, the tarmac begins, and it is five miles/eight kilometres of downhill road to Fort William and a very different world to that of the hard men of the Thieves' Road.

THE THIEVES' ROAD
Information

Distance 43 miles/68.8 kms

Maps OS Landranger 41 (Ben Nevis);
OS Landranger 42 (Glen Garry & Loch
Rannoch); OS Outdoor Leisure 32
(Mountainmaster of Ben Nevis)

Nature of Walk This is a long walk through
magnificent mountain country. It can be
completed in two or three days by fit walkers.
The route is easily followed and only two short
sections are indistinct. *Rivers need to be forded,
and crossings may pose serious problems after
prolonged rain.* The section through upper Glen
Nevis, from Luibeilt to Steall, can be very wet
underfoot. Equipment (including emergency
bivouac gear) should be for mountain
conditions. *Weather conditions are unpredictable at
all times of the year and can be very severe outside
the summer season. The route is not advised in bad
snow conditions.*

*The area through which this walk passes is very
wild and beautiful and is of great environmental
importance. Walkers are asked to treat the area with
care and respect. The route described here passes
through private estates, where selective culling of deer
for good management is carried out, the key period
being from mid-August to mid-November, though
precise details may vary from estate to estate. Before*
*going into the hills, visitors are strongly advised to
contact the TIC at Fort William for initial guidance
on stalking schedules. Individual estates can also be
contacted for advice about stalking.*

Accommodation Hotels and guest houses at
Dalwhinnie and Fort William. Youth hostel
at Loch Ossian and bunkhouse at Corrour
Station. Youth hostel and camp site in Glen
Nevis. There are mountain shelters along the
route at Culra, Staoineag, and Meanach. *The
continued availability of these voluntarily maintained
shelters is at the discretion of local estates and
landholders. Walkers should not rely on their
availability.*

Transport Dalwhinnie and Fort William are
connected to main centres by train and bus.
Trains stop at Corrour Station at the midway
point of the walk. Seasonal bus service to Fort
William from the road head in Glen Nevis.

Further Information Tourist Information
Centre, Fort William, tel. (0397) 703781.

Start Dalwhinnie Station

1 Cross the railway *with care* via the level
crossing south of the station, then follow the
lochside road towards Ben Alder Lodge. Keep
right where the road branches just before the
lodge. Continue to a corrugated-iron shed just
before Loch Pattack. (7 miles/11.2 kms)

2 Continue past the shed for a ¼ mile/
0.4 kms, then turn off left along the shores of
Loch Pattack. Cross a suspension bridge and
continue to the Culra bothy. (Culra can be
reached alternatively by following a path
leading due south from the shed. *This requires
the Allt a' Chaoil-reidhe to be forded, which may be
difficult after prolonged rain*). From Culra bothy,
follow the obvious track and path south-west
to the head of the Bealach Dubh at OS
480731. (6 miles/9.6 kms)

*Left: A red deer stag in the heart of the Ben Alder mountains.
Above right: Heading west towards Lochaber on the track to
Loch Treig.
Below right: Loch Ossian: looking back towards the
Bealach Dubh.*

3 Descend on a good track for about ½ mile/0.8 kms, then bear down right, at an angle away from the track, just beyond where a stream flows down to the right, at OS 469720. There is no obvious path until the north side of the Uisge Labhair stream is reached. The path downstream is then faint at first but soon becomes distinct. It is followed to a footbridge below the fine rocky falls above Corrour Lodge at OS 418702. (4¼ miles/6.8 kms)

4 Beyond the bridge, follow the track past a conifer plantation to reach a junction with a broad track beside a bridge over the River Ossian. From here, good estate roads can be followed to left or right down either side of Loch Ossian. The right-hand track down the north-west side of the loch is the shorter route. (4 miles/6.4 kms)

5 At the foot of the loch, at OS 366671, bear off right from the lochside track. Cross a wooden footbridge and follow the track round the hillside. Go under a railway bridge to join a broad estate track. Turn right along this track to pass Loch Treig and reach the bridge over the Abhainn Rath at Creaguaineach Lodge. (4 miles/6.4 kms)

6 Turn left beyond the bridge and follow the path alongside the Abhainn Rath past Staoineag bothy and continue for another two miles to reach a point on the river bank

opposite the ruins of Luibeilt. *The isolated building a short distance north-east of the river at this point is Meanach bothy.* (3½ miles/5.6 kms)

7 The river needs to be forded at Luibeilt. There are a number of possible crossings that all require wading. *Great care is required when the river is high after prolonged rain.* Once across the river, follow a track upstream through reedy ground to reach the banks of the tributary of the Allt Coire a' Bhinnein at OS 242693. (2 miles/3.2 kms)

8 There was a bridge over the Allt Coire a' Bhinnein at one time, but it has been washed away. It may be re-erected, but if not, the river needs to be forded. If the Allt Coire a' Bhinnein is fordable, the west bank of the Abhainn Rath should be followed for about 300 yards/270 metres before you veer off left from the river bank at OS 241694 to cross boggy ground and join a good path running west below Tom an Eite at OS 238694. *The path is very indistinct throughout this extremely boggy section until the path below Tom an Eite is reached.* If the Allt Coire a' Bhinnein is not fordable, it may be best to continue upstream along the south bank of the Allt Coire a' Bhinnein for about 400 yards/360 metres, to cross by an old sluice and an aluminium shanty. From here a faint path leads north, away from the river and through scrubby ground, to join the good path mentioned above, which leads west below Tom an Eite at

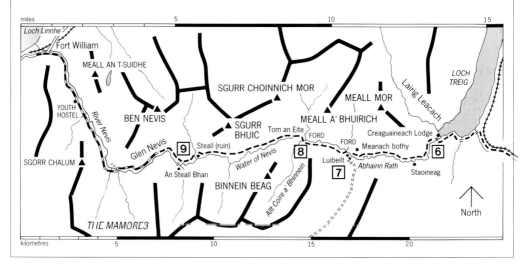

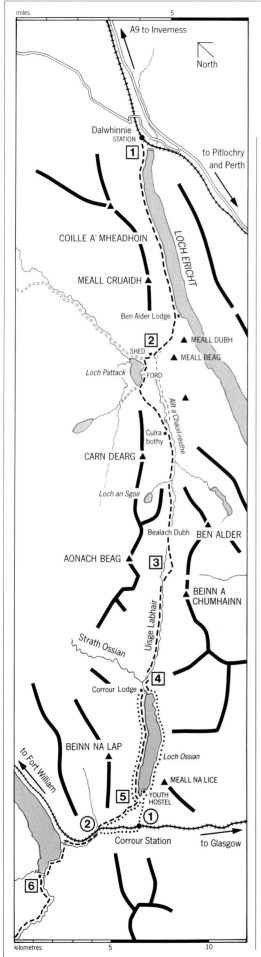

miles
5

A9 to Inverness

North

Dalwhinnie
STATION

1

to Pitlochry
and Perth

COILLE A' MHEADHOIN

LOCH ERICHT

MEALL CRUAIDH ▲

Ben Alder Lodge

2 ▲ MEALL DUBH

SHED ▲ MEALL BEAG

Loch Pattack FORD

Allt a' Chaoil-réidhe

Culra
bothy

CARN DEARG ▲

Loch an Sgoir

Bealach Dubh BEN ALDER

AONACH BEAG ▲ **3**

Uisge Labhair ▲ BEINN A
CHUMHAINN

Strath Ossian

4

Corrour Lodge

BEINN NA LAP ▲

Loch Ossian

▲ MEALL NA LICE

to Fort William

5 YOUTH
HOSTEL

② ①

Corrour Station to Glasgow

6

kilometres 5 10

OS 238694. Follow the path down upper Glen Nevis to Steall. (3½ miles/5.6 kms)

9 Continue on the rocky track through the gorge to reach the road, which is followed to Fort William. (8¾ miles/14 kms)

CIRCULAR WALKS 4½ miles/7.2 kms *or* 9 miles/14.4 kms

These routes take the walker into the heart of the Moor of Rannoch at the midway point of the main route. They are reached by a short but pleasant train journey from Fort William to Corrour Station, one of Scotland's most remote rail halts on the famous West Highland Line. Train connections can be easily worked out to allow required time for the walks, although careful note should be taken of last trains from Corrour in the evening.

Start Corrour Station

WALK A (4 ½ miles/7.2 kms)

1 Allow three hours. From the station, follow the track to Loch Ossian. At the T-junction with the lochside track, turn left for about 250 yards/225 metres, then at OS 366671, bear off left from the lochside track. Cross a wooden footbridge and follow the track round the hillside.

2 Go under a railway bridge to join a broad estate track. Turn left to return to the station. *Corrour Station was originally a passing place on the West Highland Line, and did not feature in public timetables until 1934. It was used locally, however, by such disparate groups as shooting guests bound for the nearby estates and by navvies working on the building of the dam at Kinlochleven.*

WALK B (9 miles/14.4 kms)

1 Allow four to five hours. As for above walk, to the junction with the lochside track. A circuit of Loch Ossian can then be made in either direction.

Jock's Road
Grampian

Braemar to Glen Clova 15 miles/22.4 kms

'. . . towards the summit at Jock's Road, the boulders have been cleared away, and there is a sort of ladder or staircase in the rock, such as most people are familiar with in very mountainous districts and countries . . .'

Earl of Selbourne, *House of Lords Appeal Judgement,* 1887

Jock's Road is part of a long-established route that crosses that part of the Grampian Mountains known as the Mounth. The route leads over the desolate plateau of the Tolmount and then descends through Glen Doll and into Glen Clova. The Glen Doll section of the route was made famous by a nineteenth-century court case in which a landowner sought, unsuccessfully, to deny the path's status as a right of way.

The Grampian Mountains are penetrated by glaciated valleys down which singing rivers flood onto the rich alluvial plain of Scotland's east coast. These valleys are the famous Angus Glens of Esk, Clova, Prosen and Isla. They extend into a high and lonely plateau that is crowned by the bulky mountain summits of Lochnagar, Glas Maol and Broad Cairn. For centuries they have been used as rough ways to and from Deeside and the great mountains beyond.

Such routes were used by all manner of people, in war and in peace. Iron Age settlers from Europe landed on Scotland's east coast and penetrated as far west as the Great Glen and Kintyre. It is possible that they crossed the Mounth through glens such as Clova. Amidst the rocks of the glen there is a Pictish cave dwelling called a 'weem', whose inhabitants may have crossed the intervening mountains by lines of least resistance.

The Romans built their most northerly road along the base of the Grampian foothills and established a legionary station at Inchtuthill near the mouth of Glen Isla and a fort in Clova's neighbouring valley of Glen Prosen. Agricola won a great battle in AD 84 against the Caledonian tribes at Mons Graupius near Stonehaven. It was Rome's last mark on the unrelenting north, though Mons Graupius gave its name to the Grampian Mountains.

The Caledonian chief Calgacus is credited with powerful oratory before the battle. According to the Roman historian Tacitus, the doomed chieftain told his people: 'The Romans are in the heart of our country . . . No submission can satisfy their pride . . . While the land has anything left it is the theatre of war . . . They make a desert and call it peace.' The final comment would echo down the years, and its bitterest irony is that Agricola is too often credited with making it.

Throughout the centuries, Highland warriors crossed the Mounth passes as aggressors and as fugitives. The area saw a Royal fugitive also. In 1650 Charles II escaped to Clova from the overbearing patronage of the 'Presbyterian Popes' of the Scottish Covenant. He had pretended to throw in his lot with the Covenanters in hopes of retaining Scotland from out of the chaos of the Civil War. But the Godly were too much for him. They subjected him to six hell-fire sermons a day, and scolded him for playing cards. Charles fled north on what became known as 'The Start'.

When news spread of Charles's presence in Clova, loyal clansmen came over the mountains, fired by thoughts of war and the Stuart Cause. But Charles found life in Clova as bad as life with the Godly. He sheltered in a hovel, 'in a nasty room, on an old bolster, above a mat of seggs and rushes, over-wearied and very fearful'. In such circumstances, even a deck of cards would fail to divert a Stuart sensualist. Charles made no effort to resist, when he was discovered by Covenanter troops, and he was marched back to his fate. The Start was false.

The Jacobite connection endured through the risings of 1715 and 1745. In 1745 seven hundred Highlanders crossed Jock's Road on their retreat to the north and to their own miserable fate at Culloden. Whether or not the last of the Stuarts, Bonnie Prince Charlie, was with them, has not been recorded. Fugitives from the battle sought refuge amongst these lonely hills. Their oppressor, the brutal Duke of Cumberland, described the glens of Clova and Esk as 'nests of Jacobites'.

On the descent of Jock's Road through Glen Doll. 'The narrow ravine of the glen opens suddenly into a more generous space . . .'

Wars and skirmishes apart, the cattle economy of the Highlands meant that there was always settlement in these glens, and that drovers and others travelled to and fro across the mountains. Cattle thieves from the far west came through the passes to raid the rich lowlands of Strathmore and Kincardine. In the 1740s the

authorities recorded that thieves stole cattle from these eastern plains, then drove the beasts through Glen Clova and over Jock's Road. Other illegal traffic involved whisky smugglers who are believed to have used the Jock's Road route during the restrictive excise regimes before the nineteenth century. After Culloden a detachment of soldiers was stationed in Glen Clova as part of a wide-ranging pacification of the restless Highlands.

In more ordered times, sheep and cattle were brought over from Deeside to markets at the mouth of the Angus Glens. From there the beasts were taken on to Forfar, Crieff and Falkirk, and then south on routes such as the Peebles Drove. Jock's Road was used until the middle of the last century by shepherds bringing sheep to spring and autumn sales at Cullow Market in lower Glen Clova. There is evidence also of early 'tourists' who were taken by guides along the Glen Doll section of Jock's Road.

There seems no doubt that the track through Glen Doll had been used by the public for centuries. But the legality of that use, as with so many ancient 'roads', had not been established by the time men of wealth and property began to exploit Highland estates for sporting interests in the nineteenth century. Mercenary self-interest of this kind led some landowners to oppose public access of any kind.

In 1883 a wealthy Scots emigré, Duncan Macpherson, returned from Australia and bought the Glen Doll estate for its deer stalking. Macpherson began to restrict access, not only for tourists and botanists, but also for shepherds. This last stricture was especially ill-judged. Macpherson was setting his hand against the Highlander's right to move himself and his beasts through the great lands.

He also found himself up against a formidable opponent in the form of the Scottish Rights of Way and Recreation Society. In 1885, members of the Society set out along the disputed path from Glen Doll, and erected a signpost on the way. They were confronted by Macpherson and his gamekeeper. But the Society members were accompanied by a legal officer, a 'notary public', who formally recorded Macpherson's obstructiveness. It must have been a rare piece of legal theatre.

The group was allowed to pass, but Macpherson continued to obstruct free passage through Glen Doll, and by 1887 the Society and a number of local people raised an action in the Court of Session at Edinburgh. The action was against both Macpherson and Colonel Farquharson of Invercauld, who owned the Glen Callater side of the Jock's Road route. Colonel Farquharson, who perhaps knew more of Highland tradition that did his Australian colleague, did not contest the action in relation to his own ground.

But Macpherson forged ahead and spent several thousand pounds in doing so. He won the right for the case to be tried without a jury, thus keeping it out of the public domain from which the Rights of Way Society might have gained formidable support. The case was heard in Edinburgh before the Lord Ordinary, Lord Kinnear. The Society put forward over fifty witnesses, including local people who had used the route during the previous forty years. Past owners and tenants of Glen Doll made it clear that they had believed the route to be a well-established right of way and not merely a route of 'tolerated use'. Convincing evidence of use was the existence of a publicly subscribed bridge over the White Water river at Acharn, and an ancient milestone near the mouth of Glen Doll. The ghosts of several hundred Jacobite soldiers, including some of Macpherson's ancestors, might have attested also to the military use of the road for centuries past.

Macpherson lost the pass in more ways than one. Lord Kinnear stated: 'There can be no question that the pass through Glen Doll was generally reported to be a public right of way. Those who used it did so because they had a right to use it . . .' Still Macpherson refused to yield, even when he lost an appeal to the Court of Session a few months later. Stubborn to the last, he took his case to the House of Lords in 1888, only to have this appeal soundly rejected.

The Glen Doll case has a fascination for our own times. Public leisure use of wild areas has increased greatly throughout the twentieth century, and battles for access to wild land, and to disputed rights of way, continue today. But the Glen Doll case reveals the determined spirit of the Scottish Rights of Way Society during a Victorian era when landowners had a much more powerful grip on their property, and were capable of forceful intimidation.

The result of the case is certainly an inspiration for modern walkers as they set off from Braemar on the Jock's Road route. Braemar has a wonderful Highland charm. It is on the periphery of 'Royal Deeside' but has a refreshing frontier atmosphere, albeit of the most genteel kind. To the west and north lie the great mountains of the Cairngorms. East lies Lochnagar, and south, beyond Glen Clunie, are the mountains of Perthshire. Braemar is a true crossroads of the great hills.

Our route takes us south along the A93 to Auchallater, from where an estate road leads for five level miles/eight kilometres to Loch Callater. It is an uninspiring tramp, enlivened only by the Callater Burn as it coils down the glen in a broad bed sown with rocks and

Loch Callater, looking towards the Tolmount.

striated slabs. Through Callater, in October 1861, Queen Victoria rode with Prince Albert on their last journey together. The Royal understatement was suitably dull. Her Majesty commented: 'It was beautifully clear and really it was most interesting to look over such an immense extent of the Highlands.' Especially when one owned it.

The smooth hills lie subdued to either side, as monotonously dull in the glare of the sun as they are in grey weather. But the hills ahead draw you past the lovely Loch Callater and on across grassy flats where skylarks mix their sweet song with the forlorn cry of the sandpiper and the jarring screech of black-headed gulls. The path winds through a chaos of drumlins, the morainic mounds that clutter the head of glaciated valleys. A split boulder is passed, and soon the path begins to rise towards the scooped saddle at the rim of the glen. To the right of the saddle a white waterfall, jagged as lightning, tumbles down the dark wall below the Tolmount, the unprepossessing hill that gives its name to the plateau. Right again lies the steep-sided Corrie Kander.

This is a different country in hard winter. Callater is a persuasive trap then; its flat bed allows easy passage even when under snow, its apparent shelter is deceptive when a full blizzard engulfs the plateau ahead. The glen has sucked in victims enough. There is no record of those who may have been lost on the Tolmount plateau in centuries past. But there have been tragedies enough this century. On 1 January 1959, five hikers from Glasgow set out to cross Jock's Road from Braemar. They were well equipped, but walked into a searing snowstorm with winds of seventy miles/ninety-two kilometres an hour. The five managed to cross most of the plateau, but they lost direction in the blinding drift. One by one, and separated from each other, they died before they could reach Glen Doll. One body was found soon after; the rest in the spring. In 1976 two students died in similar conditions amidst that unforgiving arctic waste.

In good summer conditions, the crossing of the Tolmount should be straightforward. But temperatures can drop quickly at this height, even on a hot July day, and rain-driven mist is tiring and deceiving. Walkers should be equipped always for survival. In fine weather, once the steep slog out of Callater is over, the crossing to Glen Doll can be a delight. From the rim of the plateau the view back west is of a vast sweep of distant mountains, speckled with snow even in high summer. Callater lies below, a perfect example of a glaciated U-shaped valley.

From the edge of the plateau the crooked line of the path is easily followed over the rocky hillock of Crow Craigies. To the north are the bare summits of Lochnagar and Broad Cairn. These hills hide their steep faces, and when viewed from the south look bland and flat-topped. But their northern cliffs are 1,000 feet/300 metres high, ribbed and buttressed and hung with beetling overhangs above gleaming lochans.

Red deer wander amongst these hills. Their brindled coats make them difficult to pick out at a distance against the dark ground. The intriguing ptarmigan is another resident. Snow-white in winter but streaked with grey in summer, this reclusive bird of the high tops blends with its background of dark hornblende and grey gneiss. The hen ptarmigan will lead an intruder away from its chicks and will feign a broken wing while doing so.

From Crow Craigies the path winds down towards the distant niche of Glen Doll, where the crags of Craig Maud and The Dounalt disturb the unremitting smoothness of the plateau. Below and to the left of the path is the sodden basin of Loch Esk glittering with fragments of water amidst the dark peat hags. It is here that walkers risk losing their way by being drawn towards the low ground when visibility is poor. But the true path leads south and follows a rocky course into the head of Glen Doll, past a stone and turf shelter and a memorial plaque to lost souls.

The shelter is now known as Davy's Bourach after a famous local character who led annual midsummer pilgrimages to the summit of Lochnagar. A previous shelter was known as Jock's Hut. But a building of sorts has stood here for centuries. It was known as the 'Shieling of Lunkard', after the rocky height above, and until the early nineteenth century it was used by travellers and as a summer home by shepherds whose beasts grazed over the heights.

The eighteenth-century shieling would have been much like the present building, though less desolate when in regular use. There may have been other buildings, each with its rough chimney issuing skeins of blue smoke into the damp air of the gloaming. Across the green slopes sheep would graze peacefully. The shepherds wore rough plaid cloaks and muddy leggings. They lived amidst a permanent odour of burning peat and heather, of human sweat and musty clothing and the smell of sheep, the whole sharpened exquisitely by the clean billowing air from the windy heights. Bad weather would make the life harsher in this unforgiving environment where even summer rain comes icy and battering, and where mist depresses.

Travellers passed regularly across Jock's Road even then: wanderers from the far Highlands heading east and south to seek work and fortune; packmen and soldiers, government officials and early tourists. The area was visited regularly by botanists. Glen Doll and Glen Clova support rare alpine plants, arctic survivors of a ten-thousand-year period. Many have become self-pollinating and all combine fragility with astonishing resilience. They attracted eighteenth-century plant hunters who would often stay at the shieling and share with the shepherds a supper of oatmeal sprinkled with boiling water and a pinch of salt, with hopefully a tot of whisky to wash it down. To the shepherds, the botanists would be familiar and welcome visitors. For their part, the botanists would find the shepherds a possible source of information about plant species, by description rather than identification.

The most notable of these early plant hunters, until his death in 1813, was George Don, a local man of impressive botanical skills. Don recorded the rare alpine sow thistle on nearby Craig Maud, and found a solitary specimen of yellow oxytropis. He discovered a small patch of alpine coltsfoot but did not reveal the exact location and left no record when he died. Fellow botanists disbelieved him and discredited him, as they had done on previous occasions. But the plant was rediscovered in 1951 within the area indicated by Don.

However, the elusive 'Jock' remains mysterious. It would be nice to think of him as one of the doughty local campaigners of the 1887 Rights of Way case, but the source of the name is not known. One suggestion is that Jock was a Clova shepherd called John Winter whose family name is already immortalized in the Winter Corrie of Driesh at the mouth of Glen Doll. Winter had angered an eighteenth-century landowner, Lord Aberdeen, during a land dispute, and is said to have hidden in the old shieling at the head of Glen Doll until the fuss died down. But a Gaelic source has also been suggested for the name, from the word for hawk, *seabhaig*, pronounced 'jowk'.

Jock's Road into Glen Doll certainly gives a hawk's-eye view. The rocky descent is steep and dramatic after the relative flatness of the plateau. The narrow ravine of the glen opens suddenly into a more generous space beyond the shoulder of Craig Rennet, from where the hill slopes seem to swoop ahead. To the right is the gulf of Corrie Fee and the slopes of Mayar. But soon the track enters the dense conifer plantation that dams the lower half of the glen. The original track is believed to have crossed the White Water near this point. It then followed the south bank of the river to re-cross at the Acharn bridge. The 1887 Rights of Way judgement recognized a confusion of routes here and called for rationalization.

Amidst the dark conifers, all that spaciousness, the airy sense of freedom, is gone suddenly, until Glen Doll merges with the more open reaches of Clova, from where the great hills on the skyline are once more visible. Their invitation to explore, to look beyond, and to travel, is compelling. That Macpherson failed to remove 'Jock the public's' right to do so was inevitable, as well as just.

Jock's Road
Information

Distance 15 miles/22.4 kms

Maps OS Landranger 43 (Braemar);
OS Landranger 44 (Glen Clova)

Nature of Walk A tough mountain route
involving a 3-mile/5-km traverse of a lonely
plateau linking two fine glens. Jock's Road
can be followed in a day by very fit walkers.
In mist, compass work may be necessary on
the Tolmount plateau, although waymarking is
generally good. *Once committed to the route there
are no alternative ways off.* Clothing and
equipment (including emergency bivouac gear)
should be suitable for mountain walking.
*Weather conditions can be severe at any time of the
year, but especially so outside the summer season.
The route is not advised in bad snow conditions.*

Accommodation At Braemar and Milton of
Clova. Youth hostels at Braemar and Glen
Doll. Camp site at Glen Doll.

Transport Bus connections from Aberdeen to
Braemar. There is a summer bus connection
between Pitlochry and Braemar. Post bus from
Glen Doll to Kirriemuir, from where buses run
to Dundee.

Further Information Tourist Information
Centre, Braemar, tel. (03397) 41600.

Start Braemar

1 Walk south from Braemar along the A93
for 2 miles/3.2 kms to reach Auchallater at
OS 156882. Go left off the road and through
a gate to follow an estate road to reach Loch
Callater. (5 miles/8 kms)

2 Where the estate road veers off right, just
past the old lodge, go left on a faint path along
the lochside, and then follow the more distinct
path along its north-eastern shore. Continue
across the sometimes marshy flats beyond the
loch to where the ground steepens towards
the head of the glen. Follow the path through
a maze of heather-covered glacial moraines.
(2½ miles/4 kms)

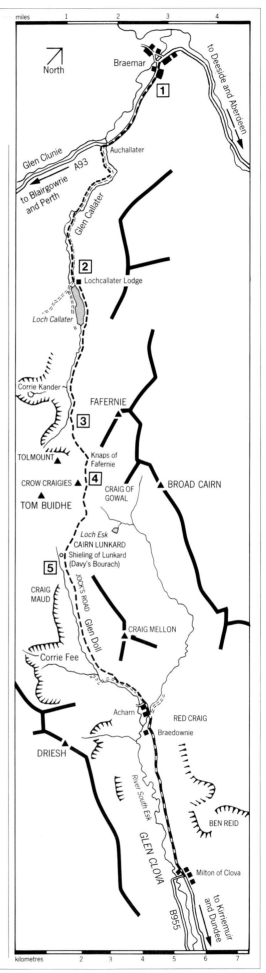

3 Climb steeply up grassy slopes past rusty iron spars. *The path becomes uncertain near the top of the slope, and care should be taken in misty conditions.* The route lies left of centre of the edge of the plateau. On gaining the plateau look for two iron spars in quick succession. Continue straight ahead from the two spars along a discernible path. After about 350 yards/320 metres, the path turns sharply right by a cairn and iron spar at OS 217807. (1¼ miles/2 kms)

4 Follow the cairned path to the left of Crow Craigies, from where it descends to pass a large peat hag. Continue across the flanks of a low hill to descend into the head of Glen Doll past a rough shelter at OS 232778. (2¼ miles/3.6 kms)

5 Follow the rocky path down left from the shelter and continue down Glen Doll to join a forestry track after about 1½ miles/2.4 kms. Continue through trees, keeping left at a junction with a broad forestry road. About ½ mile/0.8 kms further on, and just past a sandy bay on the left, a narrow track bears off left between an avenue of conifers. *This leads to the youth hostel.* The main track leads past a car park and camp site and to the start of the public road to Milton of Clova and Kirriemuir (4 miles/6.4 kms)

CIRCULAR WALKS

The Jock's Road area does not lend itself to circular walks, other than through pathless and wild country. However, a pleasant, level walk can be made to and from Loch Callater along the estate road from the A93 at Auchallater at OS 156882. (6 miles/9.6 kms) There is limited parking by the gate at Auchallater.

At Glen Doll, a good walk can be made from the car park at the mouth of the glen, at OS 284761, by following the forestry road into the glen to the junction with the track signposted Jock's Road and Braemar. Jock's Road can then be followed to the head of the glen and back (7½ miles/12 kms). Allow four hours. Alternatively, a short circular walk taking about one hour can be made by keeping left on the forestry road at the junction, and crossing the White Water. When just across the river, go left off the track along a shady track amongst the conifers and follow waymarks back to the car park. 2 miles/3.2 kms)

Above: A roe deer in the Glen Doll forest.

THE BALQUHIDDER ROAD
The Trossachs

Ledcharrie to Brig o' Turk 17¼ miles/27.6 kms

*'So far were the
Gregarach from lying
down to die as king
and Campbell planned,
that whoever attacked
one of their number had
still to reckon with
vengeance taken.'*

W.H. Murray, *Rob Roy
MacGregor. His Life and Times*,
1982

The route described here was followed for centuries by those who sought a quieter way through the Trossachs, whether on legitimate business or otherwise. It passes through Balquhidder, a village closely associated with the Clan MacGregor, the 'Gregarach', and its most famous son, Rob Roy.

When history becomes 'heritage', anything goes. And for Scotland's Trossachs area the heritage industry has fixed on Rob Roy MacGregor as the linchpin of a publicity drive that has been gift-wrapped with bloodless sentimentality. The man himself might have relished the attention. He was custom-made for it even in his own lifetime, and was famously portrayed by Sir Walter Scott, and earlier by the more cynical Daniel Defoe. Bad blood never got in the way of the Rob Roy story.

Bluntly put, Rob Roy may have been a cattle thief, an extortionist, and a dissembler. He spawned one son who seems to have been a psychopath, and who was certainly a murderer and kidnapper. But Rob Roy was also a flamboyant survivor in a brutal society that no amount of tartan tourism can reconstruct as anything other than a political and economic jungle. And his apologists cite numerous examples of Rob Roy's compassion, good sense and redeeming wit. The case rests on its merits as a great story, nicely filled out with colourful myth.

The Clan MacGregor claimed direct descent from the hereditary kings of Scotland and the Celtic Clan MacAlpin. 'S *Rioghal mo Dhream'*, My Blood is Royal', was the inscription on

*The view back north into Glen
Dochart from the pass at
Lochan an Eireannaich.*

the MacGregor arms. Such self-esteem did not guarantee survival in medieval Scotland. Gradually the MacGregors were dispossessed of lands and status by the machiavellian Clan Campbell, the Murray earls of Atholl, and the Stuarts. These senior clans were feudal and dynastic and sought to legitimize and extend hereditary landholdings by obtaining Crown Charters. Marking out land boundaries was arbitrary, and it was easy, for the Campbells especially, to include written claim to peripheral lands of lesser clans. The MacGregors might have thought themselves kings; the Campbells were empire builders.

The MacGregor response to duplicity and dispossession was vigorous, if perhaps tardy. The clan's career became bloodied by cattle-raiding, outrage and mutual betrayals as it struggled for a foothold amidst the unforgiving mountains and against its wolfish neighbours. The Campbells manipulated events through political intrigue and through false claims and charters. By the middle of the sixteenth century the MacGregors were dispersed throughout the Trossachs area from their hereditary lands of Glenorchy.

There was toleration of MacGregor lawlessness when it suited others. But in 1602 a blood feud between the MacGregors and the Colquhouns, a lowland clan, escalated from minor incident to pitched battle in which eighty Colquhouns died, and hundreds of their cattle were lifted. The incident incensed King James VI, who had been cleverly influenced by Campbell advice. The King issued an order to 'extirpate Clan Gregor and to ruit oot their posteritie and name.' It was a chilling proclamation that would be echoed ninety years later before the Massacre of Glencoe, and it proved that Stuart kings were every bit as ruthless as their own future usurpers.

Acts of the Privy Council banned the use of the name MacGregor and prohibited the clansmen from carrying arms. The King's loyal subjects were called upon to 'slauchter and mutilate them and to raise fyre'. Bounties were offered and the MacGregors were hunted down with mastiffs. The women of the clan were branded on the cheek; homes were burned; the clan chief was tricked into honourable surrender, then executed. Clan Campbell connived at all of this in spite of having allegedly goaded the MacGregors to action against Campbell's own enemy, the Colquhoun, in the first place. The politics were Byzantine, the treachery was grotesque. But it is unvarnished history, rather than heritage.

The ferocious persecution of the MacGregors is proven. The clan became known as the *Clann a' Cheathaich*, the Children of the Mist, a sentimental title that hardly encapsulates the attempted genocide of a people. It was as if the ruling parties of Scotland had decided that the MacGregors were surplus to requirement. Yet the clan survived, and by Rob Roy's birth in 1671 the Gregarach still clung to their dignity and to some land. They had survived by becoming skilled cattle thieves and by being useful to others in times of war. Blood ties with their persecutors ensured survival also. Rob Roy's mother was a Campbell.

The most famous of the MacGregors seems to have had a model upbringing, relative to the manner of the times. He was clever and personable, courageous and troublesome; and he was indoctrinated from his earliest years with the cattle-lifting ethos of his clan, that saw no crime in stealing a neighbour's beasts.

What made this eccentric cattle culture more bizarre was the system of 'black mail' by which noted fighters like the MacGregors were made official protectors, the 'Watch', of other people's beasts – for a price. The 'black' referred to the cattle; the 'mail' meant rent. It was protection money by any other name. Yet protecting their client's animals from raiders did not prevent the men of a Watch from travelling out of their own lands to raid someone else's herds. The Scots were ever audacious when it came to getting by.

The combination of a lively intelligence, cattle-driving skills, both legal and illegal, and fighting experience made Rob Roy a formidable figure. He was also a cultured man with a boisterous wit and he seems to have been trustworthy to the deserving, while tricking those who could bear it most. He kept to the romantic Stuart side during the Jacobite rebellions but trimmed to the other side when it was politic to do so, and when action was not required.

Rob Roy was always adventurous. He cocked a snook at the lordly and trounced the bureaucratic. He kept up a thirty-year feud with the powerful Duke of Montrose, who accused Rob Roy of stealing the £2,000 he had given him for buying cattle, a charge denied always by the MacGregor. Rob Roy seems to have been captured regularly by his enemies, from whom he escaped just as regularly by such *Boys' Own* devices as leaping into freezing rivers and swimming off underwater, leaving behind his tartan plaid for target practice. He was said to have exercised a Godfather-like influence, twisting the arms of local landowners who bullied poor tenants, and responding to appeals from distant kinsmen and friends who needed heavy backing in disputes. The rattling good tales are legion.

To urbane contemporaries, this was all fine romantic stuff, and the lionizing of Rob Roy MacGregor began in 1723 when Daniel Defoe published a pot-boiling pamphlet called *Highland Rogue*. Defoe had never met Rob Roy, who would have terrified him in the flesh. Like all good hacks Defoe had dined with sophisticated Scots who brimmed with anecdote and safe gossip about the

Highland rogue. The book launched an enduring myth. Rob Roy's business reputation benefited from it, and in some ways the public image of lovable rascal secured him a peaceful old age on the Braes of Balquhidder. Scott added a homelier gloss to the Rob Roy image, and our own age has made a two-dimensional parody of it.

Rob Roy lived at various homes throughout the Balquhidder area. He died in 1743 at his beloved Inverlochlarig at the western end of the Balquhidder valley. He was sixty-three, a good age for the times. For three years, during the period of the 1715 Jacobite Rebellion, his family home was at Auchinchisallen in Glen Dochart. This is a few miles/kilometres west of Ledcharrie from where our walk begins. Between the two, and close to Ledcharrie, is Luib, a grassy area that was used as a grazing 'stance' by cattle droves coming from Skye and Lochaber. The cattle were then driven from Ledcharrie to Balquhidder and on to Brig o' Turk and Aberfoyle because this route over the hills was toll-free. Rob Roy probably used the route on some of his many journeys. It is a well-attested right of way and would have been the ideal route south through the Trossachs area for anyone whose business was better conducted along unpopulated ways.

There is no continuously clear path from Ledcharrie to Balquhidder today, but the first mile/kilometre and a half of the way is obvious, where it climbs from the A85 alongside the rattling Ledcharrie Burn. In early summer the wet ground is carpeted with buttercups and starred with the blooms of white bog cotton, the lovely marsh orchid, and the elegant bog asphodel. The stream is boisterous in its higher reaches, where it pours through a series of small ravines and floods over slabby rock. Dwarf birch grows on the grassy banks, and the heather is starred with yellow tormentil.

The peace of the hills is no longer disturbed by the clatter of trains on the old Crainlarich line that now lies abandoned along the hillside. There is a lonely atmosphere where the wide basin of the upper glen is reached. Ahead, the way seems barred by the enclosing rim of the hills of Creag Ghlas and Meall an Fhiodhain on the east, and the outliers of The Stob to the south. High on the green wall of the eastern hills the cleft of the pass to Balquhidder becomes more obvious as height is gained. It is secretive enough, however, and the path to it is not well defined.

On the lower slopes of Creag Ghlas lies a scattering of ruined buildings. They are marked by a small cairn built as a shelter and they are said to mark the site of shielings, the temporary homes where women and children tended grazing cattle throughout the summer. But their form and position may suggest an older settlement. The name Ledcharrie translates as 'the plain of the monument', and there are prehistoric burial mounds in Glen Dochart. From this site there are fine views westward to the great peaks of Ben More and Stobinian, the highest hills of the area. To the north beyond Glen Dochart lie the peaks of Meall Glas and Meall a' Churain crowning a green wave of hillside.

Our route leads from the ruins along a narrow path that angles steadily up the hillside. It leads comfortably into the cleft of the pass and onto the bleak Lochan an Eireannaich. There is a dramatic change of scenery here. The smooth northern flank of Meall an Fhiodhain hides from view its spectacular southern face of Creag an Eireannaich, where glacial action has torn apart the dark rock and has spilled blocks and boulders into the grassy col beneath. Some of the blocks are massive. Predictably, the largest has earned the name of 'Rob Roy's Putting Stone'. It is more likely that the MacGregor, or his men, skulked here in rough shelter to escape the wrath of their enemies, or that they penned stolen cattle in the grassy hollows until they could be resold out of the district.

The top of the Putting Stone is bedded with heather but can be gained only by steep rock-climbing. *Eireannaich* means 'Irishmen', and it has been suggested that the loch got its name from fifth-century Irish missionaries who were active in the Balquhidder area. *Meall an Fhiodhain* means the 'hill of witness'. The old names of the Highlands are primary sources but are frustrating because they are often inexplicable.

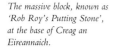

The massive block, known as 'Rob Roy's Putting Stone', at the base of Creag an Eireannaich.

From the base of the shattered cliff a path leads steeply downhill into the crammed plantations of Kirkton Glen. To the south-east

Rob Roy's grave at Balquhidder Kirk. 'Outside the ruin lies the old rascal's memorial . . .'

the blunted summit of Ben Ledi dominates the skyline. The open ground soon turns into conifer plantations, where savage felling has left a devastated landscape. The path runs down the edge of the felled area. To the right is a graveyard of broken timber; to the left, the dead lower branches of the remaining trees hang over the path like claws. You have to clamber over fallen tree trunks and tangled woods to reach the forestry track below. The track to Balquhidder now runs through featureless stands of conifers that shut out the light and discourage growth at ground level. But there is interest enough here, and roe deer frequent the edges of the trees. There is also a famous ghost – an armed huntsman with deerhounds, perhaps clutching in his fist the Hanoverian government's orders of fire and sword against Rob Roy and the MacGregors.

Balquhidder is reached at its darkly handsome church. This rather severe Victorian building of the 1850s has a pleasant interior with some fine artefacts. A large wooden cross is suspended dramatically above the altar. The church is much loved, and is cared for by a group of impressive patrons and hard-working 'Friends'.

Adjoining the present building are the sparse ruins of an earlier church, dating from 1631 but standing on twelfth-century foundations. An elaborate bell-cote crowns the surviving wall. A number of interesting memorials also survive: they are mainly of the Maclaren family who were the hereditary clan of Balquhidder and who suffered brutally, at times, at the hands of the MacGregors, although their own record was bloody enough. Rob Roy attended the old church occasionally, but true to form, stole the church bell and installed it in his sons' school on Loch Tayside, where he felt it would be of more use. The bell was returned in 1951. Outside the ruin lies the old rascal's memorial tomb. Here Rob Roy is commemorated defiantly, alongside his wife Mary and two of his sons, by a modern inscription that proclaims 'MacGregor despite them' – a slight hint of foot-stamping bravado perhaps, but in keeping with his indomitable spirit and his attachment to Balquhidder.

One meaning of Balquhidder is 'the township in the back country' a name that hardly does justice to the village's surroundings. Balquhidder lies on the banks of the River Balvag. To the west is Loch Voil, where raw mountains merge with the fluidity of water and green woods. It is back country in the best sense, however. The A84 between Killin and Callander runs busily to the west down Bonnie Strathyre, and Balquhidder has weathered its fame because of the careful stewardship of its residents.

The road that leads us south towards Ballimore continues the unspoilt theme where it rises through Glen Buckie past cottages in the characteristic single-storey Scottish vernacular style. This was a busy enough 'road' in its day. The pass into Gleann nam Meann is not a difficult one. It would have been used by local people, by cattle drovers, travelling packmen, soldiers, and, like Jock's Road in Glen Doll, by whisky smugglers avoiding punitive excise duties.

From Ballimore the path leads up Gleann Dubh through a landscape of birch and rowan trees above the Calair Burn. The burn can get into a fine old froth after rain. This whole area was once well farmed, reflecting its position on a major hill route. The upper glen is enclosed by characteristic Trossachs hills, their mottled slopes like velvet brocade blurred by soft browns and greens. It is wet county but all the more evocative for it. The air is often heavy with the scent of drenched grass and sweet decay. The hills are swathed with dark heather and bilberry, and with mint-green fern that turns red as rust in autumn.

The glen opens out into a wide basin below the rocky shoulder of Bealach a' Chonnaidh. Ruined shielings and the grey mossy walls of old sheep pens mark this as having been a valued grazing area. Today sheep still feed here. But on the river flats below the bagatelle pattern of fenced sheep pens strikes an incongruous note. Our path leads easily to the head of the glen and on into Gleann nam Meann and the long descent to the junction with Glen Finglas. The land has been subdued here by the intrusion of estate roads and by the flooding of the lower valleys to provide reservoirs.

Yet the history of the area has not been subdued. Nor has its literary use. Glen Finglas served as the background to Walter Scott's ramble of a romance, *The Lady of the Lake*, a poem that brought the first influx of tourists to the Trossachs. It was also in Glen Finglas that a band of MacGregors clashed violently with the Colquhouns in the key dispute that produced the fugitive life of Rob Roy MacGregor and the 'Children of the Mist'. Today, in spite of its reservoir and surrounding conifers, tumbling storm clouds can still douse Glen Finglas in the kind of brooding light that suffused Scott's poetry.

The hills run out at Brig o' Turk, from where connections by road can be made to Callander or to Loch Katrine and Aberfoyle. A walking route leads over the hills from a mile/one and a half kilometres west of Brig o' Turk to Aberfoyle, but it is short-lived and merges with the public road over the Duke's Pass. This is the heart of the Trossachs. To the east lie Loch Venacher and Callander; west lies the pass leading to Loch Katrine and the junction of several routes over the 'Cross Hills', the Na Troiseachan, a local name anglicized to become 'the Trossachs' and now applied to the wider tourism area. From here on, modern tourism and the motor car have captured Rob Roy's territory . . . despite him.

THE BALQUHIDDER ROAD
Information

Distance 17¼ miles/27.6 kms

Maps OS Landranger 51 (Loch Tay);
OS Landranger 57 (Stirling & the Trossachs)

Nature of Walk A varied and absorbing walk
through the Balquhidder hills. Fit walkers
should be able to complete the walk in a day.
The route is indistinct from south of
Ledcharrie to the Lochan an Eireannaich pass.
Compass work may be required here. Clothing
and equipment should be for mountain
conditions. Winter weather in the Trossachs
area can be severe. There may be shooting in
the area from August to mid-October.

Accommodation At Callander and Killin.
Some accommodation at Balquhidder and
Kingshouse. Camp sites on the A84, 1 mile/
1.60 kms north of Kingshouse, and at
Strathyre.

Transport Ledcharrie can be reached from
Callander and Killin by service buses and by
post bus. Service bus and post bus connect
Brig o' Turk with Callander, the Trossachs
and Aberfoyle. Timetables from Visitor Centre
at Callander and Callander post office.

Further Information Trossachs Visitor
Centre, Callander, tel. (0877) 30342.

Start Ledcharrie Farm OS 506281. There
is limited parking in a lay-by just west of
Ledcharrie, on the west side of the bridge.

1 Go quietly and directly through the
farmyard and through a gate. Cross open
ground ahead and follow an earthy track round
rabbit-infested hillocks. Reach a gap in a wall
and continue over wet ground. Go under a
disused railway bridge, then continue amongst
grassy knolls, and close to the Ledcharrie Burn,
to reach a wire fence where the burn runs
through small ravines. (1¼ miles/2 kms)

2 *The following section is not well defined and
directions are detailed. They should be followed
carefully, especially in poor visibility.* Go left

*Above Ledcharrie looking south towards Meall an Fhiodhain.
'There is a sweetness in the air . . .'*

alongside the wire fence for a short distance,
then go right over the fence and through a gap
in a wall. Bear up right to a cairn and then
follow a path over a heathery knoll and past a
small wooden post. Join a track and follow it
to where it fades. Bear off left along a faint
path. At this point you should be abreast of a
dry-stone wall down to your right, and should
be veering well away from the Ledcharrie
Burn. Aim for a second short post on a grassy
knoll. In clear weather the sweeping skyline
between Creag Ghlas and Meall an Fhiodhain
is prominent to your left. Your objective is the
green pass in the skyline lying 170 degrees
from the second post. Keep on this line to
reach a third short post. (¾ mile/1.2 kms)

3 About 100 yards/90 metres uphill and to the
left of this post is a prominent hollow cairn.
Make for this cairn, then continue for a short
distance uphill from the cairn to pass the low
ruin of a building, to reach a larger ruin. Just
below this larger ruin, a small path traverses the
hillside. Go right along this path, cross a small

stream, and contine on the path as it rises steadily to gain the green pass on the skyline. At the head of the pass, go through a gate in a fence and skirt Lochan an Eireannaich to reach the huge boulders below the southern face of Meall an Fhiodhain at OS 515244. (1½ miles/ 2 kms)

4 From the largest boulder, follow the path ahead for a short distance down a grassy spur, then bear sharply right to pick up a good path that winds steeply down to a stile in a forestry fence. Beyond the stile, follow the path down left to cross a stream. Continue on a path flanked by conifers to the left and an ugly cleared area to the right. Clamber over shattered trees and pass a cleft boulder to reach a junction of three forestry roads. Keep ahead down the descending road through Kirkton Glen, and continue ahead through other junctions to reach a stile in a fence. (3 miles/4.8 kms)

5 Go right along a path, then, at a junction, go left to reach Balquhidder Kirk. From the kirk keep right down a path to the public road. Turn right for about 150 yards/135 metres, then go left by the telephone box and bus

halt and cross the River Balvag. Follow the narrow road to Ballimore Farm. (2½ miles/ 4 kms)

6 Cross the fine bridge over the Calair Burn. The route goes up, right, immediately, but the steep bank here is heavily eroded. To minimize further erosion, make a short detour ahead to less steep ground, and double back to gain the path. Continue uphill to detour round a wet ditch, then go through the wider of two gates. Bear up left and follow the path steadily up Gleann Dubh, to where the path forks below the rocky height of Bealach a' Chonnaidh. Keep to the lower path and then continue above a wide green strath and on up the glen to reach a gate at the summit of the pass at OS 510150. (2½ miles/4 kms)

7 Beyond the gate descend past a cairn on the right, and follow a path alongside the stream for a short distance, then bear up right to join the estate track. Follow the track steadily downhill, keeping left at the junction with the track from Glen Finglas, and with the reservoir on your right. Join a surfaced road that leads down to Brig o' Turk. (5¾ miles/9.2 kms)

Glen Finglas reservoir above Brig o' Turk.

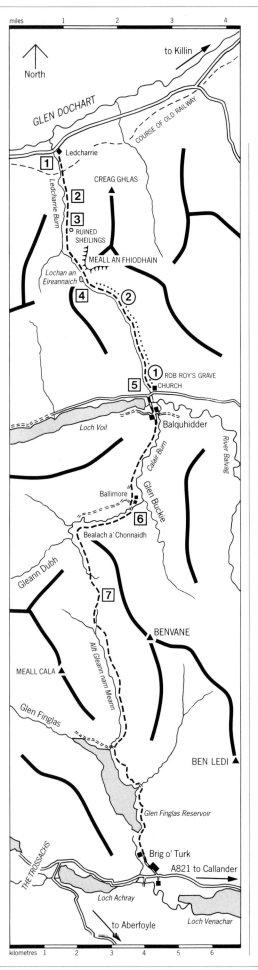

CIRCULAR WALK 5½ miles/8.8 kms

The area is poorly supplied with paths, other than forestry tracks, that lend themselves to circular walks. However, the attractive Lochan an Eireannaich and the giant boulder known as Rob Roy's Putting Stone can be reached fairly comfortably from Balquhidder, although you will have to return by the same route. Allow three hours.

Start Balquhidder. Limited parking by the church. Visitors should bear in mind the needs of church-goers, especially when services are scheduled.

1 From the west side of the church, follow a path into the woods. Turn right at a junction. A short distance along the path go left over a stile. Continue steadily uphill through Kirkton Glen on a broad forestry track for about 2½ miles/4 kms to reach an open area where the track diverges to right and left.

2 Keep ahead, leaving the track to follow a path uphill, with conifers to the right and a cleared area to the left. Fallen trees and debris obstruct the path in places. Cross a stream by a fence, and a short distance further on, go over a stile in the fence to follow a path steeply uphill. This leads to the huge boulders below Meall an Fhiodhain, and then Lochan an Eireannaich. Return to Balquhidder along the same route.

THE PEEBLES DROVE ROAD
Scottish Borders

Peebles to Ettrick 22 miles/35.2 kms

This fine walk through the Scottish Borders follows one of the main cattle-droving routes that were in use until the late nineteenth century. The route leads along a walled track onto the smooth-backed ridgeway to the south of Peebles, descends to St Mary's Loch in Yarrow, then crosses the hills to the lovely Ettrickside.

The droving trade was Britain's more sober version of the flamboyant 'cowboy' economy of the American West. It is of greater antiquity and has not been overlaid by a Hollywood gloss. Yet, in Scotland especially, there was a colourful and robust element to the trade – an element that attracted Scott and Stevenson and can still fire the imagination of the modern traveller.

The hardy cattle of the Highlands and Islands were driven to southern markets from as early as the fifteenth century. Cattle had always been the basis of a subsistence economy in the raw glens of the north, where a clan's wealth was measured by the number of beasts that speckled the green straths of the hills and grew fat on the sweet grass of summer shielings.

The harshness of the climate and the lack of winter feed meant that many cattle were slaughtered in late autumn, and the meat salted down. Those that survived struggled through the winter, and most were skeletal by the tardy spring, when they had to be lifted to their trembling feet and supported to grass. At times their starving keepers drew blood from them, and mixed it with oats and onions to produce the nutritious 'black pudding', a winter staple.

As always, the stealing of cattle was rife amongst the clans. It was a way of life in the turbulent Borders, from where raids were made deep into England. But as commerce increased, landlords and clan chiefs took cattle in lieu of rent, and began sending surplus beasts to markets or 'trysts' in the Scottish lowlands. The great trysts of Crieff and Falkirk became the autumn clearing ground for the sturdy little black or brown cattle of the north, the famous 'kyloes' that had been driven through the mountain passes and over the bulking shoulders of the Grampians during late summer, by men who were a match for such hard country and hard trade.

From the trysts, the beasts were gathered into larger droves and taken south to England. Herds could be in excess of two hundred head of cattle and the distance covered each day was about twelve miles/nineteen kilometres. The cattle grazed at overnight 'stances' so that they were delivered to the markets in good fettle. Having begun their journey in the Western Isles or the far Highlands they would reach the London markets after a few weeks recovering from the ordeal and being fattened on the rich grasslands of East Anglia and Essex. The overall trip could take several weeks.

Statistics reflect the magnitude of the trade. In 1663, state papers recorded that 18,574 beasts passed through Carlisle with toll dues paid. Many thousands more entered England across the lonely border hills and avoided customs. By the 1790s, over a hundred thousand head of cattle from Scotland, Wales and Northern England were being sold annually at London's Smithfield market. The trade was so important that legitimate drovers were exempted from the Disarming Acts that followed the Jacobite Rebellions of 1715 and 1745, and were allowed to carry arms to protect themselves and their beasts from cattle thieves.

The trade reached its climax during the early part of the nineteenth century. Thereafter, increasing numbers of beasts were transported by boat and then by rail, until modern road transport became the norm.

The drovers followed lines of least resistance across the great hills. But their routes were controlled by other factors. They needed good grazing on the way, and sought to avoid toll bridges and other charges imposed for grazing. Over time, free passage became constrained by local farmers and landowners who resented their improved ground being grazed by passing cattle that ranged widely and 'streamed' across the land. Thus, on the foothills south of Peebles the drove road was contained between stout stone walls, known as 'raiks'. These walls enclosed a droving space of between sixty and one hundred feet/eighteen to thirty metres. They survive today and can be seen from the heart of the town as grey walls enclosing a broad ribbon of green that snakes up the eastern slopes of Glensax, as tempting a sight for the walker as any open road.

Peebles is a confident town, in line with its history as one of the great textile centres of the Southern Uplands. Its broad High Street retains the irregular pattern of a Borders' market town. Many of its buildings are of rough-cheeked whinstone, as resilient and reassuring as the citizens themselves. At the bottom of High Street stands the imposing Old Parish Church with its castle-like crow-step gables and crown steeple. The River Tweed glides sweetly below.

Peebles was a walled town in the sixteenth century; its history has been as hot-blooded as that of other Border towns; its citizens have been distinguished. William and Robert Chambers of publishing and encyclopedia fame were born in the crooked little street of Biggiesknowe. The explorer Mungo Park practised medicine in chambers in Peebles High Street, and the novelist John Buchan was closely associated with the town.

The natives of Peebles are known as 'gutterbluids', while 'stooryfoot' serves for dusty-footed incomers, a description that might have fitted the passing drovers and their charges. It is likely that the fastidious yet hard-headed burghers of Peebles would have coped efficiently and profitably with the rough-skinned droving trade. The town would have been less salubrious than it is now, its streets a satisfying welter of muck and blowing straw and raucous humanity. There was a richer texture to its townscape and to the misty riverside flats of Walkers Haugh and Ninian Haugh and the ancient 'Tuede Grene', the traditional overnight grazing stances used by the herds.

From Peebles, the drovers followed the line of the present Springfield Road to where it divides at the mouth of Glensax. From here the modern walker follows a wooded path through Gipsy Glen. It is a stiff climb to the high ground on a grassy incline that two hundred years ago would have been mired or dust-stirred by the scrabbling feet of cattle, full of grass from a night's grazing. Steam would be rising from their shaggy flanks and the air would be filled with lowing complaint and the hoarse shouts of the drovers, themselves sore-headed and round-bellied from the Peebles' ale houses. The drovers were described as 'great stalwart, hirsute men . . . shaggy and uncultured and wild' – a fair match for their charges. Their clothing was coarse linen and homespun

On the drove road looking north towards Peebles.

tweed. Some went barefoot or were roughshod, and they smelled of cattle and the damp open air. Modern walkers might follow timidly in such footsteps.

Today, the way is more easily managed than in the wake of fractious cattle. The path soon levels off on the ridgeway shoulder of Craig Head, from where the views back north are splendid. Peebles lies comfortably in its wooded setting with the swell of the Pentland Hills beyond. For the Highland drover, a last backward glance would have been unsettling as he turned his face reluctantly to the south, keen to finish the drove, but never prepared to push the cattle too hard.

It is along this first stretch of the route that the form of the drove road is best preserved. The flanking walls twist and turn across the shoulder of Kailzie Hill, their linear pattern a delight to the eye. They cease abruptly at the conifers of West Cardrona Forest, from where there was less need to contain the cattle as they streamed across the rough hilltops ahead.

From Kailzie the route winds satisfyingly over the broad tops of Kirkhope Law and Birkscairn Hill. There are sweeping views across the deep trench of Glensax to the Heights of Hundleshope and Glenrath. The mottled slopes of the hills are imprinted with geometric shapes of bright green, where the ground has been burned to improve growth. This is grouse country, and the sharp, whirring flight and rasping croak of alarmed birds can be a sudden intrusion from underfoot. On these heathery tops, the hen harrier and the golden plover are also present.

The drovers struck south from the line of the ridge at Stake Law, where the pale white heads of the mountain windflower nod amidst the heather and blaeberry sward. Our objective lies beyond the head of the Quair Water and the steep-sided Loch Eddy that lies below the green den of Glenshiel Banks. Ahead lies a rolling sea of border hills, featureless yet exhilarating because of its spaciousness. This is the heartland of Yarrow, of Ettrick and Teviotdale, a land that for centuries was hauled in and out of border disputes between England and Scotland, until the Act of Union in 1603 imposed a political boundary at least. The land remained lawless still, its leading families bred in the bone as 'reivers', the robbers of goods and cattle, and as moss troopers, the border bandits who were as hot-blooded as any Highland clansman in their defence of pride and of territory.

From the high ground, the drove road swings south through the fleecy conifers of Brakehope Rig and into the windy strath of the Douglas Burn. Here, five thousand years ago, dripping woodlands of oak and birch, alder, willow and ash, deep-filled the valley. There are no rough slopes or shattered crags in this land of sedimentary rock that has been worn down and smoothed by glaciation. But the rounded hills bulk large enough; they drew from the border clans a fierce possessiveness.

At Blackhouse stands the ruin of the sixteenth-century Blackhouse Tower, now invaded by ivy and twisted trees. These towers or 'peels' are a characteristic of the embattled land of the historic borders; their simple but effective defences were easily drawn round the warring factions. This one was the scene of a legendary slaughter, a story too casually retold, but irresistible and long-enshrined in a famous border ballad, *The Douglas Tragedy*. A Douglas daughter fled here with her lover, in the face of her family's disapproval of the match. They were pursued by her father and her seven brothers, and in the ensuing carnage, of 'bloody wounds that were redder than wine', all ten were killed. Today, the serenity of the hills seems to repudiate such awfulness.

From Blackhouse, the route south lies along the signposted Southern Upland Way. The route is well maintained: wooden walkways now span the boggier sections of the Hawkshaw Rigs, where the old drovers would have ploughed ankle-deep through the mire while the cattle ranged widely ahead. Isolated on the green slopes stands a circular sheep pen or 'stell', a common feature of these border hills. Curlews and lapwings forage on this wet ground, their haunting complaint matching the lonely space. Soon the path rises, and at the top of the slope a magnificent view of St Mary's Loch appears ahead.

The drovers would have drawn breath here, while the cattle bellowed uneasily at the sudden distance, before stumbling down the winding way to Dryhope. There is another ruined tower at Dryhope, roped and swathed in ivy and tangled branches like the Blackhouse ruin. Dryhope was the birthplace of the Flower of Yarrow, the beautiful but bellicose Mary Scott, ancestor of the novelist Sir Walter.

From Dryhope, the drovers would have crossed the river flats at the mouth of St Mary's Loch. From here, one route led over the rising ground of Peat Law and Altrieve Rig to the east of the loch to join the line of the modern road to Tushielaw in the Ettrick Valley. Today, there are no clear tracks or rights of way along this line. Instead, our route follows an alternative droving route that leads down the east side of the loch to Tibbie Shiels Inn.

There is level walking along this section, and it is made more pleasant by the nearness of the lapping water and by the elegant birch trees that frame the larch plantings of Thorny Rig. Scott enshrined the beauty of St Mary's Loch in *Marmion*: 'Far in the mirror bright and blue, Each hill's great outline you may view . . .' He was describing the rounded tops of Bridge End, Bowerhope

The drove road on Craig Head: 'grey walls enclosing a broad ribbon of green . . .'

Law and the Oxcleuch Rig, the glaciated hills that frame the head of the loch.

This is writers' country. Scott was a regular visitor to Tibbie Shiels Inn, along with many of Edinburgh's literary figures – great chatterers all. But the true native son was the Border poet James Hogg, the Ettrick Poet, whose effigy stands beside the busy main road just down from Tibbie's. Hogg's memory haunts the entire area. He was born at Ettrick, was shepherd at Blackhouse for many years, and died at Altrieve just over the hills from St Mary's Loch.

Tibbie Shiels was run by Isabella 'Tibbie' Richardson, née Shield, a redoubtable lady who survived into her nineties. The old building retains its nineteenth-century style and offers welcome refreshment before the next stage of the walk. It is probable that an inn stood here before Tibbie's day, and did brisk business with the droving trade. The grassy river meadows between St Mary's Loch and Loch of the Lowes would have made a good overnight grazing stance. They were deep with sweet grass and slaking water, and the drovers could bed down alongside the quieted cattle until the pale, misted dawn brought a ripple of movement through the herd. Dark nights were favoured. In moonlight, the kyloes wandered further afield and the drovers lost sleep.

From here, the line of the old drove road followed the south-eastern bank of Loch of the Lowes towards Riskinhope, then climbed steeply between Peat Hill and East Muchra to traverse the broad back of Pikestone Rig. There is a path and track along this course today, but it is indistinct by Riskinhope, and the recommended route from Tibbie Shiels is via the Southern Upland Way.

This route leads to the ruined buildings of Riskinhope Hope, from where there is a stiff climb onto Pikestone. There is a cruel atmosphere of abandonment here. The wrecked house stands dangerously decrepit amidst its skeletal copse of pines. On the eastern slopes, the fine stone walls of the inbys and sheep stells have proved more resilient. From the hard-won rim of Pikestone the neat geometry of the walls can be nicely viewed. Behind them the combed-back conifers of Fall Law rise to the skyline.

From beyond Riskinhope Hope, the route follows a broad-backed ridge to rejoin the drove route to Peniestone Knowe on the green crown of the lonely hills. Below lies the shallow trench of the Whithope Burn with its sheep pens and its scarred drainage channels. Beyond the col ahead our route bears off left along the old kirk path to Ettrick, once followed by mourners from Yarrow as well as by the drovers. There is no surviving evidence of path or track across this brimming waste. It was the kind of ground that the cattle would have ranged across freely, and disuse by cattle and people would lead to rapid resettlement of the shifting ground.

However, the route is obvious in clear weather, and the descent alongside the Kirk Burn leads pleasantly down towards the green strath of Ettrick and to Ettrick Kirk with its fine external staircase and its leafy churchyard. Here, amidst the damp grass and mouldering leaves, lie the graves of Tibbie Shiels and James Hogg. Tibbie lies just west of the church tower, and the Ettrick Poet lies several yards to the south. Some distance along the valley road, towards Ettrick post office, stands a rather formal memorial to Hogg, its stiffness quite out of keeping with the softness of Ettrickside.

From Ettrick, the drovers would have taken their beasts east by Deephope and the Hazel Rig to Buccleuch, and then south through Craik and Teviothead towards the English border. But Ettrick is a fitting place to end this walk. Vast conifer plantations carpet the southern hills and mask the lie of the land, and besides, the quiet hills of Ettrickside suit the memory of the little Highland cattle and their keepers. To the south lay the old enemy, and even in the peaceful heyday of the drovers, a Highlander would have felt uneasy as he drew south towards England and away from the enfolding security of the Border hills.

St Mary's Loch.

THE PEEBLES DROVE ROAD
Information

Distance 22 miles/35.2 kms

Maps OS Landranger 73 (Peebles & Traquhair); OS Landranger 79 (Hawick & Eskdale)

Nature of Walk The route is mainly through open, hilly country. *There are a few steep sections. Paths and tracks are good, but some indistinct sections may require compass work in misty conditions.* The route to Tibbie Shiels Inn can be walked comfortably in a day, and the whole route, as described, should be possible in a day for strong walkers. Clothing and equipment should be for hill conditions. *The weather can be wet and windy at any time, and may be severe outside the summer season.*

The route passes through sheep-rearing country and sections of grouse moor. Walkers are asked to bear this in mind at sensitive times of the year. Visitors are advised to contact the TIC at Peebles for initial guidance on grouse-shooting schedules from 12 August onwards.

Accommodation At Peebles. Pub and hotel accommodation at St Mary's Loch. Camp sites at Peebles; limited camping at Tibbie Shiels Inn, where refreshments are available and where there is a seasonal café on the A708. Accommodation at Ettrick. Caravan and camp sites near Ettrick.

Transport Peebles can be reached by bus from Edinburgh and from other main border towns. Bus connections further south are scant. Bus connections to Selkirk and thence to Peebles can be made from Tibbie Shiels Inn. A school bus runs from Ettrick to Selkirk during term-time. Timetables can be obtained from local TICs.

Further Information Tourist Information Centre, Peebles, tel. (0721) 720138 (seasonal); Scottish Tourist Board, Edinburgh, tel. (031) 332 2433.

Start Peebles

1 From Peebles High Street, go down the lane to the right of the TIC to reach Tweed Green. Bear left to cross the River Tweed by a footbridge. Cross the busy B7062 and bear left through Victoria Park along a surfaced path. Where the path ends, go up right to Springfield Road and turn left. Keep ahead to where the public highway ends at the entrance gateway to Glensax at OS 260393. (1½ miles/ 2.4 kms)

2 Keep ahead along a rough lane, signposted to Yarrow by Gipsy Glen. Cross the Haystoun Burn and continue up steps. Climb steeply uphill to reach open ground through a gate, then follow the walled drove road round the east side of Craig Head to another gate. (1½ miles/2.4 kms)

3 Follow the drove road steeply left, then continue across Kailzie Hill where the drove walls cease. Continue on a good track past a cairn and go over Kirkhope Law, Yellow Mire Hill and Birkscairn Hill, then descend past a signpost. Follow the fence on the left to where it ends and to where a wall comes in from the left. (3½ miles/5.6 kms)

4 *Throughout the following section, the route of the old drove road is not well defined in places.* Leave the main track and go left down the line of the wall for about 200 yards/180 metres, then go south towards the head of the valley below. In clear weather the objective is a green track seen crossing the flat ground to the south. In misty weather keep south and downhill to pick up the start of the track above Glenshiel Banks. Follow the green track for about 1 mile/ 1.6 kms until it is lost amidst peat hags. Bear right across some very wet ground to enter a conifer plantation. (1½ miles/2.4 kms)

5 Follow a faint path through grass, going south-west along the top edge of the conifers. (Note the round sheepfold down to the right.) The path veers left and uphill to reach a signpost to Craig Douglas. Turn right to reach

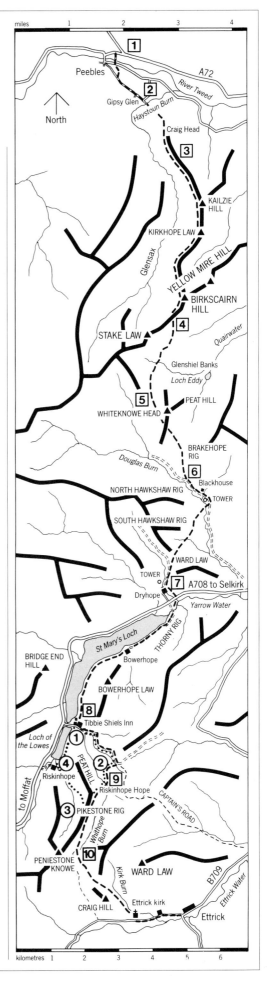

a yellow-arrow post, then go down a grassy ride and on to reach a stile. Continue down a heathery ride to reach a track going right. Follow this improving track to a junction with an estate road alongside the Douglas Burn at OS 273278. (2 miles/3.2 kms)

6 Turn left down the estate road to reach Blackhouse. Join the Southern Upland Way just past the ruins of the tower, by going right over a stile and footbridge. Turn left and follow a rough track uphill to where a signposted path veers off left. Follow the well-defined route to Dryhope over the eastern flanks of South Hawkshaw Rig. (1¾ miles/ 2.8 kms)

7 Where the Dryhope track reaches a gate in sight of the remains of Dryhope Tower, go left over a stile and follow signs to the A708. Cross the road and then a footbridge to follow the bank of the River Yarrow west to join the track across the foot of St Mary's Loch. Turn left across a bridge and follow the unsurfaced road along the southern shore of the Loch. Continue past Bowerhope Law on good paths to Tibbie Shiels Inn. (4 miles/6.4 kms)

8 Turn left outside the entrance drive to Tibbie Shiels and follow the track up past Crosscleuch and through trees to merge with Captain's Road. After about 1½ miles/2.4 kms, a sign points to Riskinhope Hope. The route leads out of the forest and down to the ruins of Riskinhope Hope. (1¾ miles/2.8 kms)

9 Cross a footbridge over the Whithope Burn and climb steeply uphill following guideposts. Continue along the broad back of Pikestone Rig via guideposts to where the Southern Upland Way merges with the old drove road at the foot of a grassy knoll at OS 243176. Go left along the side of Peniestone Knowe towards a low col, to reach a signpost to Ettrick Kirk and Scabcleuch. (1½ miles/ 2.4 kms)

10 From the signpost, bear left off the main track of the Southern Upland Way and follow a faint path across wet ground to a signpost and a stile in a fence. *The route to Ettrick kirk is indistinct from here.* Beyond the fence, bear up left 145 degrees, keeping quite low and then contouring the hillside to pass above a round sheepfold. Continue to a solitary post in the saddle ahead at OS 248154. From the post, go east-south-east downhill between Craig Hill on the right and Ward Law on the left. In clear weather, a prominent cairn on the southern flank of Ward Law is a useful identifier. Pass below a sheepfold to the right of the Kirk Burn, and pick up a path down to Ettrick Kirk and Ettrick. (3 miles/4.8 kms)

CIRCULAR WALK 5 miles/8 kms

The walk starts at Tibbie Shiels Inn and follows the main route to Riskinhope Hope and on along the Southern Upland Way to the junction with the old drove road. The drove road is then followed north to Loch of the Lowes and back to Tibbie Shiels Inn. The walk should take about three and a half hours.

Start A708 by Tibbie Shiels Inn (parking by A708)

1 Walk up the side road past Tibbie Shiels Inn and follow (8) as for main route to Riskinhope Hope.

2 Follow (9) as for main route to where the path merges with the old drove road at the foot of a grassy knoll at OS 243176.

3 Turn right and follow the track of the drove road north for about 2 miles/3.2 kms until the perimeter fence of Riskinhope above Loch of the Lowes. Turn right to follow the line of the fence above a plantation. At the end of the fence, strike off left and downhill to join the path leading off right alongside the loch.

4 Follow the path to a gate and then across a wooden bridge. Follow the river bank to a gate onto the approach road to Tibbie Shiels and turn left for the main road.

The graveyard at Ettrick Kirk.

HIGH STREET
Lake District

Penrith to Ambleside 25 miles/40 kms

This is an airy walk along the majestic ridge of High Street in Lakeland's eastern fells. The route follows the line of the Roman road that connected the forts of Brocavum at Penrith and Galava at Ambleside. This was the highest road that the Romans built in Britain, and its stony course survives today amidst a powerful and evocative landscape.

The Romans were nothing if not direct when it came to road building. Yet their famous road along the great ridge of High Street poses unanswered questions on several counts. There is still unresolved debate about the course of the road's northern section, and about the steep and untypical line of its southern descent into Troutbeck. But excavations have shown, unquestionably, that a road of typical Roman construction ran across the rising ground east of Ullswater and then struck unerringly along the great ridge to the south. It gave the name of High Street to the 2,719-foot/ 3,216-metre summit that lies alongside its highest point.

The Romans imposed control rather than conquest on Cumbria. They consolidated their grip on Southern Britain by the middle of the first century AD, and then subdued a menacing hinterland through military occupation of Wales and Northern England. The Lakes' area lay within the territory of the Brigantes, a loose coalition of British tribes that had submitted to the governor Cerialis in AD 73. But it was Agricola who established Roman control over the whole of Northern Britain. In AD 79 the Twentieth Legion, under his command, advanced north from Chester as part of a tripartite thrust into Scotland. Forts such as Brocavum were built along the line of that advance.

Brocavum guarded the crossing of the River Eamont at a junction with the trans-Pennine Roman road from York. The original fort was of timber and earthwork, but by the second century AD a more substantial fort had been built to house a thousand *auxilia*, the support troops recruited from Rome's client-tribes in Europe and South Britain. These auxiliaries were hardened campaigners though less well trained than the men of the legions who comprised the main fighting force of the Roman army. The auxiliaries' job was to maintain the rule of the Empire, and to garrison the frontier.

Far to the south of Brocavum, the fort of Galava at Ambleside was a later addition to a military network that was extended under the emperors Trajan and Hadrian. Forts were built at Ambleside, Ravenglass and Hardknott during the early years of the second century. They were part of a chain of coastal defences that were linked to Hadrian's Wall. Galava, like Brocavum, would have been a typical fort of timber buildings within turf ramparts. Such forts were later rebuilt in stone. Galava housed five hundred soldiers; they were part of a formidable force of ten thousand men who garrisoned twenty forts throughout Cumbria, an indication that the native Brigantes were not only restless but numerous, and that Rome feared the unknown outer darkness of Ireland, a short distance away across the water.

The bare foundations of Galava are all that survive today, and though unremarkable when compared with Hardknott and other sites, the uncovered sections, sunk amidst pale grass on the lakeside meadows of Windermere, have a forlorn dignity. The fort was frequently out of commission during the second century, when its troops were redeployed for service in Northumbria or Scotland – those troublesome 'reservoirs of savagery' so aptly described by the historian G.M. Trevelyan. But Galava was reoccupied each time the Lakeland Brigantes rose in their own savage revolts.

The Roman occupation of Lakeland was at its peak during this time. But Roman politics were in turmoil by the century's end, and troops were withdrawn wholesale from the north to support the British governor Clodius Albinus in his struggle with Severus in Gaul. The Caledonian tribes broke through Hadrian's Wall and struck into Cumbria. A triumphant Severus later recaptured the north, but further rivalries within the Roman hierarchy saw more neglect by the end of the third century and again in the fourth. Inexorably, the Empire lost its grip on Britain, and by AD 407 the last troops were withdrawn and the Lakeland forts abandoned.

After the withdrawal, the fabric of Roman occupation was unpicked ruthlessly across the land, although forts such as Galava and Brocavum were used in some form throughout the Dark Ages. Galava had a civilian population that would have remained within the environs. But the fort soon lost its significance as a central focus of the community, and its walls were quarried for use elsewhere. Brocavum was used for longer because of its strategic position at the crossroads of busy routes. But part of the fort was later incorporated into the entrance way and moat of Brougham Castle, and its stone was used in later extensions to Brougham.

Of all Rome's imprints on the north, Hadrian's Wall remains the most impressive survivor. But the Roman roads are perhaps the most enduring, and modern roads now often follow their courses. In the Lakes, the mountain route from Galava along the great ridge of High Street is a marvellous indication of Roman certainty. The route was a direct link from south Lakeland to the main Roman road to Carlisle. It followed a natural ridgeway that had probably been in use since prehistory.

The route would be little used by the Romans outside the summer campaigning season. Its twenty-five Roman miles, each one the famous *mille passus* of 1,618 yards/1,456 metres, were well within the capabilities of Roman soldiers for a day's march. But High Street was probably unpopular with the troops. It was longer, and in parts steeper, than the normal day's march of fifteen to twenty miles/twenty-four to thirty-two kilometres, and Roman soldiers were unlikely to view their surroundings with the same leisurely appreciation that we do today. To them this was simply hard marching country in a brutal landscape of often swirling mist and buffeting winds.

The pace would be a military one. The auxiliaries wore leather jerkins and half-trousers, light mailed tunics and iron helmets. They marched in sturdy leather boots and were armed with the *gladius*, the short fighting sword, and they carried two javelins. On the march their personal gear, which included a crescent-shaped trenching and turfing tool, was carried on a staff slung over the shoulder. On a route like High Street, maintenance was often carried out by soldiers on the march. Their hard work and the skill of the Roman engineers are reflected in the substantial fragments of road that survive today.

For the modern walker the journey along High Street is best started from Brougham Castle on a southbound route that leads through cultivated country and thence into the heart of the eastern fells. Brougham Castle is open to the public and is a splendid relic of medieval work. From its airy heights the outline of Roman Brocavum can be seen on the adjoining private ground. The Roman road struck west from Brocavum, along what are now modern lanes and highways.

A more enjoyable route for walkers today starts a short distance north of the castle, where a footpath leads west along the banks of the River Eamont. This is twentieth-century pastoral, although rafts of white-flowered crowfoot sprawl across the stream's surface as they might have done in Roman times, when the unhedged river meadows were grazed by sheep or cordoned off for the growing of wheat and barley.

The route leads over the medieval Eamont Bridge, a site steeped in history. It was here in AD 927 that Athelstan of Wessex reasserted Saxon power over the King of the Scots and over Northern Britain. He may have done so at the nearby Bronze Age earthwork known fancifully as 'King Arthur's Round Table'. The Scottish army of Charles II camped beside this earthwork in 1651, en route to annihilation by Cromwell at Worcester, and equally ill-fated Jacobite armies later marched through Eamont. Of the elusive 'King Arthur' there has been never a sign.

The Round Table earthwork may date from the Bronze Age

like the neighbouring Mayburgh Henge. Our riverside route passes close to Mayburgh – an impressive earthwork that once bristled with internal standing stones. Though Saxon in name, Mayburgh is certainly prehistoric. The Romans may have made use of the site, although the suggested line of their road passed several hundred yards/metres to the south. The road led on through the villages of Yanwath and Tirril before it turned south-west by Celleron towards the rising ground of the fells. This is the accepted line today, although some authorities suggest that a more direct eastern line from Brocavum to the open fells would have fitted the traditional straight alignment of Roman roads. For our purpose the route through Celleron is the most convenient. Above Winder Hall Farm, open ground is reached at last, and the track passes below the dwarfish scarp of Heughscar Hill. From here the first breathtaking views of Lakeland can be enjoyed.

The contrast with the dense pattern of cultivated ground already covered is startling. In the immediate distance lies the bland sweep of Moor Divock and Barton Fell, where the Roman road runs. But the eye is drawn to the west, down the gleaming tongue of tree-fringed Ullswater and its enfolding hills of Martindale and Matterdale, with the mighty Helvellyn beyond.

From Heughscar Hill the route descends to cross the old track that links Pooley Bridge to Helton. It then leads south across the grassy slopes to the stone artefact known locally as 'The Cockpit', a substantial remnant of a Bronze Age double-ringed circle. The site contains four burial mounds and has rocky projections at three cardinal points. The Cockpit is part of the extensive scattering of prehistoric relics on the peaty basin of Moor Divock. Most are related to burials, and the area was probably the sacred ground of a Bronze Age community based at the fortified camp on the summit of Dunmallet, the tree-covered conical hill above Pooley Bridge.

Such burial sites in high places resemble the barrow mounds of the Exmoor Ridgeway, and are of the same era. They strengthen the argument that the ridgeway line of High Street may have been used in pre-Roman times by carriers of the stone axeheads knapped at the Langdale outcrop on Pike o' Stickle at the heart of Lakeland. High Street was known during the medieval period as 'Brettestrete', the Briton's Road, an odd but significant label, harking back to pre-Roman times. What the Romans thought of the Moor Divock artefacts is not known. But in keeping with the Empire's sophisticated politics, such native sacred sites were generally left unscathed. The Romans conquered as much by assimilation as by military force.

The Roman road ran south-west from The Cockpit, following

a rising line over the cold green shoulder of Barton Fell. It is indistinct on the ground today, although sections of a raised embankment, known as an 'agger', can be identified, and at certain times of the year a strip of lighter-hued grass marks out the route. About two thirds of a mile/one kilometre along its track, excavations have revealed typical Roman construction. There was a foundation of flaky stones laid to a depth of two feet/sixty centimetres. The stones were about six inches/sixteen centimetres long and two inches/five centimetres thick, and were probably taken from the moorside quarry of Loadpot Hole on the summit of Loadpot Hill. These stones were covered by a layer of compacted peat that had a final top dressing of gravel. There were also kerbstones on either side of the road, although excavations some few miles/kilometres ahead revealed none.

The authentic line of this road is now difficult to follow through the chaotic ground, especially in misty conditions. The better option is to bear right from The Cockpit along a good track to where the high ground is regained over Arthur's Pike. The line of the Roman road is rejoined on The Dodd and Loadpot Hill, where the ruined chimneybreast of an old shooting lodge, Lowther House, points the way south.

From here the route is satisfyingly direct, a glorious tramp along the narrowing switchback of the High Street range, with the ever-changing skyline frieze of Lakeland's central peaks ahead. Half-wild ponies, black-skinned and breezy-maned, roam across the green spaces round Loadpot. At speed, they race arrow-straight

On Moor Divock: 'the eye is drawn to the west down the gleaming tongue of tree-fringed Ullswater . . .'

Looking south to Windermere from the Roman road across High Street: 'its course runs like a dried-up river bed across the plateau . . .'

ahead, covering in minutes distances that take us a plodding half-hour.

There is an exhilarating spaciousness about High Street. The eastern fells lack the craggy atmosphere of the Langdales, or of Helvellyn or Great Gable, and the flattened ridge retains a moorland form at first. But where the Roman road leads onwards across Wether Hill and High Raise, the deeply incised valleys of Haweswater, Ramps Gill and Hayeswater Gill, and the great bight of Riggindale Fells, lend a nice sense of the precarious. As height is gained by High Raise, the western fells unfold in all their glory. High Street itself is a massive hogs-back hill. From the nipped waist of the Straits of Riggindale the line of the Roman road strikes up High Street's western flank. Its rocky hardcore is still intact; its course runs like a dried-up river bed across the plateau south of High Street summit. It skirts the cairned 'beacon' of Thornthwaite, where you take in great gulps of the bubbling air.

This can be a windy place. On the edge of the Hayeswater cliffs, even in midsummer, a savage wind can roar out of the north-west. But a park-like peace can reign here also. The flat crown of High Street is known locally as Racehorse Hill. It was here that nineteenth-century shepherds gathered each summer to exchange wandered sheep, a ritual that grew into festival, complete with pony-racing and picnicking and incomparable views.

To the south, Windermere gleams in the distance. South-west is the far top of Coniston Old Man and the sweep of summits running north through the flat-topped Pike o' Blisco to Bowfell, Scafell and Great Gable fifteen miles/twenty-four kilometres away, beyond the striking bluffs of the Langdale Pikes. In the western foreground is the round-topped Stony Cove Pike, and directly below are the interlocking valleys of Hayeswater, Threshthwaite and Troutbeck.

The Roman road is said to have descended steeply from Thornthwaite into Troutbeck, down a stretch of track known as the Scot Raik. But on the high ground, a broad-backed ridge continues from Thornthwaite over the shapely summits of Froswick, Ill Bell and Yoke, and several authorities suggest that the Roman road may have followed this ridge, rather than descending into the Troutbeck Valley. A map of 1838 marks stretches of track across Yoke as 'Roman Road', and the ridge route does lead conveniently to the Garburn Pass, from where a rocky road continues towards Troutbeck or Windermere. This pleasantly mountainous route can be followed from Thornthwaite as an alternative to the accepted descent that we now follow into Troutbeck via the Scot Raik.

The Raik is a steep descent, and its gradient and sudden

divergence from the ridgeway do not readily suggest Roman planning. Roman engineers would surely not have abandoned high ground so quickly. The name 'Scot Raik' is enigmatic also. Most commentators suggest that it was named after a skirmish between local people and Scottish cattle raiders in the eighteenth century. A Scottish influence certainly extended to Penrith at the time, and the Border reivers of Annandale, of Ettrick and Teviotdale might well have lifted the fat cattle of the lakeshore. But the path was used also by cutters of peat and furze, and the old English word 'scot' means to score or gouge, and may explain the meaning of 'Scot Raik' better. 'Scot' is used elsewhere for natural features. There is a small stream below Troutbeck village known as the Scot Brook. No one has yet claimed that it ran red with the blood of Scottish cattle thieves.

Whatever its name, or its credentials as a Roman road, the Scot Raik gives a rapid descent down the steep sides of Froswick and into the delightful Troutbeck Valley. It has been suggested that the steep and precipitous way once traced more of a zigzag path, and that subsequent use and landslides have seen corners cut and the line of the track distorted. In wet weather the descent can be awkward and unpleasant.

The Raik drops over one thousand feet/three hundred metres in less than a mile/one and a half kilometres. At the bottom of the slope, the change of environment from bare upland to valley floor is emphatic. Ahead, tree-covered slopes enclose the valley of Hagg Gill. On the right is the high rounded hill of The Tongue. Reeds and bracken choke the wet ground where the Hagg Gill drains onto the flats. The path soon joins a broad track flanked by a good Lakeland wall.

A mile/one and a half kilometres further on, the track leads abreast of the spoil heaps of the abandoned Park Quarry, where we bear down left to cross a wooden bridge over the stream. The old workings slice into the hillside and are now choked with trees. Lakeland slate-quarrying reached its peak in the mid eighteenth century, when the expansion of English cities and towns led to increased demands for roof slates. Cumbrian 'tuffs' yielded a thick-grained slate of a greenish-purple hue. It was carried towards the coast by packhorse trains along the route that we now follow. Many Lake District quarrymen prospered elsewhere. One of North Wales's most successful quarry owners was William Turner, whose father was a Troutbeck slateworker.

The path from Park Quarry leads between the fellside and the tree-fringed river. Bustling streams drain from the slopes above. Where the ground opens out south of The Tongue, the handsome house of Troutbeck Park stands amidst trees on the opposite side

The remains of the Roman fort at Galava, Ambleside.

of the valley. Troutbeck Park was owned for a time by Beatrix Potter. Our route merges with a more substantial track that leads on to Long Green Head Farm, and across the grassy slopes of Moor Head and Sour Howes. The track here is level, undeviating and solid underfoot, and has been skilfully built up and embanked in places.

Looking back north from here, the domed hill of The Tongue fills the head of the valley, and the summits of Yoke, Froswick and Thornthwaite crowd the skyline. If the Roman soldiery did use this steep approach to High Street, then they must have dreaded the march north, especially in wild weather, when the fellside becks gushed down the slopes from out of the creeping mist, and the Scot Raik was awash with mud and loose stones.

The track continues south to Fusethwaite Yeat, from where some authorities believe the road would have continued to a junction with a Roman road between Kendal and Ambleside. But for a pleasant alternative we branch off below Sour Howes and follow a right of way through the Limefitt caravan and camp site, to reach the busy A592. From here, a left turn leads to Troutbeck's Jesus Church. An original church stood here in the late fifteenth century, its name reflecting the medieval devotion to sacred names. The present church has a fine stained-glass window designed by William Morris in the nineteenth century. Troutbeck was favoured by the pre-Raphaelites and their associates, and Ford Madox Brown and Sir Edward Burne-Jones are said to have contributed to the design of the window while on a visit to Morris.

There is no evidence that our route from here is a continuation of the Roman road. But it does follow part of the old road through the lovely Troutbeck village, then leads via the wooded Jenkin Crag to emerge close to the fort of Galava beside the reedy flats of the former bed of the River Rothay. The site of the fort, just south of Ambleside, lies within an area now called Borrans, a Scandinavian word for 'pile of stones', and possibly an indicator of the fort's decline during the Dark Ages. The foundations of the central section of the fort containing the commander's house, the headquarters and granaries, have been excavated, but the remains of the barracks are below grass. From this once busy place, the 'poor bloody infantry' of the Roman army set off for the fells, and the long haul over High Street, on a road that has endured for far longer than the Pax Romana ever did.

HIGH STREET
Information

Distance 25 miles/40 kms

Maps OS Landranger 90 (Penrith, Keswick & Ambleside); OS Outdoor Leisure 5 (The English Lakes – NE area); OS Outdoor Leisure 7 (The English Lakes – SE area)

Nature of Walk A challenging walk that follows field paths initially, then rises to traverse Lakeland's eastern fells before descending to the shores of Windermere. The route is best done over two days, but it can be split conveniently only at Pooley Bridge. Fit walkers can complete the route in a day if it is joined from Pooley Bridge, from where the distance to Ambleside is 21 miles/33 kms. Tracks and paths are good. Clothing and equipment should be suitable for mountain walking. *Weather conditions can be severe at any time of the year, and especially outside the summer season.*

Accommodation At Penrith, Pooley Bridge, Troutbeck and Ambleside. Youth hostels at Troutbeck and Ambleside. Camp sites at Pooley Bridge and Troutbeck.

Transport Rail and bus connections to Penrith from main centres. Bus connections to Ambleside from main centres. There is a summer bus service between Penrith and Ambleside via Keswick. Timetables from local rail and bus stations and TICs.

Further Information Tourism Information Office, Penrith, tel. (0768) 67466; National Park Tourist Information Centre, Pooley Bridge, tel. (07684) 86530.

Start Penrith

1 Brougham Castle and the remains of the Roman fort of Brocavum can be reached from the centre of Penrith by going down King Street, then by following Old London Road and Carleton Road to cross the A686. Continue down the road and lane beyond the Cross Keys Inn, and beneath an underpass. Turn up left for Brougham Castle. The notional course of the Roman road can be followed from Brougham Castle along the B6262 and the B5320, through Eamont Bridge and Yanwath to Tirril. A pleasant alternative is

The slopes of Hayeswater Gill from High Street.

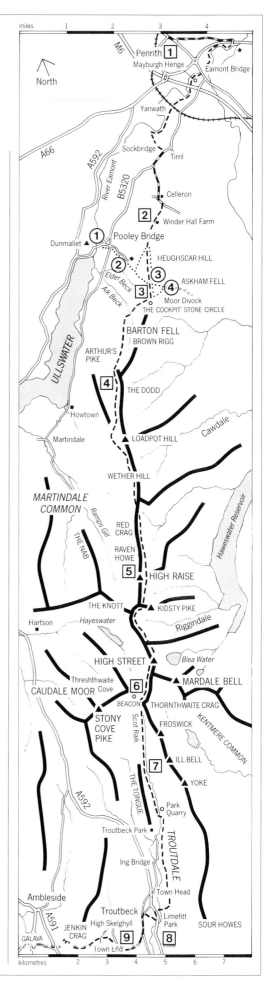

to go over the stile directly opposite the exit to
the underpass already mentioned, signposted
Eamont Bridge. Go along the left side of the
field to the River Eamont, then follow the
river upstream by delightful field paths through
Eamont Bridge, Yanwath and Sockbridge to
Tirril. The route is well signposted. From
Tirril, go west along the B5320 for ½ mile/
0.8 kms, then go left along a lane signposted to
Celleron. Turn left at a T-junction to reach
the entrance to Winder Hall Farm. (5½ miles/
8.8 kms)

2 Go up the drive to Winder Hall Farm, and
keep right of the farm buildings to follow a
stony track to open ground. Where the track
bends up left, leave it and keep ahead alongside
an old wall bordering the wood on the right.
Keep ahead where the wood ends to follow a
path towards the small limestone scarp of
Heughscar Hill. Join a good track by a cairn
and go right. (1 mile/1.6 kms)

3 Cross a junction with the track coming up
from Pooley Bridge, and follow the path
bearing left to reach the remains of the stone
circle known as The Cockpit. *From here the true
line of the Roman road veers off left and over Brown
Rigg. The line is indistinct, although there are signs
of a raised 'agger' here and there. The going is rough
and the alternative route described here is the better
option.* From the stone circle, bear right over
the Elder Beck and continue along a stony
track that becomes grassier. The track dips
down to cross the rocky bed of the Aik Beck,
and soon reaches a cross junction. Turn left
and go up a broad grassy track to pass to the
left of the rocky top of Arthur's Pike. At OS
461200 join a sunken track that comes in from
the left. (2½ miles/5.6 kms)

4 Go right for a few yards, then bear off left
up a rising path that contours round the side of
Loadpot Hill for 1¾ miles/2.8 kms to reach
the meagre ruin of Lowther House at OS
456177. Continue due south on the grassy
track that leads over the twin mounds of
Wether Hill, then pass two small tarns at Red
Crag, to follow the track where it runs

between a line of old fence posts and a drystone wall. (4 miles/6.4 kms)

5 Where the wall ends and the line of posts veers off right, go right for a short distance then bear up left round the west side of High Raise. Descend to a col and go left where the track forks. Follow the faint track to where it joins a well-worn track, and turn right. Descend to a T-junction with another track and a flanking wall at the Straits of Riggindale. Turn left downhill, then go right through a gap in the wall and follow the stony track of the Roman road uphill and across the western flank of High Street. (Alternatively, the wall can be followed on its left-hand side to reach the summit of High Street. It is then followed to rejoin the Roman road just before Thornthwaite Beacon.) (3 miles/4.8 kms)

6 Continue to the beacon cairn at Thornthwaite. Go left from the beacon for about 200 yards/180 metres, then bear off right by a curved iron spar set into a boulder. Keep right of a rocky outcrop, and follow the line of the Scot Raik on a steep descent into the Troutbeck Valley. (2¼ miles/3.6 kms)

7 Go through a gate at the valley bottom, and continue through reedy ground to join a good farm track. At OS 425064 and abreast of the quarry spoil heaps on the left, go left through a gate. Cross Hagg Gill, then branch right, and continue south to pass Long Green Head farm. A mile/1.6 kms further on, above Limefitt caravan park, keep right at a fork in the track, go through a metal gate and go right by the Haybarn Inn. Continue through the caravan park to emerge onto the A592. (3¼ miles/ 5.2 kms)

8 From here, a pleasant route via Troutbeck can be followed to the site of the Roman fort at Galava. Go left down the A592, then, just before the church, go right up a stony track to Troutbeck village. Turn left; then, just past the post office, turn up right, then left, to follow a walled lane for ¾ mile/1.2 kms. (1½ miles/ 2.4 kms)

9 Leave the lane by a gate on the left, signposted Skelghyll and Jenkin Crag. Continue past High Skelghyll and into the trees of Jenkin Crag. After ⅓ mile/1 km follow a path down left to reach the A591. Cross the road *with care*. Go past the Water-head Hotel, then right along the lakeside road to reach the recreation park, beyond which is Borrans Field and the remains of Galava. (2 miles/3.2 kms)

CIRCULAR WALK 4½ miles/7.2 kms

A pleasant walk taking about two hours can be made from Pooley Bridge to Moor Divock, where the Roman road crosses a landscape which contains numerous prehistoric remains.

START at Pooley Bridge, OS 473245

1 Go left along the B5320 from the TIC at Pooley Bridge, then turn right along the lane signposted Howtown and Martindale. Keep ahead at a crossroads, and go up the lane signposted Roehead.

2 From the road end at Roehead, follow the rough track signposted Helton, onto the moor for a short distance, then turn up left on a grassy, rutted track to pass a large boulder after 50 yards/45 metres. Pass a stand of pines and reach a T-junction with a broad track. Turn right and follow the track downhill. *This is the line of the Roman road.*

3 At a cross-junction with the Pooley Bridge–Helton track, keep ahead and follow a grassy path to reach the double stone circle known as The Cockpit. From The Cockpit, go north-east across ground that can be very wet to reach the Pooley Bridge–Helton track by a signpost. *The area north of the Helton Track is particularly rich in prehistoric remains, including stone circles, burial cairns and stone rows.*

4 Turn left and follow the track back to Roehead and on to Pooley Bridge.

THE MONKS' TROD
North York Moors

Guisborough to Whitby 27 miles/43.2 kms

*'Bridging the
uncultivated wild
between England's
villages and little towns
ran the road trodden by
growing numbers of
men and horses.'*

Sir Arthur Bryant, *The
Medieval Foundation*, 1966

The theme of this walk is the paved causeway or 'trod', along which packhorses and people travelled dry-shod through the often muddy countryside of the North York Moors. The route crosses areas of open country and then leads through the green heart of Esk Dale.

Before the nineteenth century, travellers in Yorkshire had no need of waterproof boots or gaiters. When they wanted to keep their feet dry they laid miles of sandstone slabs across wet and muddy country. Reducing erosion was an added bonus. Tracks became 'trods', the paved causeway became the high and dry way.

The practice of 'paving' across wet ground dates from earliest times. Planks of alder and oak were used in some areas. In the Somerset Levels the Neolithic tracks that snaked across the mire were constructed of thousands of split logs, which were pegged into wooden crutches and laid on a bed of tree trunks and peat. It is mainly in North Yorkshire and the South Pennines area that paved flags were used to line pathways. The geology of these districts met the demand for manageable rock. In the Peak District millstone grit was readily available, and in North Yorkshire softer sandstone was easily quarried into slabs.

The use of paving stones in North Yorkshire increased during the monastic period, when the great abbeys of Whitby and Rievaulx, and the priories of Gisborough and Mount Grace became involved in agriculture, commerce and the transport of goods. The monastic houses were held by different orders: Whitby by Benedictines; Gisborough by the revivalist Augustinians; Rievaulx by the Cistercians. Abbeys and priories established routes linking them to their outlying farms, properties and churches. The abbeys also traded with each other, and monks travelled great distances on foot to buy wool and other commodities.

Gisborough Priory and Whitby and Rievaulx Abbeys are said to have had a monopoly on the breeding of the Chapman, Jaeger and Galloway horses used for pack-carrying. In the late fourteenth century Whitby had a team of sixty packhorses with which the abbey's fisheries distributed their catches throughout the district. Rievaulx had salt pans on the coast from where local areas would have been supplied by packhorse. From the twelfth century there were iron-smelting 'bloomeries' in Esk Dale. Raw ironstone and ingots were transported by packhorse. Lime and coal were also carried, and the traffic in farm produce was extensive. Whitby had markets and an annual fair from the middle of the twelfth century, and in 1263 Gisborough Priory was granted a weekly market and annual three-day fair. The markets depended on regular traffic, by packhorses and travellers, from the moorland villages.

Opposite: Lovely Lealholm.

It seems certain that an extensive network of paths and trackways existed during the monastic period. Many of them were paved. After the Dissolution of the monasteries, paved ways became more common as secular trade developed. The enterprising monks had set the pattern. Agriculture and industry grew, transport of goods expanded, and new products such as alum emerged.

Alum was used in a number of industries, including fulling, tanning and dyeing, and it was distributed widely by packhorse trains. By the seventeenth century, the processing of alum shale was well established round Guisborough town, and the story of its production in Yorkshire is a colourful one. Until then, the Pope had held a monopoly of alum production and had forbidden Christians to buy alum from any other than Italian producers. The method of production was complex and secret. During a 'Grand Tour' of Europe, Sir Thomas Chaloner, whose family had bought Gisborough Priory in 1550, noted that the vegetation and geology around Italian alum pits was similar to that of the Guisborough district. The enterprising Chaloner is said to have smuggled Italian workmen, and their production secrets, to Guisborough, where he was soon turning out good Yorkshire alum from local shale.

This early example of industrial espionage must have been particularly galling to Papal pride and purse, and Papal fire and brimstone were directed at the perpetrator. But Chaloner carried on with his profitable burning of Guisborough shale, and the industry was soon producing thousands of tons of alum, keeping the packhorse trains busy along the paved ways.

Such ways ensured all-weather passage throughout the North York Moors. Regular use of unpaved ways often resulted in serious erosion as the characteristic 'hollow way' or sunken lane of the English countryside demonstrates. John Farey, in his review of Derbyshire roads in 1807, complains of the poor state of the highway and of the habit that waggoners had of 'stranding' a route by forming new tracks alongside a badly rutted one. It became the practice to lay paved causeways along the raised edge of waggon routes so that foot travellers and packhorses could avoid the often flooded holloways. Flagging was extended to fields and woodlands and to routes between villages. Hundreds of miles of paved causeway were established during the seventeenth and eighteenth centuries in those parts of the country where slabby stone was available, and especially in North Yorkshire.

The causeways fell into disuse when roads and wheeled transport improved, and when railways made the packhorse redundant. Most of the paved ways were either ripped up for building stone, or covered by road surfacing. Steep pathways that are now staggered with broken edges and muddy pits are the emptied beds of old causeways, and in grass-choked combes handsome slab bridges are often all that are left of once continuous trods.

But many miles of paved causeway do still survive, sunk beneath the encroaching peat or overgrown by damp moss and matted vegetation. Some exposed stretches are famously known; others have been recently uncovered by the hard work of the National Park authorities. Still more survive precariously alongside metalled lanes, or wriggle their way across fields. Where these paved causeways punctuate the line of a route they are immensely appealing to the walker.

This walk seeks out surviving paved causeways along the course of a notional route between Gisborough Priory and Whitby Abbey – a route which may or may not have monastic provenance. The section betweeen Grosmont and Whitby was known as the Monk's Trod and is believed to be the line of a route that linked Whitby Abbey with Grosmount Priory.

The walk starts at the ruined Gisborough Priory. The priory's ruins are overpowered by the surviving arched east wall, which was retained by the Chaloner family as a gateway to the estate. The mouldings of the façade are intricate, and though eroded in places, they still reflect a gothic elegance that is typified by slender half-shafts. The surviving gatehouse is also impressive, and is a good starting point for our walk.

The west-facing scarp of Gisborough Moor must first be climbed through a tortuous web of forestry tracks from which deliverance onto the open moor is a relief. The path then leaves the gloomy wall of conifers behind, and runs through swathes of heather and bilberries. There are signs of adjoining sunken paths that run parallel to each other all the way to where the distinctive Hob Cross perches on its heathery mound. The cross is one of many such artefacts throughout the North York Moors.

Crosses and pillars were erected as waymarks, and many have distinctive inscriptions carved into them. Most were erected after 1711, when Justices ordered 'guide posts' to be set up at strategic points throughout North Yorkshire. Many stones have destination names carved into them, and there are some with quaintly carved hands pointing the way. Initials usually represent the names of adjoining parishes or the names of surveyors who erected the stones.

Beyond Hob Cross the moorland begins to dominate. This can be a bleak quarter when sheeting rain slices across the peat hags. There is no real shelter then, and the yielding ground becomes quickly waterlogged. The advantages of paved ways in such conditions is illustrated when the causeway known as the Quakers' Trod is joined on the crest of High Moor. Even in dry conditions progress along the slabs is a delight. The name Quakers' Trod is said to relate to regular use by the Society of Friends, whose members travelled from the Esk Dale villages to their meeting house in Guisborough during the early eighteenth century. The stone work is in good condition and does not suggest heavy use by horses. But trods were often turned over once they had become worn or 'dished' in the middle.

The moorland seems as featureless as the sea. But like Exmoor it has the sea's openness and symmetry with the sky. The real features are space, airiness and the freedom of uninterrupted distance. You travel optimistically across this sweeping landscape. To the north-east lies Lockwood Beck Reservoir, a mere blink of water against the backdrop of the sea. In the middle distance is the sprawling fringe of industrial Teesside. South-west are the Cleveland Hills merging eastwards with Westerdale and Danby High Moor and the scarp-like edges of the valleys that feed into Esk Dale.

The paved trod unrolls beneath your feet. Around the causeway, the heather moor is marred by machine-cut channels dug to assist drainage and the healthy growth of heather for grouse-breeding. The cuttings have been here for several years, and seem unlikely to merge with the landscape they seek to preserve.

The Quakers' Trod between Guisborough and Commondale. 'The paved trod unrolls beneath your feet.'

Where the paved section of the way ends, our route continues past the Bronze Age tumuli of Black Howes, and then follows another section of paved trod down to the village of Commondale. This section of causeway runs parallel to an overgrown sunken way. Commondale is a moorland outpost. Here at the head of the Esk Valley there was once a thriving weaving industry that was based on piece-work by cottagers. A bleachery was established at Commondale in the mid-seventeenth century, and the packhorse traffic to and from the village must have been extensive.

Today, the Esk Valley railway passes through Commondale. The route of this wonderful rural line is a close companion of the rest of our walk. The clatter of occasional trains punctuates the quiet of the countryside without being too intrusive. From Commondale our route is drawn into the gentler confines of Esk Dale, along good tracks and paths that lead past the villages of Castleton and Danby. At Danby the National Park has an excellent visitor centre that can be reached from our route by continuing along Briar's Lane from the Duke of Wellington Inn.

From Danby, the way leads onto the high moorland to pass Danby Beacon and its broken tumuli. In autumn these moors are suffused with the deep purple of heather. The Beacon is a high viewpoint from where the sea is visible at Whitby fourteen miles/twenty-two kilometres to the east. The line of an ancient ridgeway is followed from the Beacon past numerous tumuli and the rather forlorn, and well-named, Stump Cross. The way joins a fine paved trod that leads towards Lealholm and the enfolding valley.

This is the last of the moorland walking. Our route is now absorbed into a countryside that is more English pastoral than upland wilderness. The Esk glides quietly by, its banks shaded with beech, sycamore, hawthorn and golden broom. Deep grass fringes the riverside meadows, its greenness stitched with the yellow flowers of buttercup, the blue of meadow crane's-bill and the white foam of cow parsley. The woodland coverts hum with insect life in the thick summer air. But the characteristics of an ancient way remain. At one point, where the river is crossed by a modern

The stepping stones across the River Esk at Egton Bridge. 'The stones are nicely regular, although a touch coffin-shaped.'

footbridge, there is a paved ford. The surface of the underwater slabs are smooth and flat beneath the glassy flow of the water. And at Glaisdale, by the entrance to East Arncliff Wood, is Beggar's Bridge, a famous feature preserved in its seventeenth-century form.

The bridge was built in 1619 by a Yorkshiremen, Thomas Ferris, to commemorate the difficulties he had in courting. There was no bridge over the Esk at that time and Ferris had to swim across the river to meet his sweetheart, whose wealthy father scorned the poor suitor. Ferris decided to try his fortune at sea. The night before he left, the Esk was in spate and the lovers could only wave goodbye. Had this been anywhere other than canny Yorkshire our hero would have chanced a crossing and been swept away and drowned. His lover would have died of a broken heart, and a wheezy folk ballad would be their legacy. Instead, like a wise tyke, Ferris went off to sea, made his fortune, returned, and married his sweetheart – and then built a bridge to prove the point.

The sweethearts may well have swanned through East Arncliff Wood along the delightful paved trod that leads high above the Esk, and snakes its way beneath the shady canopy. In autumn its flags are speckled with russet leaves. It is easy to imagine the swaying packhorses moving through these woods, bulky with panniers, their dark mottled hides merging with the dappled shade, their metal shoes ringing on the flags.

Beyond Arncliff a lane leads to Egton Bridge where stepping stones span the Esk. The stones are nicely regular, although a touch coffin-shaped. Egton Bridge is a village that is gracefully surviving the price of its prettiness and accessibility. The way east from here is by the rather dull, but convenient, old toll road of the Egton estate. Part way along the road, the 1948 charges board has been preserved on the wall of the old toll house: carts were charged by the number of horses and wheels; motor vehicles were charged one shilling; and the toll was reduced to sixpence for hearses – half-price when you were wholly dead.

Beyond Grosmont the route climbs onto the high ground along some excellent stretches of paved way. It passes the modest but handsome Newbiggin Hall, which stands on the site of a fourteenth-century moated building. From Newbiggin the route continues through fields, with paved sections tucked in alongside the hedges and beneath bunched grass. This is the part of the way that is still known as the Monks' Trod. The paved sections are sporadic but regular, and there is a persuasive sense of antiquity along the high ground where the views recapture some of the moorland flavour. To the south is the steep edge of Sleights Moor, and to the north broad fields rise to Egton Low Moor.

Soon the ground drops away towards Sleights Bridge and the busy main road, from where the line of the old route towards Whitby has been overpowered by the B1410. It is possible to follow paths to the north of this road, but the detour is artificial and very steep in places. There are sections of paved way that lead to Whitby from St John's Church, which lies on the A169 about a mile/one and a half kilometres south of Sleights Bridge. But this too is something of a diversion.

Instead, the modern 'paved way' of the B1410 heads unerringly to Ruswarp. From here, stretches of dressed flags lead on towards Whitby, along a path that winds through increasingly suburban countryside to emerge above the town quay. Whitby is a likeable town that is nicely wrapped round the narrow seaward channel of the River Esk. The modernized west side is balanced by the old quarter, where the narrow canyon of Church Street leads to famous stone steps. The steps rise endlessly to the Church of St Mary and to the ruins of the abbey above a cold sea.

St Mary's Church is intriguing. It has an Alice in Wonderland interior that is crammed with high-sided box pews and is overlooked by galleries. Its walls are lined with huge wooden tablets bearing scriptural texts. There is a gorgon of a stove, and a three-decker pulpit in full sail. Clamped to the pulpit are long-stemmed hearing trumpets that were installed early last century for the partially deaf wife of the vicar. This is a seagoing church of a shipbuilding town that is comfortable with its past. 'Our days pass like a shadow' proclaims the inscription on the church's sundial. But St Mary's stands four-square and substantial.

The church's graveyard sprouts dark thickets of slate. Such grim-faced headstones must have appealed to the novelist Bram Stoker who drew Whitby and St Mary's into his immortal *Dracula*. Beyond the church lie the gothic ruins of the abbey. The original building was founded in 657 on this high place, then known as 'Streoneshalh'. It flourished until its brutal sacking by Viking invaders in 794. After the Norman Conquest the tumbled ruins were incorporated into a Benedictine monastery, but this building was in turn ruined at the Dissolution.

Today, there is a certain bleakness about the abbey ruins. The sandstone mouldings of the recessed entrance way have been wonderfully eroded by the North Sea winds, and there is an airy dignity about the towering walls of the north aisle and transept. But overall this is a devastated building that is somehow more naked, exposed and ruined than land-locked Gisborough Priory where our journey began.

THE MONKS' TROD
Information

Distance 27 miles/43.2 kms

Maps OS Landranger 94 (Whitby & surrounding area); OS Outdoor Leisure 26 (North York Moors Eastern Area); OS Outdoor Leisure 27 (North York Moors Western Area)

Nature of Walk The route is best done over two days. The going is generally easy and firm underfoot, though sections can be muddy during prolonged wet weather. Weatherproof clothing should be carried. Parties should be properly equipped for a winter crossing of the moorland sections.

Accommodation At Guisborough and Whitby and at the villages along the way. Youth hostel at Whitby. Camp sites near Guisborough and Whitby.

Transport Guisborough and Whitby can be reached by bus from main centres. The Esk Valley railway betweeen Whitby and Middlesbrough connects Whitby to all the villages along the route as far as Commondale.

Further Information Tourist Information Centre, Guisborough, tel. (0287) 633801; North York Moors National Park, The Moors Centre, Danby, tel. (0287) 660654.

Start Gisborough Priory

Hob Cross.

1 From the Church of St Nicholas, walk past the priory gates and turn left down the street, signposted to Whitby. Turn left along Whitby Lane for about 250 yards/225 metres, then turn right up Butt Lane. Follow the rough lane for about 1 mile/1.6 kms, to cross an old railway, and reach the edge of the forest. *The next section is waymarked with blue arrow posts but is indistinct in places.* Follow the posts to reach the rim of the quarry. Keep ahead and look out for a path going left into the trees (*no waymark*). There is an old stone gatepost a few yards into the trees. Go up this path. (2 miles/3.2 kms)

2 Cross a broad track and go up rough stone steps opposite, to follow a path. At a T-junction with a broad track, go left, then after a few yards go right by a boulder and through a gate. Continue along a path. At the next junction (*no waymark*), go left down a track by a big boulder, then right at a T-junction. A short distance further on, where the track divides, keep left and downhill to bear off right by a tree. Follow the path out of the trees and uphill. Continue to Hob Cross at OS 645134 (1¼ miles/2 kms)

3 Go sharp left, when abreast of Hob Cross, towards a field wall and past inscribed stones. Continue on a path across the moor, and beneath power lines. Join a paved way and continue right, to a road. Go right round a sharp bend in the road, then bear off right before the traffic warning posts end. Follow a path across the moor and on down the side of a conifer plantation to reach a road. Turn left for 200 yards/180 metres, and where the road bends, go sharply right to follow a path and paved way down to Commondale. (3¼ miles/5.2 kms)

4 Go left and up the lane towards the station. Follow the lane round left, past a bungalow, and continue for 1¼ miles/2 kms, to emerge at a bend in a road above Castleton. Go downhill for about 200 yards/180 metres, then go left along a track signposted Danby. Continue behind a row of houses and keep ahead where the track divides. Reach a road and continue,

Stone trods through the woods above Fotherley's Farm, north of Grosmont.

with care, for 300 yards/270 metres into a dip. Go off right over a stile and then up through small fields to emerge via a neatly kept lawn alongside houses. Turn left and follow stone trods past a quoits pitch and down to a road. Turn right and reach a crossroads by the Duke of Wellington Inn. (3½ miles/5.6 kms)

5 Cross over and go up Briar Hill opposite. At the top of the slope go off left and follow a surfaced road up and round to the right. Where the road goes left, continue ahead along the lower of green tracks and through a gate. Where the track bears off left by a solitary hawthorn tree, leave it and keep ahead alongside a wall. Go through a gate and bear down left past a telegraph pole, then turn left along a track. Go down right by trees and over a stile and footbridge. Go up a bouldery slope, then bear up left alongside the boundary wall of the wood. Where the trees end, go over a wooden boardwalk and keep alongside a wall, to reach a road at OS 725087. Turn left and follow the road to Danby Beacon. (2 miles/3.2 kms)

6 At the road corner, by the Beacon, turn right along a rough road. Pass a junction at OS 763092 and, 100 yards/90 metres further on, bear off right along a grassy track by a footpath sign. Reach a stone post at a junction with a paved way. Turn right to reach a road corner. Turn left, then right at the main road, and go down into Lealholm. (3 miles/4.8 kms) Turn left just past the car park and follow the lane to Under Park Farm. *The route from now on is occasionally signposted with the leaping salmon motif of the Esk Valley Walk.* Go right at the farm, then left alongside the River Esk. Cross a stile and a wooden bridge, then turn right to follow a track. Cross a river by a footbridge and climb steeply up to join a road. Keep straight ahead for about 200 yards/180 metres, then go left through a well-kept garden between houses. Continue over stiles and through the woods, pass Mill Wood cottage, and go uphill to a road. (1¾ miles/2.8 kms)

7 Turn left and follow the road for ¼ mile/0.4 kms to a T-junction by the Arncliffe Arms. Cross over and go down a stony path to

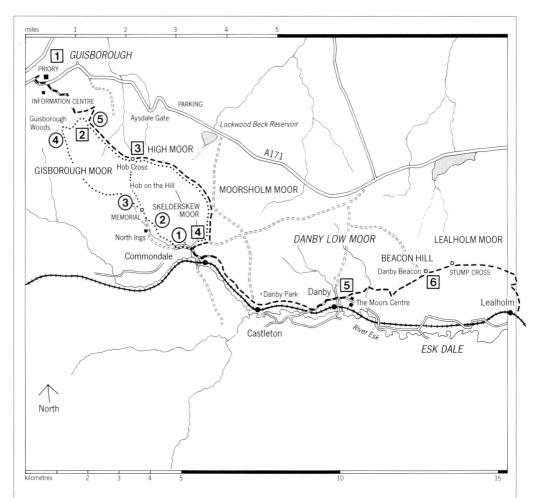

the left of the pub. At a T-junction by a house, go left, then up wooden steps. (Beggar's Bridge is to the left.) Follow the path and paved trod through East Arncliff Wood to reach a road. Turn left down the road to Egton Bridge. (2 miles/3.2 kms)

8 At the junction with a road, signposted Goathland, and just past the Horseshoe Hotel, turn left down some steps, then cross the Esk by stepping stones to reach a road. Go right down the road through Egton Bridge and, just round the left-hand bend, by St Hedda's Church, cross over, then follow the Egton estate road to where it emerges at a public road above Grosmont. (1½ miles/2.4 kms)

9 Turn left for a few yards, then go right along a farm road through Grosmont Farm, and on to Fotherleys Farm at OS 833066. Part way up the steep cobbled drive to Fotherleys, bear up left through a gate, and follow a paved trod steeply up through the wood. At the top go through a gate into a field. Continue to join a lane that passes Newbiggin Hall, then continue in the same direction, keeping field edges to the right until reaching a gate. Beyond the gate, keep the field edge to the left. Reach an

area of scrubland where the paved trod ends. (2¼ miles/3.6 kms)

10 Follow a rutted path downhill. Cross a lane, then several yards down the path opposite, go down left and cross a footbridge. Follow overgrown trods through several fields to reach a lane. Go right and, just before buildings, go right and follow trods through fields to reach a road. Follow the road down to the A169 at Sleights, then go along the B1410 to Ruswarp. (2¾ miles/4.4 kms)

11 Turn left past the church at Ruswarp, and 150 yards/135 metres ahead, cross over and go down an alleyway. Follow the paved way, go up some steps and bear right at a fork. Go along a field edge, then cross an old railway cutting. Cross a school playing field. Go left past the school entrance and, before the main road, keep right along a path that leads under the road. At the top of some steps, go right, then down a slope to a road. Go along the road to Whitby town centre, or keep right and cross the railway line, with care, to the quayside. (1¾ miles/2.8 kms)

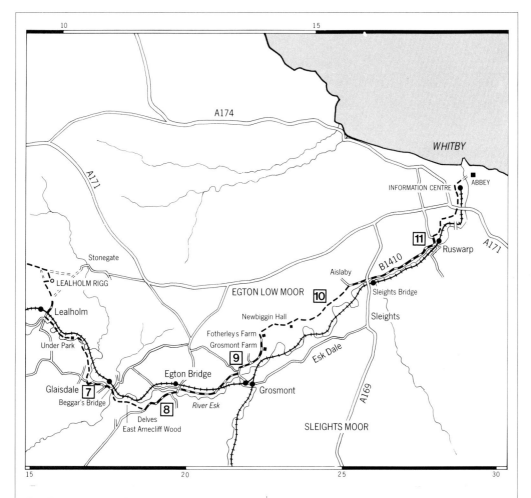

CIRCULAR WALKS 8 miles/12.8 kms *or* 5 miles/8 kms

A choice of routes takes in the attractive stretch of paved trod known as the Quakers' Trod, and follows shorter sections of paved causeway.

Start at OS 656106 by a stand of conifers about ⅓ mile/1 km along the road running west from Commondale. There is some roadside parking.

WALK A (8 miles/12.8 kms) Allow four to five hours.

1 Go north-west along a track, then after 50 yards/45 metres, turn off right along a path signposted Guisborough. Follow a section of paved way onto an unpaved path that merges with a broad track.

2 Continue past an old railway waggon, then bear off left along a path to pass by a memorial stone.

3 Continue to a T-junction with a broad track. Cross over and follow a sandy path to reach a gate at the edge of a conifer plantation.

4 Keep ahead through the wood and at a T-junction with a broad track, turn right. *This is the Cleveland Way.* Keep ahead for about ½ mile/0.8 kms and look out, to the right, for a blue waymark by the rough stone steps described in (2) in the main route directions.

5 To return, follow (2) and (3) on the main walk, and on reaching Commondale, follow the road west to the starting point.

WALK B (5 miles/8 kms) Allow two and a half hours.

1 As for (1) and (2) on Walk A as far as the memorial stone.

2 Just past the memorial stone, at OS 646118, bear off right 352 degrees. Pass a line of grouse butts on your left to reach the stone pillar of 'Hob on the Hill'. From here bear 350 degrees for just over ½ mile/0.8 kms to reach Hob Cross. Follow (3) on main walk to reach Commondale.

JAGGERS' GATE
Peak District

'Edale, sited in a shallow and fertile valley and mentioned in Domesday Book, was evidently at one time a place of some importance as five packhorse ways converge there . . .'

A.E. and E.M. Dodd, *Packhorse Ways in Derbyshire,* 1974

This delightful walk follows old packhorse ways through the High Peak. It crosses the Midhope Moors by the ancient Cut Gate track, then passes down the western side of the Howden and Derwent reservoirs, and into Edale by Jaggers Clough. From Edale Head, the way climbs across the southern edge of Kinder Scout to Hayfield.

There was always great business done in Derbyshire and Yorkshire.

Wherever there was industry, raw materials and manufactured goods were carried to and fro. The desolate and difficult ground of the High Peak moorland was no barrier to such enterprise. Prehistoric ridgeways traversed the limestone plateau of the southern White Peak, between the valleys of the Derwent and Dove, and converging trackways met at the great Iron Age hill fort on Mam Tor above the Edale Valley. The Romans too left their mark on the 'waste'. Their roads lay along direct lines that crossed such formidable heights as the Snake Pass between Melandra, near modern Glossop, and the Roman settlement of Navio at Brough. From Navio a Roman road, the Long Causeway, struck east over the stony reef of Stanage Edge and across Hallam Moor to Sheffield.

Post-Roman paths and trackways threaded their way through the limestone valleys of the southern White Peak, and by the medieval period the wet and difficult ground of the Dark Peak was crossed by numerous tracks that had been cut through the swamping peatlands. Large areas of the Peak District were granted to abbeys after the Norman Conquest. The monks employed packhorse trains to carry goods along routes that were consolidated in the following centuries by merchants, packmen and local people.

Packhorse or 'pannier' teams of up to forty horses, tied nose to tail, and veiled with tinkling bells as warning of their approach, travelled throughout the Peak District. The men who drove the teams were called 'jaggers'. They took their name from the dialect word 'jag', meaning 'a load'; although an alternative source might have been the sturdy little German Jaeger ponies that were widely used as packhorses, along with Scottish-bred Galloways. These last were described by Daniel Defoe as being 'good pacers, strong easy goers, hard, gentle, well-broken and above, all, they never tire'.

The horses were certainly tough, agile and sure-footed. They stood about fourteen hands high (4 ft 8 in/1.4 metres), the ideal height for loading the slung wicker panniers carried to either side. The panniers varied, depending on the type of load. Special baskets known as 'hottes' had hinged bottoms and were used for materials

Opposite: The packhorse bridge at Grindsbrook Booth, Edale.

like turf, coal and stone that could be dropped quickly at journey's end. Each packhorse could carry up to four hundredweight (two hundred kilogrammes). Saddles with high peaks were used for carrying long sacks that were filled with coal; leather girth bands called 'wanters' were used to strap down cloth. Other goods carried by the packhorse trains included salt, fish, timber and lead.

The packhorse trade is remembered through the names of numerous pubs, not least the Old Nag's Head at Grindsbrook village in Edale, and the Pack Horse Inn at Hayfield. Its characteristics are revealed in the subtle line of packhorse ways on steep slopes, and in the narow hump-backed bridges that had parapets low enough not to impede the slung panniers.

Jaggers have been immortalized by such surviving place names as Jaggers Clough. Other packhorse users were known as 'badgers', the merchants who bought and sold corn. Their name is derived from a dialect word meaning to haggle or to argue over a price. Other names for the solitary 'commercial' travellers of the time were 'swailer', 'huckster', 'chapman', 'trowman' and 'higgler'. Whatever the title, these enterprising characters kept open the lines of communication through desolate regions of the Midlands and Northern England. They were a crucial element of commerce from the earliest times.

Our route starts from the heart of Penistone at the handsome eighteenth-century building that once housed the town's cloth market and shambles. Penistone prospered during the eighteenth century, after its inhabitants petitioned successfully for a weekly market. It was a centre of the textile industry and gave the name 'peny stones' to a type of cloth. Packhorse teams travelled to and from the town across the western moors, and the people of the Derwent Valley area crossed the Cut Gate to Penistone with goods that included cloth, cream and hazelnuts. Derwent farmers drove stock to Penistone's important beef market, and cattle were still being driven over the Cut Gate early this century when local farmers maintained the track.

Our route leads from the outskirts of Penistone over Hornthwaite Hill to Hill Side, from where it follows a typical holloway that has all the characteristics of an old cart track and drove road. The way loses its identity amidst the swathes of bilberries in the rough brakes of Hartcliff Hill, but the line of the route leads on through fields to Langsett and the busy A616.

Before the building of Langsett Reservoir the way would have continued directly to Brook House Bridge at the crossing of the Porter or Little Don River. But the walker now diverts to Langsett Visitor Centre, from where a pleasant path leads through the conifers along the reservoir's northern shore. The handsome barn at Langsett dates from the seventeenth century, and was used for storing corn and hay. The building has been beautifully restored through joint action by a number of bodies, including Yorkshire Water and the Peak National Park. It is now a visitor centre and a local community hall – a happy combination in keeping with the National Park's community ethos.

Langsett Reservoir, which was completed in 1904, has a Victorian solidity about its stonework. It is encircled by spruce, larch and pine and has merged with the landscape, especially by Brook House Bridge at its western end. Beyond the bridge the rocky way rises to Hingcliff Hill and the Midhope Moors. Ahead, the moorland lies dark and bare. Ragged walls, their rough stone stacked like cut peats, mark off old grazing boundaries.

This is a dour and grudging landscape. Yet, to the west, the shallow valley of Hordron Clough is a green enclave, deluged with streams that drain from Howden Edge. Blinks of sunlight reflect off the glittering threads of water and illuminate the emerald daubs of sphagnum moss. Soon our path reaches the rim of Mickleden, another green oasis where the clean-cut beck flows through a remarkable sequence of tight meanders. The slopes of Mickleden are dotted with birches, and at the head of the clough the trees are densely clustered. The path runs arrow-straight along Mickleden Edge, its rocky bed fringed by purple heather.

The Edge is a windy place. It draws you on through a dark and sodden landscape where bitter blood seems to ooze from the peat hags and from the dark trenches called 'groughs' that slice through the blanket bog. These were famous grouse moors and are still managed for the breeding of that wonderfully raucous bird.

Hard usage of the Cut Gate by modern walkers has eroded the peat cover to the bare rock in places. Yet by its very name the 'Gate' reflects its origins. It was dug through the peat for men and beasts to pass, and it is of great antiquity. The way was known also as Black Dike. Carts used it as well as pack trains, and it was referred to as 'Cart Gate' in sixteenth-century documents.

People have used this fragile landscape to the extreme. The post-glacial woodland of the high moors was steadily reduced by burning and felling. The process began during the Mesolithic period, from about 6,000 BC. A change from a dry regime to a wet westerly climate encouraged the spread of blanket bog across cleared ground. Heavy grazing by sheep and cattle brought added pressure that was intensified during Saxon and Norman times. The peat itself was cut for fuel throughout the centuries, and the acid rain of our own industrial pollution has had an insidious and damaging effect on the core ecology of this truly fragile landscape.

Physical damage is all too obvious. During World War II these moors were used for tank training and artillery practice. Today, the yielding ground seems devastated, especially on the stranded track across the northern shoulder of Margery Hill, where too many walkers detour outwards to avoid the wetter sections. The dilemma facing the hard-pressed National Park Authority, and walkers themselves, is brutally evident, although such erosion is localized and less insidious than the widespread effect of landscape exploitation and pollutants.

When moving through the heart of the bog the view ahead is restricted. But once over Howden Edge the way runs in a free-wheeling descent towards the deep trough of the Derwent Valley. Now the eye is absorbed by the great wall of moorland to the west, and the high points of Grinah Stones and Bleaklow Hill beyond. To the south-west is the massy ridge that runs east from Kinder. Immediately south of the path is the scarp of Howden Edge, with the velvety green banks of Upper Hey tumbling down towards the valley.

The path leads down into Cranberry Clough and to Slippery Stones at the River Derwent. The last part of the descent is ragged and steep, and its clumsy line reflects modern use. Packmen and their wise beasts sought a longer but gentler way up and down steep slopes. To the left of the present path there is evidence of an old

The Cut Gate path: 'once over Howden Edge the way runs in a freewheeling descent towards the deep trough of the Derwent Valley.'

holloway that slants along the slope of the clough, then climbs through a series of zigzags. The pack trains would have toiled gently uphill here, or eased downwards, the tinkling bells of the horses as unobtrusive as birdsong.

Packmen would not recognize the Derwent Valley today. This is a drowned landscape, with its surviving slopes mopped up by dense plantations of conifers. The great reservoirs of Howden, Derwent and Ladybower were built to supply the domestic needs of Sheffield, Derby, Leicester and Nottingham. They were built at the expense of an ancient pattern of human settlement. Beneath the passive surface of Ladybower lie the drowned villages of Derwent and Ashopton. At the water's edge, paths, tracks and byways have been cut off, their edges now trimmed by the lakeside road and by the dense curtain of pine trees. The result is an exquisite chocolate-box landscape that is admired by huge numbers of car-bound visitors.

For some time after the flooding of Ladybower the tower of Derwent Church protruded from the water – an unbearable reminder. It was demolished in December 1947. But some artefacts did survive the deluge. The stolid packhorse bridge at Slippery Stones dates from 1683 but stood originally by Derwent village. In *A tributary to the River Derwent near Slippery Stones.* 1939, when the Derwent area was scheduled for flooding, thoughtful people raised enough cash and commitment to have the

bridge dismantled into 900 numbered pieces. The stones were placed in storage and the bridge reassembled at Slippery Stones in 1959.

Beyond Slippery Stones our route enters Derbyshire and follows a mangled forestry track to where the surfaced road begins. Three miles/nearly five kilometres of road lead to a forest path that climbs steeply to the high ground of Gores Heights and Lockerbrook, and on to a splendid viewpoint at Hagg Post. In clear weather the great bulk of Kinder is seen to the west beyond Seal Edge, Blackden Edge and the twin tors of Crookstone Knoll. Across the Woodlands Valley is the graceful line of the Lose Hill to Mam Tor ridge that encloses Edale. South-east lies Win Hill, with the long sweep of the Derwent Valley running into the distance.

It is an inspiring view that may or may not have engaged the jaggers as they toiled uphill from Woodlands or began their steep descent from Hagg Post. Downward-bound packhorses would have been eager to reach the watering place at Hagg Water Bridge on the River Ashop. Once across the river there is a stiff climb to a junction with the Roman road from Glossop, at a point just west of Hope Cross. A quick descent to Jaggers Clough leads on into Edale and a delightfully level ramble through this loveliest of Peakland valleys.

Edale lies at the heart of the transition zone between the White and Dark Peak. To the south is the limestone shield of the ancient carboniferous seabed; to the north is the dark gritstone delta that formed as the flood plain of the great rivers of the ancient Caledonian mountains. Around Edale lie the unstable shales and siltstones that have formed the 'shivering mountain' of Mam Tor. The valley is a gentle contrast to the bare uplands. It is drained by the River Noe, and throughout its length cultivation of the softer soil has produced a pleasing pattern of small farms at the famous 'Booths'. These booths originated as shepherds' shelters strung out along the base of the valley slopes. Everything is linear in Edale. Even the railway seems to merge with the lie of the land as soon as it makes its sudden entrance to Edale from Cowburn Tunnel beneath the high ground of Colborne.

The packhorse route leads satisfyingly through Nether Booth and Ollerbrook Booth to the chequered shade of Grindsbrook Booth, where a lovely packhorse bridge leads across the tree-hung stream to a street of medieval style. Here the packhorse drivers would have stopped for food and drink while the horses clattered their hooves uneasily on the stone ground, in a sunny haze of corn dust amidst the rich smell of leather and sweat. From Grindsbrook the route continues west on sections of paved path along the 'alternative' Pennine Way. It leads to Upper Booth and then to Lee

Farm, where the National Trust has an imaginative information shelter.

Soon, Edale relinquishes its green hold, imperceptibly at first, where the head of the valley rears up at Jacob's Ladder beneath the rim of the rock-beaded moors. The River Noe floods quietly by, amidst graceful woodland where the National Trust is carrying out excellent regenerative work. To the right, smooth green sheepfolds rise to the skyline, their territories divided by ancient walls.

There is a renewed sense of challenge where the moorland edge presents its rougher face. Beyond the handsome packhorse bridge at Edale Head, the broad stony staircase of Jacob's Ladder curves uphill. The Jacob of this singular short cut was a tenant of the nearby Edale Head House past which the carefully engineered packhorse way still climbs. Jacob's Ladder has been cushioned against the pressure of Pennine wayfarers by excellent stone-work. The packhorse way is less used, and elbows its hollowed way past the ruins of the old farm with its walled pastures, where the packhorse trains may have stopped for the night.

At the top of the rise a brutally stony track leads on across the level moor to reach Edale Cross and its strange little enclosure. The cross is medieval and was known originally as Champion Cross, named from the Peak Forest ward of Champagne, the rich grassland area to the south. The cross marks the junction of the medieval wards of Champagne, Longendale and Ashop-Edale. The 1810 inscription records a later restoration. Edale and Hope Crosses and similar Peakland monuments were probably erected by the medieval monks of Welbeck and Basingwerk Abbeys, who used these moorland tracks for transporting wool and other goods until the Dissolution opened the way to secular trade.

This is the western edge of the High Peak. To the south and west the land declines into the middle distance round Chapel-en-le-Frith and Whaley Bridge. Our way lies downhill through Oaken Clough and Coldwell Clough, and on along a surfaced road past the small quarry near Bowden Bridge, from where walkers set out on an April day in 1932 to trespass deliberately on Kinder Scout for the cause of 'freedom to roam'.

Our walk ends at Hayfield. In the narrow streets of this charming village, packhorse trains once lined up with their loads of wool and other goods, before heading onto the moors. Hayfield was always a busy place, counting amongst its industries, cutlery-making, woollen and cotton manufacturing, quarrying and farming. The village is hedged in today by the A624, but its heart lies on the moorland side of the road, and its Pack Horse Inn is a reminder of the great days of the jaggers and their tough little horses who made of the High Peak a manageable 'waste'.

JAGGERS' GATE
Information

Distance 25 miles/40 kms

Maps OS Landranger 110 (Sheffield & Huddersfield); OS Outdoor Leisure 1 (The Peak District – Dark Peak area)

Nature of Walk A mix of moorland and valley walking. The route can be spread over two days, although very fit walkers could complete it in a day. Clothing and equipment should be suitable for mountain walking. *Weather conditions can be severe at any time of the year, and extreme snow conditions may be encountered during winter.*

Accommodation At Penistone, Langsett, Edale and Hayfield. Youth hostels at Langsett and Edale. Camping barns in Edale at Cotefield Farm and Upper Booth. Camp sites at Edale and Hayfield.

Transport Rail connections from Sheffield and Manchester to Penistone and Edale. Bus connections to Hayfield from Glossop and New Mills railway stations.

Further Information Tourist Information Centre, Barnsley, tel. (0226) 206757, National Park Information Centre, Fairholmes-Derwent Valley, tel. (0433) 50953.

Start Penistone Old Market House

1 Walk down St Mary's Street, and where the road bends right under a bridge, follow a lane round left, then go right along Stottercliffe Road. Keep ahead across the recreation ground to a gap in the far wall, then continue to Cross Royal Head at OS 230029 where a stile leads right to a road. (1¼ miles/2 kms)

2 Turn left, then branch right down a lane to Hill Side. Turn up left opposite Bank House Farm, and follow a rough lane uphill. Continue through a field and on round the wooded flank of Hartcliff Hill. At a road, turn right, then left down a drive to pass a farm. At Nether House Farm, go through the yard and over a stile into a lane. A few yards down the lane, go right over a stile and then down through fields and over stiles, passing just left of a big pylon. Cross a disused railway and reach the busy A616. Turn right and walk along the road, with care, to the Langsett Barn car park, from where a signposted path leads through a gate into the pines. Branch left at a wooden post and follow a track, via signposts to Brook House Bridge. (3¼ miles/5.2 kms)

3 Beyond the bridge, turn left and follow the track onto open moorland. Keep right where the track forks at OS 197000. Continue on an obvious track via Mickleden Edge and the Cut Gate to the old bridge at Slippery Stones. (4½ miles/7.2 kms)

4 Beyond the bridge, turn left and follow the forestry track to the road head at Howden Reservoir. Follow the road for 3½ miles/ 5.6 kms, then bear off right on a path at OS 167910. Continue amidst trees and along a stony track to pass Lockerbrook Farm. (5¼ miles/8.4 kms)

5 Reach a junction of tracks above a steep descent at OS 164890. Keep ahead and downhill on a zigzag track, signposted to Hagg Water Bridge. Cross the A57 Snake Pass road, and go down a shaded holloway to cross Hagg Water Bridge. Beyond the bridge turn right for a short distance, then bear up left through a staggered barrier, and continue up a stony track through mixed woodland. Go right at the next T-junction, and follow the track onto open grassland to reach a cross junction of tracks. Keep ahead, signposted Edale, and descend a rough track to Jaggers Clough. (1¾ miles/2.8 kms)

6 Cross the stream at Jaggers Clough, and go right through a gate to follow the track up left. At a fork at OS 149868, just before Clough Farm, take the path bearing off right to pass above the farm. Continue to Rowland Cote Youth Hostel. Pass the front of the hostel, then go down the drive, bearing right to join a grassy path leading off right. At OS 135862 bear down left to the right-hand field corner.

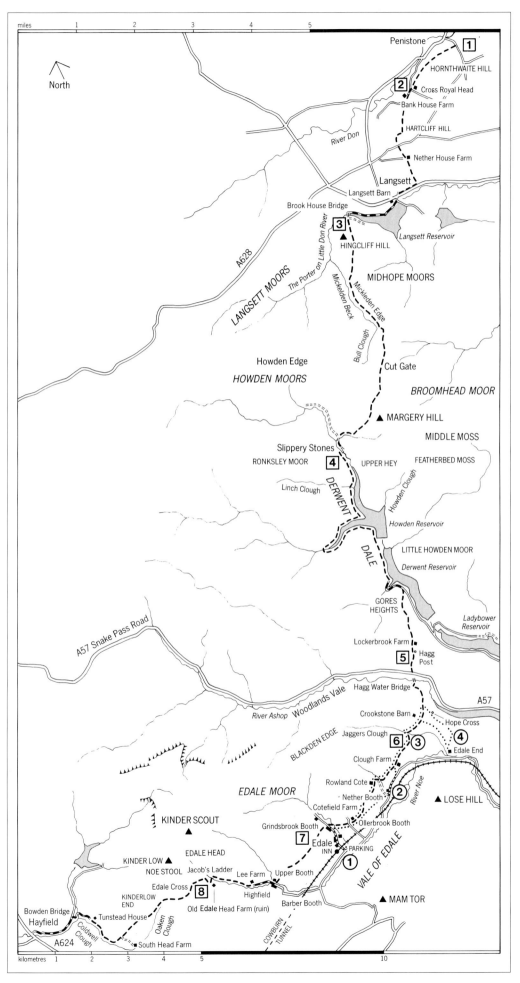

Go right over a stile and continue below Cotefield Farm. Continue to Ollerbrook Booth and, where the track divides, keep to the right of a Dutch barn. About a ¼ mile/ 0.4 kms ahead, go left through a stone squeeze and down a narrow path to cross a packhorse bridge. Continue up past the Old Nag's Head. (2¾ miles/4.4 kms)

7 Cross the road and go over a stile between cottages to follow a sunken track. Continue on good paths along the alternative Pennine Way route to reach Upper Booth. Turn right out of the farmyard by a phone box, and continue to Lee Farm and on to Jacob's Ladder. (2¼ miles/ 3.6 kms)

8 Cross the packhorse bridge and bear up left away from Jacob's Ladder, to follow the packhorse way past the ruins of Edale Head House. At the top of the slope, continue along a very stony track, and where the Pennine Way goes up right at OS 081861, keep ahead through a gate. Pass Edale Cross and continue downhill. The track eventually becomes a surfaced road that is followed to the car park and camp site at Bowden Bridge and on to Hayfield. (4 miles/6.4 kms)

CIRCULAR WALK 5½ miles/8.8 kms

The route goes east from Edale to Jaggers Clough, then follows a Roman road past the ancient marker of Hope Cross, before returning via Jaggers Clough. Allow three hours.

Start car park at Edale

1 Go down the steps to the left of the toilet block, and turn right to pass Fieldhead information centre. Turn right by the cemetery, and keep straight ahead to Ollerbrook Farm and on past Cotefield Farm and through fields to reach Nether Booth Farm and the public road.

2 Go left along the road for a short distance, then turn up left by a 1905 public footpath and bridleway sign. Follow a hollow lane to Clough Farm. Cross the stream and go through a gate and up right to join a broad track that leads east to Jaggers Clough.

3 Go through the gate at Jaggers Clough and cross the stream. Follow the rough track uphill to a cross junction of tracks at OS 160876. Turn right, and follow the line of the old Roman road past Hope Cross. *Hope Cross is a restored guidestone of medieval origin. The inscribed place names on the pedestal are Victorian.* A ½ mile/0.8 kms beyond the cross, go right over a stile and descend steeply alongside a well-made wall. This is a National Trust path.

4 At the bottom of the slope go over a wooden step-stile, then turn sharp right to reach a metal gate. Go right through the gate and then, at a junction by a National Trust stone waymark, keep right up a sunken track to reach the descending track to Jaggers Clough. Go down left and through Jaggers Clough. Follow the directions for (6) on main walk to reach the Old Nag's Head at Edale, from where a left turn leads to the car park.

A road like a river. Looking east from Old Edale Head Farm near Jacob's Ladder.

THE SLATE ROAD
Snowdonia

Bethesda to Blaenau Ffestiniog 19 miles/30.4 kms

'By its nature the work was violent.'

Merfyn Williams, *The Slate Industry*, 1991

A tough but absorbing walk through Snowdonia, along old roads and tracks used by miners and quarrymen. The quarried mountain areas of North Wales are stark but compelling, and the wild country between them, through which this route leads, is always magnificent.

Snowdonia is a rough, rocky place and is impervious to the two hundred inches/five hundred centimetres of rain that pours onto its mountains each year. The rain can be softly persistent, or it can pour. When it pours, the hard muscle of the mountains throws off all that water in white torrents that spring up within minutes. Even the light has a watery mutedness about it. Yet through all that sodden gloom, the sun can strike a blow. When it does, the torrents gleam in response, the rocks blur into softer greys, and the dripping sedge and moor grass turn emerald green.

But in the slate quarries of Snowdonia, the sun struggles to make an impression. This is where men have violently exploited the land and left a permanent shadow. The quarries lie uneasily alongside the loveliness of the National Park. In the higher mountains the ground is deep with the shattered spoil heaps of glaciation and frost. The tumbling ridges of Glyder Fach bristle with fragmented rhyolite; on Tryfan, you pick your way through bruising mantraps of jagged rock. But out of this chaos there emerges a naturalness of form and substance that is beautiful and awesome and in balance. It is in the wrenched landscape of the quarries that the eye struggles to find such balance and beauty.

Welsh slate is practical rather than beautiful, though in use it can be aesthetically pleasing. The word slate derives from the Old French *escalater*, to 'splinter', 'shiver', or 'burst'. Slate began as silt that was deposited beneath ancient seas; it was later altered to shale that had a horizontal bedding plane. During the great mountain building frenzy of the Caledonian earth movements, the shale came under massive lateral pressure and its structure was re-formed into a plane of cleavage that allows easy splitting into slabs and tiles.

Slate was used for building from the earliest times; the Romans had slate roofs and floors, and the Welsh people broke out blocks and tiles from local outcrops for their own use. But it was the Industrial Revolution and the expanding urbanization that accompanied it that increased the demand for roofing tiles.

Those who turned domestic slate working into a major industry came mainly from outside Wales. The first of these archetypal landowning businessmen was Richard Pennant, whose family originated from Flintshire but had been long established as Liverpool merchants. Through marriage in 1765, Pennant

The Miners' Path leading towards Llyn Bochlwyd.

acquired the slate-rich Penrhyn estates at the mouth of the Nant Ffrancon valley. He began the systematic development of the Penrhyn Quarry, using vast profits from his family's sugar plantations in the West Indies; from slaves to slates in a generation. Having learned the value of money, though perhaps not of men, Pennant bought out the leases of the fifty or so local quarrymen who worked the mountain slate; he paid £160 for the privilege. Soon he became Lord Penrhyn, though the title was conveniently lifted from an estate in Ireland.

Development of Dinorwic, at Llanberis, began some years after Pennant set the example. Others opened the slate-rich areas at the head of the Vale of Ffestiniog, where the rock is finer grained and more slate-blue than the predominant purple of Penrhyn, and where the pitch of the veins has led to mining, rather than to the quarrying of terraced galleries.

From the beginning of the nineteenth century the slate industy expanded rapidly. It was at its most profitable between 1825 and 1870, and by the 1870s there were over 14,000 quarrymen working in Snowdonia. They maintained a healthy independence from too much wage slavery, the traditions of rural Wales having bred a contempt for autocratic managers and employers. But, as the industry matured and as those early quarry owners, who were hands-on workers themselves, faded from the scene, quarrymen began to lose their independence, and with it their grudging respect for those they had recognized as being fair masters.

Industrial relations in the quarries were complex and, in retrospect were fascinating. Militancy and political anarchism emerged within the workforce as the tensions of the maturing industry and of implacable market forces became at times unbearable. There were also irreconcilable differences between the social, political and religious biases of the quarry owners and the workers. These were differences that went as deep as the veins of slate. At heart the conflict was between Welsh and Anglo-Saxon.

The differences evolved into disputes about wages, work practices and bad management. At Llanberis's Dinorwic Quarry in 1885 a dispute turned into a lock-out. At Blaenau Ffestiniog's Llechwedd in 1893 a dispute was more amicably resolved. At Penrhyn there was a protracted dispute and a lock-out during 1896 and 1897. But the most bitter confrontation of all was the Penrhyn lock-out of 1900 to 1903. It split the community like the slate itself. Men worked away from home to sustain their families. Others agreed to work at Penrhyn and were reviled by their neighbours. The most reviled were those who spied on strikers and militants and identified them to the managers. In Bethesda the savage epithet 'bradwr' meaning 'traitor' may still be heard as the worst of all insults.

The Penrhyn lock-out heralded a decline in quarrying that the structural changes of the twentieth century were to make inevitable. What is left from heavy industry in a rural location is usually a bleak landscape, both natural and human. But in Snowdonia the beauty of the mountains absorbs some of the bleakness. At Llanberis, the Dinorwic Quarries are plain to see, but are somehow diminished by the crowding in of the mountains. At Blaenau, the old Oakeley, Llechwedd, Votty and Bowydd slate workings are heaped up with spoil tips amidst a landscape that can still be strikingly beautiful in the blurred air of early morning. At Bethesda, the great growling pit of Penrhyn Quarry is hidden behind innocuous spoil heaps and needs to be viewed from its western rim to appreciate its vast scale. From the same high ground, the mountains beyond are glorious.

Today, the road out of Bethesda, to the south, leads quickly towards those mountains through Nant Ffrancon. In Pennant's time there were two horse tracks up the valley to the alpine shelf at Rhaeadr Ogwen. Pennant built the Penrhyn Road up the west side of the Afon Ogwen in 1791. In 1808 an east road was constructed through Nant Ffrancon, but it was a poor effort; its gravel surface sank alarmingly. Telford soon took it in hand, flattened the inclines, and laid stone foundations. The road was part of the main route from Shrewsbury to Holyhead, a rocky enough road to Dublin in its day. Pennant's old Penrhyn Road survives. It sees little traffic now, and makes for a pleasant walk in the face of those glorious mountains at the valley head.

At the road head is the bustle of Ogwen, where we follow the crowd onto the Cwm Idwal track as if locking onto a conveyor belt. Ogwen is astonishing. It is the epitome of accessible tourism; an irresistible attraction like Land's End or Avebury. We are all responsible for this conspicuous tourism, and it says everything for the hard work of the National Park Authority that the pressure is still manageable.

We leave the Idwal track, where it swings right towards the magnificent Cwm Idwal and its tumbling cliffs of Y Garn and Glyder Fawr, to keep uphill on a path that is initially boggy and treacherous. It leads past the trim little Bochlwyd Buttress on the left, and climbs steeply to Llyn Bochlwyd within its glaciated basin. This was a route used by copper miners from Bethesda on their weekly trek to the Glaslyn Mine on Snowdon. The miners were of the same calibre as the quarrymen, their life in the high mountains perhaps even harder. Their journey to work was a long slog when, full of Sunday meat and Methodism, they climbed through the rocky heart of the Glyderau.

Today, walkers thread their way up the same track for pleasure, though the unrelenting steepness until Bwlch Tryfan is reached can be exhausting. The Bwlch is remarkable. It is a ragged chaos of splintered rock from which Tryfan and Glyder Fach rise to either side. A boundary wall snakes up the crest of both mountains until it is absorbed into the muscle of the ridges. The great bounding ridge of Glyder Fach is the most spectacular; it soars skywards to Castell y Gwynt, 'the castle of the winds', a desolation of naked rocks. Beyond the col our path winds on across the head of Cwm Tryfan, with always the great shoulder of Tryfan itself looming ahead. Far below, the ribbon of the A5 snakes through Nant y Benlog. The final rise to the watershed moor by Llyn y Caseg-fraith, 'the lake of the pied mare', is steep but short-lived.

From here the path runs across a yielding landscape that brims with water most of the time. Behind lie the ragged mountains of the Glyderau and Tryfan, making, in fine weather, a dark contrast between the bronze grass of the moor and the piercing blue of the sky above. Ahead the moorland edge suddenly declines into the great tumbling slopes that run down to Nant Gwryd. The view south from here is tremendous. Snowdon's main peak of Yr Wyddfa dominates, but reclusively, behind its bulwarks of Lliwedd and the great ridge of Crib Goch. Due south, Nantgwynant winds into the hazy distance, the stream of the Afon Glaslyn a glittering thread drawn through the needle's eye of Llyn Gwynant. South-east are the softer crowded hills of Carnedd Y Cribau and Yr Arddu and distant Cnicht.

From here, sure-footed walkers can descend like a bouncing

stream to the road at Pen-y-Gwryd, although steady progress is best advised. The miners would have gone down quickly, their boots sparking on the stones. At the road, frenzied traffic accompanies us for a short distance past the famous Pen-y-Gwryd Hotel and the junction with the Llanberis road, to where the old road through Nantgwynant slants down into the valley bottom. From Pen-y-Gwryd, the copper miners went west, contouring round Moel Berfedd to take the track that led to the Glaslyn Mine barracks, under Snowdon, on the bleak shores of Llyn Llydaw.

It is a pleasant walk along the old road, where it slips easily down the fall of the valley slope towards Llyn Gwynant. Up to the right, lie Cwm Dyli and the big shoulder of Lliwedd. The only flaw in this fine balance of valley and mountain is the giant drainpipe that slides down from Cwm Dyli to feed the power turbines in the bed of the valley. The fall of the neighbouring Afon Glaslyn points up the contrast between Nature's eye for a line and Man's insensitivity.

Nantgwynant is a beautiful valley, reminiscent of Lakeland or Scotland's Trossachs, its beauty marred only by the bustling main road. But our route takes us quickly south, above the youth hostel at Bryn Gwynant and into a charming area of mixed woodland and rhododendrons. There are good hedged lanes that run through the overhanging greenness of the woods and the glossy shrubs, where it is cool and lovely in the early morning, mellow at dusk, and, in stormy weather, rich with the smell of the damp earth.

The path leads across the western slopes of Moel Meirch, where a chaos of overlapping hillocks, wooded, and dense with heather and ferns rises in waves towards muted skylines that are much less bare and rugged than those of the Glyderau. To the south, the vast bulk of Craig Wen and Yr Aran frame the gap of Nantgwynant, where the hills close like a vice at Beddgelert. Ahead is the castellated ridge of Moel y Dyniewyd with its blunt-headed outliers, and with Yr Arddu and the great shoulder of Cnicht to the left. In the middle distance, small fields, plantations and tumbling meadows fit like the pieces of a mosaic.

Our path leads into Nanmor, a delightfully quiet valley. From here, quarrymen walked across the mountains to the Rhosydd Quarry above Blaenau Ffestiniog and Tanygrisiau, and the path they used is the one we now follow. The path has been built up in places, and rock steps have been cut and rough kerbs laid. The way rises steadily to reach the dark waters of Llyn Llagi within its cirque of rough cliffs. From here the path leads uphill into the bottleneck ravine at the northern end of Craig Llyn Llagi, from where it climbs very steeply over a narrow col. To the north-west, the vast mountain wall of Snowdon looms over Nantgwynant.

Rhosydd on Bwlch Cwmorthin: 'a sea of tumbling slate that washes up against the ruined buildings'.

The quarrymen would know this scene well, from backward glance or from a welcome homeward view as they crossed the high ground. Quarrymen and miners in the nineteenth century wore white fustian coats and trousers, with thick flannel undergarments. Their favoured headgear was a bowler hat, and they carried umbrellas – which would have been of little use in the tearing winds of the plateau. Over their shoulders the men carried their week's food in white sacks called 'walats'. They would have made ghostly figures in the driving mist of this bleak mountain landscape, where today we trudge by, wrapped in rainbow colours.

The path soon reaches the high lake of Llyn yr Adar. This is the heart of the mountain. Coarse grasses and dark reeds and sphagnum moss fringe the lake shore. The great shoulder of Cnicht rises to the south, and our path heads for a long terrace-like ridge that flexes its way towards the crest of the mountain. But we bear south-east along a tumbling track that slides down over great whale-backed ribs of rock that flow down into the cupped valley of the Afon Cwm-y-Foel. Hidden below the path, and overlooking the lake, there is an adit shaft that slices into the rock. Adits are horizontal tunnels driven into the side of a mountain in order to extract slate from a deep vein. Adits such as this lonely relic were probably worked by a handful of local people before the full-scale industrialization of the slate industry began. The adit is flooded now, its walls furred with moss and sprouting the rich green fronds of hard fern.

The path leads past Llyn Cwm-corsiog, the 'lake of the bog', unadorned in name and in nature. Cwm-corsiog was dammed to supply water for the Rhosydd Quarry. Below here, where the stream gushes down by Clogwyn Brith, there was a smaller lake, now a dank hollow where the remains of wooden planks that once lined the face of the dam litter the ground, and the pipework of a siphon and pump still survives.

The Rhosydd Quarry is still a remarkable place. At over 1,600 feet/480 metres, on Bwlch Cwmorthin, it was one of the highest workings in Snowdonia, a successful smaller mine on the fringe of the bigger Ffestiniog concerns. Today, the flat mountain plain of the Bwlch is like a sea of tumbling slate that washes up against the ruined buildings of the quarry's main complex. In the last century this area would have been a mass of machinery, a web of pipes and wooden launders on slate pillars, carrying water to drive the great wheels that powered the massive cutting saws in the mill, to cool them, and to douse the clouded dust. Beyond the buildings the cables of the tramways and inclines shrieked and rumbled as the raw slate was carried down from the workings.

Good slate was discovered here in 1830 by two Croesor men,

but full-scale production did not begin until the 1850s. The main feature of Rhosydd was the vast open pit, the West Twll, that was developed from the 1840s. It lies on the high ground to the south of Bwlch Cwmorthin. The West Twll is nearly five hundred feet/one hundred and fifty metres across. Another open working called East Twll suffered a disastrous collapse known as the Great Fall in 1900. From these vast pits, working levels, adits and galleries were thrust into the heart of the mountain. The quarry produced 220,000 tons of finished material, 222 million slates in all. The price for this was the two and a half million tons of waste that now squat in the mountainside tips. The slates were carried by pack ponies down to Tanygrisiau, until acccess was gained to the famous tramway incline of the adjoining Croesor Quarry in 1864, giving transport all the way to Porthmadog.

Rhosydd employed an average of two hundred men, most of whom lived in the *baracs*, the ruins of which still survive. These barracks were noisome places where the men paid up to three-pence a week for a share of a double bed and a lice-ridden mattress, in dark rooms that were hardly ever ventilated and rarely cleaned. But the spirit of the workers was remarkable. Their dark humour christened the barracks as *Llety'r Llaban*, 'lout's digs' and *Ffau Dwll*,

Llyn Cwmorthin above Tanygrisiau.

'den hole'. The quarrymen were wonderful singers and the Rhosydd choir was famous. The men were said to gather on the rim of Cwm Croesor on fine summer evenings to sing their heart-stopping Welsh songs and hymns. The swelling chorus could be heard far down that lovely valley to where the green trees and the sweet grass marked a softer world than the sea of slate. The Welsh talk was rich also; debates on all subjects were held, and *barac* poets emerged. One, Edward Lloyd, who died in 1922, wrote of his life at Rhosydd in the 1860s, a time when his 'muse ran as lively as a free pretty girl'.

It was a way of life that could not survive technological, social and economic changes. Rhosydd operated into the twentieth century but struggled to keep going after closure during World War I. It closed for good in 1948, although a syndicate of Llanberis men pirated slate from the walls of the buildings until 1954. Their crude methods included toppling the walls, and the flattened gables can still be seen. But the ruins of Rhosydd speak eloquently of generations of quarrymen and their families, whose values and energies demand our respect, though we can hardly regret the passing of the hard life that went with them.

The memorials of that life line the way from Rhosydd to Llyn Cwmorthin, on a track that was ancient before quarrying began and that was once a cattle-droving road from Croesor. The track leads past the gaunt walls of cottages and the proud ruin of Y Gorlan, the Calvinistic Methodist chapel that was built on Llyn Cwmorthin's shore in 1867. The shell of the building survives, its roof timbers intact, its floor littered with broken stones, and the stucco of its walls wonderfully scripted with whorled fungi and lichen, like a relief map of the great mountains above. Wooden pews once filled the chapel, and the pulpit stood between the round-arched doors and windows. Slate fence posts, like broken spears, line the track outside the chapel and gaunt pine trees stand braced against the mountain winds. From here the track leads down towards Llyn Cwmorthin. Its surface is studded with slate fragments; the pale, saffron-coloured moor grass sweeps away to either side.

Beyond Llyn Cwmorthin, the way descends through a chaos of old buildings and strewn slate, alongside the bounding Afon Cwmorthin, to Tanygrisiau, 'the place under the steps'. To the south is the Vale of Ffestiniog, where the grim buildings of the Trawsfynnydd power station can look like a gothic castle in the white mist of first light. To the north-east, Blaenau lies like some dark old stronghold amidst its rocky bluffs, with the great terraces and spoil heaps rising above. It may not be the smiling face of Snowdonia, but it is a compelling one.

THE SLATE ROAD
Information

Distance 19 miles/30.4 kms

Maps OS Outdoor Leisure 17 (Snowdonia – Snowdon Area)

Nature of Walk A strenuous walk that crosses two mountain ranges, involving steep ascents and descents. Tracks and paths are continuous except for a few short moorland sections *where careful route-finding and compass work may be required in poor visibility.* Very fit, experienced walkers could complete the route in a day. Clothing and equipment (including emergency bivouac gear), should be suitable for mountain conditions. *Weather conditions can be severe at any time of the year, but especially so outside the summer season.*

Accommodation At Bethesda and Blaenau Ffestiniog. Hotel at Pen y Gwryd. Youth hostels at Ogwen and Bryn Gwynant.

Transport Rail connection to Blaenau Ffestiniog from Porthmadog. Bus connections from main centres to Bethesda and Blaenau Ffestiniog. Summer bus service throughout Snowdonia area. Limited service in off-season.

Further Information National Park Visitor Centre, Bettws y Coed, tel. (0690) 710426; National Park Visitor Centre, Blaenau Ffestiniog, tel. (0766) 830360.

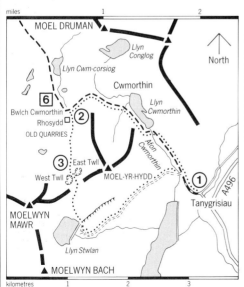

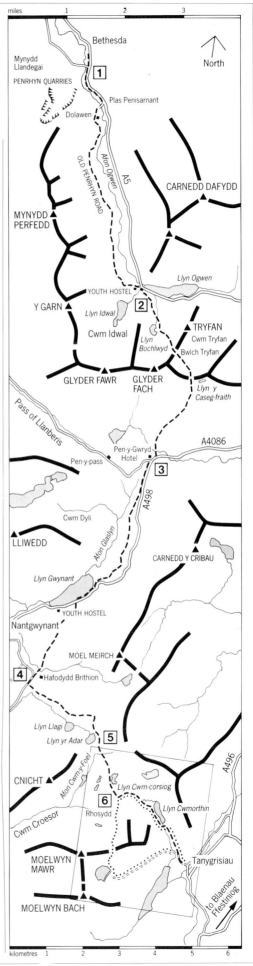

Start Bethesda

1 Follow the A5 south for about 1 mile/1.6 kms, then go off right at OS 631652 and down a drive past Plas Penisarnant. Cross the Afon Ogwen and follow a path alongside trees and past Dolawen. Continue across some boggy ground to a stile, then follow a wall to bear off right, passing between trees to the left of a house. Reach a gate onto the old Penrhyn road, and continue south to the Ogwen car park. (4¾ miles/7.6 kms)

2 Just past the toilets, turn right up the main Cwm Idwal track. Soon, where the track bends sharply right, keep ahead and follow a path into Cwm Bochlwyd and up to Bwlch Tryfan. Go over the step-stile in the wall, and continue on a rocky path to climb onto the moorland plateau at OS 667583. Llyn y Caseg-fraith is down to the left. Keep to the path that leads due south across peaty ground towards a small outcrop. Bear right just before the outcrop, and follow the path downhill to

Looking back to the north from Bwlch Tryfan: 'a ragged chaos of splintered rock . . .'

reach the road at Pen-y-Gwryd. (3½ miles/ 5.6 kms)

3 At the road junction, keep left down the A498. After about 300 yards/270 metres, bear off right at a rough lay-by, and follow the old road down Nantgwynant. Just before the A498 is rejoined at OS 650522, keep ahead past a barn, and follow a muddy waterside path to join the road. Go down the road for a ¼ mile/0.4 kms, then go off left, through a gate and along a track. Just past an open-sided barn, at a right-angled bend, bear off the track and follow a stony path uphill alongside trees. Continue along a walled lane. Pass an old building down on the right, and keep ahead towards thick stands of rhododendrons. Go through a gap in a wall, and continue alongside an old wire fence. Follow a winding path through rhododendrons, to reach a gap in a wall at a T-junction with a good path. Turn left, and continue through conifers; the path can be very muddy underfoot. Emerge onto open ground, and follow paths south to a wooden footbridge. Beyond the bridge, go left and reach a road corner at OS 637495. (4¾ miles/7.6 kms)

4 Follow the road south for a ¼ mile/0.4 kms, then go left at a signpost. Keep ahead, east, over grass, to pass to the left of a cottage. Cross a stream, bear up left to pass in front of a house, then go sharp right up a stony track. Keep alongside a fence, and reach a gate in a wall. Beyond the gate, keep ahead through a rocky section, and follow a path alongside a stream. Continue upstream, and at a wire fence bear sharp left. Go over a wall by a step-stile, and cross a flat boggy area. Bear up left, but do not go too high. Pass above a stone sheepfold, and follow the path as it climbs above Llyn Llagi. Where the path leads into a hollow at the top of a ravine, at OS 655486, there is a cairn. Go sharp right (south) and follow a very steep rocky path to where it levels off through a rocky hollow, then bear left (south-east) at a col, to reach a rocky outcrop on the shore of Llyn yr Adar. (2½ miles/4 kms)

5 *The next section is not well defined.* From the rocky outcrop on the lakeshore, follow a grassy track along the east side of the lake, for about 200 yards/180 metres. Just by a reedy patch, bear off south and away from the lake. *There is no obvious path at first.* Step over a low peat bank, and keep south across wet ground to cross a stream. Keep south to reach a large cairn on a low ridge at OS 658477. From the cairn, cross the ridge and continue south-east on a good path, descending some steep rocky sections, to reach Llyn Cwm-corsiog. Continue south to where the ground descends, and keep downhill, passing through a broken fence and keeping right, to reach the ruined buildings of Rhosydd at OS 665463. (1½ miles/2.4 kms)

6 From the ruined buildings, follow the track east and down steeply to Llyn Cwmorthin. Continue along the west side of the lake, past the ruined chapel, then cross a slate bridge at the head of the lake, and follow the track down to the road head at Tanygrisiau. Follow the road through the village and on to Blaenau Ffestiniog. (2 miles/3.2 kms)

CIRCULAR WALK 3¾ miles/6 kms

This three-hour walk leads through a complex area of old quarry workings and past very large open quarries. *Great care is advised with children and dogs. Ruined buildings should not be entered. Adits (mine shafts) should not be entered under any circumstances. The final descent to Llyn Stwlan is very steep.*

Start Tanygrisiau. There is parking at OS 684454.

1 Go up the track alongside the Afon Cwmorthin to reach Llyn Cwmorthin. *The track was originally a quarry tramway.* Continue along the west side of the lake, past the old chapel and other ruined buildings. Continue steeply up left to reach the slate-strewn plateau and the impressive ruins of the Rhosydd quarry buildings and barracks.

2 Behind the ruined buildings, continue along a slaty track past the mouth of an adit on the left. *This adit runs through the mountain to the huge quarry pit of West Twll. It is dangerous to enter.* Continue up a steep incline, bearing left at the top by the ruins of a winding house, then go right and up another incline. At the top, go between walls, then turn sharp left to continue between slate heaps. Pass more ruins, and continue steeply on a slaty path to a wide level area. Go right, south, past ruins along a broad raised track, to reach the edge of West Twll.

3 Go left along the edge of West Twll, and where the rim of the quarry swings right, keep ahead, south-east, across a short section of boggy ground to reach a cairn. *The collapsed workings of East Twll Quarry lie down to the left of this section. Care should be taken not to wander off the line.* Turn right at the cairn and follow a causeway track for about 300 yards/270 metres. Bear down left off the track, and pick up a poorly defined path that leads increasingly steeply down towards Llyn Stwlan. *The final descent is very steep and requires care.* Follow the road from Llyn Stwlan to regain the car park.

Offa's Dyke
Welsh–English Border

Monmouth to Sedbury 18 miles/28.8 kms

This lovely walk follows surviving sections of the eighth-century earthwork known as Offa's Dyke, where it runs along the rim of the eastern escarpment of the valley of the River Wye in south-east Wales. The route follows field paths and woodland tracks above the great limestone cliffs of the Wye, to emerge on the banks of the River Severn.

Offa's Dyke is not an ancient 'way' in the accepted sense of being a route between places. It is a unique 'ancient monument', the remains of a great frontier work that ran for one hundred and fifty miles/two hundred and forty kilometres between Anglo-Saxon Mercia and Welsh Wales. Eighty miles/one hundred and twenty-eight kilometres of the frontier incorporated earthworks; the rest was made up of natural barriers such as rivers and dense forest. Most traffic flows were through 'checkpoints' in the dyke, but it seems probable that a continuous track ran alongside the sections of earthwork, and along the line of the frontier where it comprised natural boundaries. The authority on Offa's Dyke, Sir Cyril Fox, believed that there was 'unhampered lateral movement along the frontier', and that, where there was no earthwork, a broad ride was cleared through forest and scrub to maintain continuity.

Offa's Dyke was built between AD 784 and 796; it was a remarkable engineering achievement for its time and place, and it has survived to prove the point. The man who conceived it is more difficult to assess. Offa emerged from the misty turmoil of the Anglo-Saxon world as an opportunistic and enterprising ruler. Achieving status of any kind in those dangerous times marked out a person as ruthless. Yet Offa achieved more than local dominance. He was the first 'king' consciously to establish boundaries to a large territory.

Offa was one of a line of Mercian kings who dominated the heart of Anglo-Saxon England. The Mercians came to power through the aggressive policies of great leaders such as Penda, Wulfhere and Aethelbald. These were the *bretwaldas*, the 'wide rulers' to whom lesser kings paid tribute by attending the *bretwalda*'s court and by supporting him in wars. Offa came to power in 757 after the assassination of Aethelbald, a murky deed in which he may have played a part. He then won the throne by force, usurping Aethelbald's heir, Beornerd.

Offa was content at first to consolidate his power. He travelled about his kingdom, visiting the thirty or so tribes of Mercia, and forging bonds of loyalty while suppressing any potential unrest. During the winter months, Offa and his court stayed at Tamworth, in modern Staffordshire, in a 'royal hall' with attendant services that included a mill and farms.

By the 770s Offa had welded Mercia into one kingdom. He then invaded neighbouring territories, defeating the people of West Sussex before striking unsuccessfully at Kent. In 778 the Mercian army invaded Wales, where the recalcitrant Britons had resisted Saxon advance since the end of the Roman era. Offa wasted the countryside of the border and then withdrew. The following year he defeated the King of Wessex and annexed a large part of modern Berkshire. By 785 Offa at last won control of Kent, and thus became the most powerful *bretwalda* in the country. It took him from the bone-strewn royal table at Tamworth to the heart of Europe, and to an alliance and friendship with the Holy Roman Emperor, Charlemagne, and with the Pope. But wild Wales remained forever at his back.

The first great King of Mercia, Penda, had been helped by the Welsh kings of Gwynedd during his struggles with Northumbria in the seventh century. But it was an uneasy alliance, and sporadic raiding of Mercia by the Welsh continued. Penda began a programme of dyke building by erecting short sections of defensive earthwork across river valleys and ridges, where the Welsh had found easy access to the frontier farms of the Mercians.

By Aethelbald's reign, the Mercian king was styling himself Rex Britannia. But relations with Wales had deteriorated and it is thought that Aethelbald built the large earthwork known as Wat's Dyke to block an increase in raiding by the Welsh. Wat's Dyke set a precedent for Mercian earthworks, though the example of Roman works such as Hadrian's Wall influenced dyke building generally. Wat's Dyke ran for just over forty miles/sixty-five kilometres, from the banks of the Dee Estuary to a point south of Oswestry, and it protected the vulnerable north-western flank of Mercia from Welsh attack.

However, contemporary records show that the Welsh continued to raid into Mercia, even during the height of Offa's powers in the 780s. Offa won control over southern England by 785, and he may have ordered the building of his dyke at that time. It would be a gesture typical of one who had triumphed over his Saxon rivals, yet had failed to subjugate Wales. A great physical boundary was the next best thing. Offa may have negotiated territorial agreements with the border Welsh, especially in Powys, over the siting of the dyke, because many of the earlier Mercian short dykes, and the land they protected, were abandoned deep inside Welsh territory.

Offa's Dyke was built quickly thanks to efficient engineering and to a large local labour force, augmented by Mercian regular soldiers. Clearance work through the forests of mid Wales and along the border hills was the first stage. Surveyors first planned the course of the dyke. Then local workers began the hard work of building the embankment and strengthening it with stone facing and timber work. In areas where planning was difficult, the dyke was pushed forward blindly at times. There are many erratic realignments, as well as dramatic differences in building style, that seem to indicate changes in work gangs and surveyors. At times the dyke is high, then suddenly becomes vestigial. But generally its line is regular and its proportions massive.

Once completed, Offa's Dyke was patrolled and garrisoned at key crossing points by small groups of regular soldiers. These 'border posts' controlled passage out of Wales of the legitimate traders and cattle dealers who operated even in times of war. A watch on the border would also have been kept by local Mercian farmers and conscripts, and reinforcements could be quickly summoned from the well-populated Mercian borderlands.

Offa's Dyke was successful militarily as well as politically. Skirmishing between Welsh and Mercians continued apace, but there was no large-scale invasion of Mercia during the rest of Offa's reign. The great king died in 796, and as so often happened in the wake of a powerful ruler, the Mercian leadership weakened. By the 820s, Mercian power had waned before the ascendancy of Wessex, whose King Ecgbriht also established greater control over Wales.

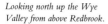

Looking north up the Wye Valley from above Redbrook.

Soon, Offa's Dyke became redundant as a frontier and as a defensive work, especially when a unified Wales developed closer political alliances with Saxon England and with Europe. But the dyke survives as a symbol of the intellectual change that transformed Saxon kings from being overlords of fragmented kingdoms to rulers of a 'national' territory.

The concept of the dyke was bold and self-confident. It was a man-made feature that sought to change a landscape. Yet the dyke's appeal today lies in its natural form. Offa would have been happy, probably, to erect a Mercian 'Berlin Wall' of concrete and steel, had the technology been available, but he had only natural material at hand, and his great earthwork was an extension of nature's own boundaries.

Most of the dyke's sections of earthwork are followed today by an official long-distance footpath. But the route diverges from the main line of the dyke at Rushock Hill above Kington. From here, the 'Offa's Dyke Path' follows an attractive course to Hay-on-Wye, then traverses the great ridge of the Black Mountains to follow field paths south to Monmouth. From Rushock, Offa's frontier probably ran in the form of a cleared way across the densely wooded Plain of Hereford to the banks of the River Wye at English Bicknor and Symonds Yat.

The surviving embankment of Offa's Dyke in Highbury Woods.

There is no evidence of earthworks across the Plain of Hereford, which confirms Cyril Fox's belief that a clearance line was all that was needed where natural boundaries such as forests existed. Then, at English Bicknor, an earthwork was again begun, and fragments of this survive today. South of Symonds Yat, however, it seems that the great river became the border and remained as such until the point at Highbury above Redbrook, downriver from Monmouth, from where our walk along the final sections of Offa's Dyke begins.

Monmouth is a convenient starting point for the walk, although there is no physical connection between the town and Offa's Dyke, and there is no definite evidence that the site of the present town was a Saxon settlement. Monmouth was a Norman town, fortified as a border keep, and its main street retains the random outlines of a medieval market that widens from the splendid Monnow Bridge and then narrows again at Agincourt Square. Our route south from Monmouth makes for pleasant walking and offers alternatives. One route can be followed down the east bank of the River Wye; another by the official Offa's Dyke Path that winds up over the high hill of The Kymin.

We leave Wales at Redbrook, and enter England and Offa's domain. The path leads up a broad flight of sixty-seven steps and on through fields to the edge of Highbury Wood, four hundred and fifty feet/one hundred and thirty-five metres above the Wye. From here a view back north reveals the narrowing of the valley gorge, where the sandstone cliffs have been deeply cut by the river. Beyond, lies the open apron of the flood plain where the Rivers Monnow, Trothy and Wye meet. Offa's Dyke is massive in Highbury Wood. Fox suggested that the dyke showed a downward trend towards Redbrook, and that its line was purposefully absorbed into the slope of the valley. He concluded that, from opposite Monmouth to Redbrook, the east bank of the Wye had been used as the frontier, after which it followed the rim of the escarpment, where another section of earthwork began.

Fox questioned why the Mercians did not simply use the east bank of the Wye as a natural boundary all the way to the Severn. He concluded that the eastern bank of the river was left open to allow Welsh traders landing points during their trafficking upriver. Fox cited this as an example of Mercian diplomacy that emphasized the civil role of Offa's Dyke. But the high profile of the dyke may also have reflected Mercian pride. The rim of the escarpment was bare of trees in the eighth century, and the crowning glory of a man-made rampart would have been dramatically visible from west of the river.

Fox traced the line of the dyke through Highbury Wood in

1931. His fieldwork was robust. He and his colleagues forced their way through the dense undergrowth. 'This was the first time that movement along the line of the dyke was found to be physically impossible without the use of a billhook,' reported Fox, with a hint of some excitement beneath the academic restraint. In Saxon times, Highbury Plain, as its name implies, would have been an area of open ground. The plain was farmed until late in the last century, after which it reverted to woodland.

Highbury is now a National Nature Reserve and a protected area. It is richly endowed with a leafy mix of oak, beech, ash, lime and hazel, and the blossoming wild cherry. On summer mornings there is an exquisite mistiness in these woods; leaves are glossy in the wet, the ground is drenched with dew, and the air is heavy with the scent of damp and mildew. There are fallow deer and tiny muntjac deer in the area. The latter are nocturnal and rarely seen, but fallow deer move rapidly through the crackling undergrowth when disturbed, and quick glimpses of them are possible at dusk and in the early morning.

Offa's Dyke is constant company here. It is massively steep on its western face where the slope drops away towards the valley bottom. In places, the stony bones of the embankment show through, and twisted yew trees tangle their great roots with the core of the dyke. After about a mile/one and a half kilometres, the dyke swings downhill and declines where our path crosses Coxbury Lane. A few yards further on, by a ferociously gnarled lime tree, the dyke takes on a changed alignment past Coxbury Farm, where it is clearly seen as a low grassy bank. There are lovely views to the Wye Valley from here. Beyond Coxbury, the path leads on towards the leafy acres of Creeping Hill Wood and Quicken Tree Wood on Wyegate Hill, where bluebells lie in drifts in early summer. On Wyegate, Offa's engineers struck high to take the dyke to a height of over five hundred feet/one hundred and fifty metres, as if asserting once more the dominance of the frontier above the Wye.

But as always, landscape dictated, and the dyke descends rapidly on the south side of the hill to where the valley of the Mork Brook descends to Bigsweir Bridge. Our path leaves the course of the dyke here, although the earthwork survives in places where it crosses the valley, climbs through the nicely named Mocking Hazel Wood, and crosses a sunken lane that runs west down to the river at Bigsweir. This lane has some embanked features but is essentially a holloway. It is medieval, probably, although it is marked on maps as Offa's Dyke.

Our path takes us down to the A466 at Bigsweir Bridge, and a choice of routes. The riverside route to Brockweir is pleasant and uncomplicated. It winds downriver through the ferny woods and hugs the river bank where the Wye nudges a rounded elbow at the village of Llandogo, lying on the opposite bank between the wooded heights of Cuckoo and Bargain Woods. Trees overhang the river, and occasional bursts of white water breach the quiet glide of the mainstream.

The inland route follows more properly the course of Offa's Dyke, through a complex landscape of small fields and rural suburbia, where the dyke has become fragmented and eroded in places. Initially, the way lies steeply uphill through a wooded landscape where massive oaks and sweet chestnuts cloud the air with their greenness. Sections of the dyke are often seen in close consort with walled hedges across St Briavels Common, where the dyke was known locally as the Devil's Ridge. The views down the interlocked valley of the Wye are splendid.

Beyond the riverside village of Brockweir, the merged route regains the high ground of the eastern bluffs above Tintern Abbey. From here, it maintains height as far as Chepstow, through the woods of Passage Grove and Shorn Cliff. For the walker, the way through the woods is glorious enough, the dyke being massive and steep-faced. By the rock outcrop known as the Devil's Pulpit there is an exhilarating view down to the ruins of Tintern. The abbey was founded by the Cistercians in 1131 and survived until the Dissolution of 1538, after which it decayed and was robbed of stone. But even in ruins, Tintern was magnificent, and the 'sublime' appeal of its ivy-clad gothic architecture and of its picturesque setting attracted Wordsworth and Turner, among many other literary and artistic figures of the Romantic Movement.

How the Devil must have laughed at all this from his eponymous pulpit on the high ground, where the picturesque is overshadowed by twisted trees and wickedly sinister outcrops. From here, the course of the dyke snakes along the leafy crest of great cliffs and escarpments. It reaches its highest point of seven hundred feet/two hundred and ten metres in Shorncliff Wood, where its eastern side has been faced with stonework as a hedge boundary of a much later date than Offa's time. Now, the path winds on through woods that seem to crowd in ever more tightly, and where, in heavy rain, there is some shelter at first, until fat beads of water begin to spill from the dripping leaves, and the stony, root-matted path becomes glassy and treacherous underfoot.

Our way soon diverges from the dyke where it strikes across Dennel Hill towards the clifftop of Ban-y-gor. Land development and building force a diversion to the B4288 and then on towards Woodcroft and the spectacular viewpoint of Wintour's Leap, from where the distinctive Lancaut Peninsula can be seen. The line of

Offa's frontier struck across the neck of the peninsula, and possibly incorporated the embankment of its Iron Age promontory fort. From Wintour's Leap the path leads along the edge of impressive limestone cliffs, then veers inland and follows a tortuous course past the outskirts of Chepstow.

The Romans bridged the river near modern Chepstow, but the town was established by the Saxons, its name deriving from the Old English *ceap* for market and *stow* for place. The Welsh name for the site was Ystraigyl. It had a richer sound but was just as prosaic in its meaning of 'the bend of the river'. By Offa's time the site must have been abandoned to the Welsh, probably by agreement. It was the Normans who gave Chepstow its real stature, not least by building the magnificent Chepstow castle, their earliest stone-built fortress.

Beyond the A48 the line of the frontier was well served by the limestone cliffs on the east bank of the Wye. But where the Offa's Dyke path skirts a modern sewage works at Tallard's Marsh, an earthwork was raised once more. On this final section, the dyke has been breached and destroyed in places, but is impressive enough along its rather well-kept way past the houses of Pennsylvania Village and across suitably named 'Saxon' streets. The Sedbury to Beachley road cuts through the dyke at a section of bank known as Buttington Tump, where a memorial stone commemorates the Silver Jubilee of 1977.

To the south lies the Severn Bridge, which links to the shorter Wye Bridge via a viaduct across the tip of Beachley Point. Over one thousand years separate the twentieth-century marvel of the Severn Bridge from the eighth-century marvel of Offa's Dyke. The design of Offa's Dyke may be simplistic by comparison, but the dyke takes the honours for length. Here on the banks of the Severn it reaches its end at Sedbury Cliffs. Trees line its course from the main road, and the ground can be miserably wet and muddy at times. At the end of the dyke, on the sandstone edge of the cliff, there is a memorial stone. Below, lies the wide sweep of the Severn, with its central banks of Oldbury Sands and the inshore channel of Slime Road, where vessels that missed the tide could safely ground on the soft sand until high water.

Sedbury Cliffs is not the most spectacular ending for the great Mercian earthwork which has traversed so much high ground and cliff edge in its long journey down the Welsh Marches. But the sense of place is inspiring. Cyril Fox finished his six years' survey of Offa's Dyke at this spot, and may be indulged for his reflection: 'Memories . . . flooded the mind, for the place seemed to be to an unusual degree characteristic of the Mercian frontier line as a whole and to evoke the very spirit of its creator.'

Offa's Dyke
Information

Distance 18 miles/28.8 kms

Maps OS Landranger 162 (Gloucester & Forest of Dean); OS Outdoor Leisure 14 (Wye Valley & Forest of Dean)

Nature of Walk A lovely walk following the course of the great Mercian earthwork known as Offa's Dyke. The route can be completed in a day by experienced walkers. It is part of a National Trail and is well signposted throughout. There are a few steep inclines, and sections of the route may be wet and quite muddy at times. Clothing and equipment should be for country walking.

Accommodation At Monmouth and Chepstow and at villages en route. Youth hostels at Monmouth, Chepstow, and at St Briavels, just off the central section of the route.

Transport Rail connections to Chepstow from main centres. Bus connections to Monmouth. There are buses between Monmouth and Chepstow along the A466 on the western bank of the Wye, although Offa's Dyke can only be reached from the A466 at Tintern, Brockweir, and from points north of Bigsweir Bridge.

Further Information Tourist Information Centre, Monmouth, tel. (0600) 713899.

Start Monmouth

1 Cross Wye Bridge and keep ahead where the A466 branches right. Cross with care where the A4136 swings left and uphill by the Mayhill Hotel. Follow a railed path uphill to reach a road. Continue uphill to a bend, then leave the road along a path, signposted Beaulieu Wood. Follow waymarks to the summit of The Kymin. Go right, keeping left of the Round House, and continue down a drive to go left through a kissing gate. Follow a path through open fields, and then go down a rough lane to a road at Upper Redbrook. Go down right, then cross over, just before an incline bridge, to follow a lane to reach the A466 at Lower Redbrook. (3½ miles/5.6 kms)

2 Go left, then turn up left before the Bell Inn. Climb steps, then follow waymarks to Highbury Farm, where a right turn leads to the entrance to Highbury Wood. Follow the earthwork of Offa's Dyke to reach a road at OS 543055. Turn right, to reach the A466 at Bigsweir Bridge. *A footpath from this road leads the 1½ miles/2.4 kms to St Briavels. (3¼ miles/5.2 kms)*

There are alternative routes to Brockweir from Bigsweir Bridge.

3a The Inland Route Just before the bridge, go left through a gate by a lodge. Follow waymarks on a path across fields and through woods to reach a road opposite Birchfield House at OS 541039. Follow the road right, and in 200 yards/180 metres, go off right down a lane, then continue along a stony path and a track to reach another road. Turn right, and after 200 yards/180 metres, go left over a stile and into a field. Reach a farm lane, go left for 50 yards/45 metres, then turn right down an enclosed path. After 100 yards/90 metres, take the right fork, ignoring the waymarked stile on the left. Reach a road, continue to a T-junction, and turn left. Go off right down a path at a sharp left bend. Cross a lane, then reach a road. Go left, then immediately right down the drive to the gate of Brook House, from where a path down to the right is followed across a stream to reach a rough road. Continue, to emerge at the Brockweir road opposite the Mackenzie Hall. *(Brockweir village is ½ mile/0.8 kms downhill to the right.)* Cross the road diagonally right, and follow a path downhill to cross the Brockweir Brook. Go steeply uphill to a large signpost. *The riverside alternative comes in from the right here. (3¼ miles/5.2 kms)*

3b The River Route Go left over a stile, just before the traffic lights at Bigsweir Bridge. The path follows the river bank closely, and is well waymarked. At Brockweir, turn off right, just past the inn, then turn right down a surfaced lane. At the stables, turn sharp left and go uphill to the large signpost described above. (3½ miles/5.6 kms)

4 From the large signpost, bear uphill and follow waymarks to enter Caswell Wood. Follow fine sections of Offa's Dyke, passing the Devil's Pulpit, and continue to the B4228 at OS 553977. (3 miles/4.8 kms)

5 Go right for ⅓ mile/0.5 kms, then go left over a stile and follow waymarks to regain the B4228 at OS 545966. Go left along the road for ⅓ mile/0.5 kms, then cross over at some houses. *The viewpoint of Wintour's Leap is on the right.* Follow a path going off right behind the houses to reach the B4228. Turn right along the road, with care, for 50 yards/45 metres, then go right and follow waymarks to pass the distinctive Twtshill Tower to reach a road. (2½ miles/4 kms)

6 Turn right and go down to cross a road. Continue down a surfaced lane between walls, then at a junction turn left up a steep path. Fork right down a narrower path to reach a drive where a right turn leads to a road. Turn right, and cross the railway and the Chepstow bypass. In 80 yards/72 metres go right into Wyebank Avenue, then turn left at the first side road, and a few yards further on, go right down a narrow fenced path. Follow waymarks, passing a sewage works, to continue through the housing of Pennsylvania Village, and on across a field to reach Buttington Tump and the Sedbury–Beachley road. Cross the road *with care,* and go up the lane opposite for about 15 yards/13 metres, then go right over a stile and follow the path to reach the Offa's Dyke Stone. *By following a path down right from here, to the foreshore, a path leading inland can be followed back to the road.* (2½ miles/4 kms)

Near Buttington Tump on the final stretch of the Offa's Dyke path.

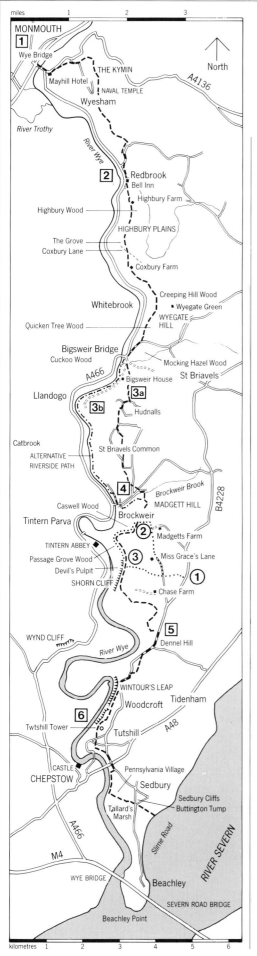

Above: Tintern Abbey, where 'the picturesque is overshadowed by the twisted trees'.

CIRCULAR WALK 4 miles/6.4 kms

A pleasant walk that includes the section of the Offa's Dyke path that runs through the woods high above Tintern Abbey. A short diversion to the Devil's Pulpit can be included. Allow about two hours.

Start Car park on the B4228 south of St Briavels at OS 558995

1 Follow a path through the trees to pass a trig point. Continue to reach a track at OS 554993. This is Miss Grace's Lane. Turn right along the track.

2 At Beeches Farm follow waymarks round the buildings, and go down a slope to a gate. Beyond the gate, turn left to reach a stile by a large boulder. Go over the stile, and join the Offa's Dyke Path. Turn left, and follow the dyke through Caswell Wood.

3 Just before the Devil's Pulpit, at OS 544995, go left over a stile, and follow a path through fields to reach Miss Grace's Lane. *The Devil's Pulpit is worth visiting for its views down to Tintern.* Retrace the route back to the car park.

THE PEDDARS WAY
East Anglia

Knettishall to Holme next the Sea 46½ miles/74.4 kms

The Peddars Way is a lengthy but undemanding walk through the quiet countryside of Norfolk. The route follows the line of a Roman road that sliced through the territory of the Iron Age Iceni tribe, whose last doomed leader was the formidable Boudica. What the route lacks in dramatic landscape features it makes up for with its engaging sense of isolation and its rural peace.

The relentless flatness of East Anglia can be unnerving. Yet the area has ancient landscape forms that were shaped by the tidal seas and by the glaciers that once surged across the vast fields of its heartland. Planning a Roman road through this landscape was like firing an arrow across the sea. Nothing got in the way, least of all people. Before the great road, now known as Peddars Way, was built, the Romans had found little need of military control of the area. It was the territory of the Iceni, a client tribe of the Empire, subservient and pliable and passive until Boudica.

The Iceni was one of the earliest of the Iron Age tribes to settle in Britain. The tribe had centres at modern Norwich, Caistor St Edmund, and at Thetford, Snettisham, and King's Lynn – all close to the Peddars Way. Their farming settlements of thatched huts and wickerwork stockades were scattered throughout the countryside, a pattern of Iron Age development that was archaic by the time of the Roman invasion.

Caesar's exploratory invasions of Britain in the first century BC met with united British resistance. But eventual divisions between the British tribes led to five of them, the Iceni included, surrendering to Rome. The pattern of capitulation was established. Roman influence was in the land.

During the one hundred years between Caesar's invasions and the Claudian Conquest of AD 43, there was trading and cultural interchange between south-east Britain, Roman Gaul and Italy. When the invasion of AD 43 took place, many of the British tribes were eager for peaceful association with the conquerors. The Iceni especially were happy to become a client kingdom, a device used skilfully by the Romans in all of their conquests, as a way of stifling native resistance. In Britain, the fire of native independence burned still, but it lay with the fanatical Druid priesthood of the old religion, and with the western tribes.

Roman forts and settlements were established at such sites as Camulodunum near Colchester, and Verulamium, the modern St Albans. Romanization of the Britons of the south-east continued. But resentment smouldered, especially over the system of *colonia*, by which retired legionaries and others of Rome's servants were given land and an unspoken superiority over the Britons. At Camulodunum a great temple deifying Claudius was built after the

Emperor's death in AD 54. The Druids seethed; they had retreated to the refuge of far Anglesey but their influence in fermenting hostility against the conqueror was still potent.

The catalyst of British revolt was the breakdown of the client kingdom arrangement between Rome and the Iceni. Rome's custom was to take full control of a client kingdom at the death of its king. This would have been the expected course of events with the Iceni, whose clienthood was now anomolous in a Britain under more or less total Roman control, and where the tough military governor, Suetonius Paullinus, eschewed diplomacy for the sword. Paullinus arrived in Britain in AD 58. Within two years he had extended Roman influence to the north and west, and was poised to attack the Welsh tribes and to penetrate the last refuge of the Druids on Anglesey.

The King of the Iceni, Prasutagus, died in AD 60, leaving a declaration that his two daughters, were to be co-heirs to Iceni territory, with Nero, Claudius's successor. It was a doomed hope. Roman loans to the Iceni were withdrawn (economics being at the heart of politics), and Roman administrators conducted a heavy-handed inventory of all Iceni property and wealth. It was attended, probably, by crooked dealing and by the barefaced theft of goods. Ex-soldiers and minor officials descended on the royal palace of the Iceni, and began to pick over the very stuff of tribal identity. Prasutagus's wife Boudica resisted, and in a notoriously savage response, she was stripped and lashed. Her daughters were raped and brutalized by soldiers and officials alike, and the villages of the Iceni were vandalized. Tribal lands were seized by *colonia*.

Meanwhile, Paullinus and the bulk of his forces were well advanced into Wales. The governor believed that the south-east was secure from unrest. But an outraged Boudica joined forces with the disaffected Trinovantes and other tribes to raise a revolt. Roman confidence was such that Camulodunum was undefended. Boudica's army advanced on the city and sent a separate force to ambush the Ninth Legion, which Paullinus had dispatched from the north-west to deal with what he believed was a minor revolt.

The Ninth was ambushed while the cohorts were in an extended line of march. The legionaries were annihilated, native blood lust was loosed, and in the name of blood-smeared deities, Camulodunum, and then Londinium, were savagely destroyed. At Londinium, Boudica's horde committed horrific atrocities, especially against women, in revenge for the humiliation she and her daughters had suffered. There was no mercy. According to Tacitus, it was *'caedes, patibula, ignes, cruces'* – 'sword, gibbet, fire and cross.'

But the British lingered too long at Camulodunum, in typical native dalliance brought on by the euphoria of success. It allowed Paullinus first to reconnoitre and then to force march his entire army down from the north-west. He marshalled them at a point on Watling Street on a battlefield that was to his advantage. From Londinium, Boudica and her hectic army swept north-west, sacking an abandoned Verulamium on the way, and massing before the Roman forces at last.

The numerical odds against the Romans were formidable. One chronicler claimed that there were 230,000 Britons to the Romans' 15,000 foot soldiers and cavalry. But the numbers were more likely to be about 100,000 Britons – odds enough. Men and women fought together in the British forces; they were driven by a primitive hysteria and excitement, but had no coherent battle plan: their most famous device was the lightweight chariot, symbol of Boudican glory.

Paullinus had chosen a position that gave the trained and disciplined legionaries the advantage of close-quarters fighting, in which the short sword, the *gladius*, was used to devastating effect against the clumsy long swords of the Britons. But first, thousands of Roman javelins rained down on Boudica's berserk fighters with terrible effect; then the legionaries charged, spearheading in a series of phalanxes, with shield walls guarding their flank. Tens of thousands of Britons were cut down in the ensuing rout. Paullinus's cavalry increased the carnage. Roman losses were said to run to the hundreds only.

It is from this battle that the mythic image of Boudica has come down to us, thanks to the embroidered reportage of the Roman historian Dio Cassius. Boudica was described as belligerent and 'huge of frame', heroic in her iron-clad scything chariot hauled by great horses. In fact, the British chariot was a lightweight, wheeled vehicle of wickerwork, without wheel scythes, which would have hampered movement. Descriptions of Boudica's death are equally mythical. She is said to have been poisoned or to have killed

herself, but we do not know with certainty. She was doomed, of
course, as was this last great rebellion against the implacable might
of Rome, though it shocked the Roman govenment and led to a
reappraisal of policy towards Britain.

For Paullinus, the hard-bitten, impulsive soldier, the immediate
policy was ruthless reprisal. The British revolt had humiliated him
and had cast aspersions on his judgement and marred his successes
in the eyes of the politicians of Rome. The Iceni, especially, were
brutally treated; their lands were devastated, and famine –
augmented by the fact that the Iceni had failed to sow crops in their
year of revolt – was allowed to spread unchecked. Paullinus's
vengeful reprisals caused concern in Rome, and by AD 61 a more
conciliatiory governor, Petronius Turpilianus, was appointed. But
as well as reconciliation and diplomacy, the Romans shrewdly
increased the militarization of the area, which included extending
the road network of East Anglia.

It was during this time that the road now known as the Peddars
Way was pushed north from Stane Street, near Colchester, to Long
Melford, Ixworth and Knettishall – where the National Trail now
begins. The road had no recorded Roman name, and the word
'Peddars' may simply have been adopted from a standard word for
path or track. It is thought that the Romans used the road mainly
for transporting troops to the shores of The Wash at Holme next
the Sea, from where ferries ran to Lincolnshire. But the road was
also garrisoned with watch towers and small forts, as military
control was imposed on the Iceni and on a land effectively lost
forever from the native British.

But Boudica's name was not lost (in spite of being misspelt as
'Boadicea'). The name means 'Victoria' – a cruel irony – and it was
the Victorians, of a very different Britain, who resurrected the
doomed Iceni queen as a symbol of their own imperialism, and
gave pride of place on London's Embankment to a monumental
sculpture of queen and stylized chariot, scythes and all.

The start of the modern Peddars Way pays fleeting respect to
Suffolk, but the line of the road south of Knettishall is now lost and
lacks convenient footpaths. At Knettishall, the route north plunges
immediately into woodland, then crosses the Little Ouse River
into Norfolk to reach the A1066 Thetford to Diss road through tall
reassuring beeches. Beyond, is a wood of mixed conifer and beech
where the earthwork, the agger, of the Roman road is clearly seen
to the left as a grassy embankment crowned with thorn bushes and
trees.

At the River Thet, wooden boardwalks have been laid along the
marshy river banks. To the right, there is a wide stretch of wetland

that is wholly characteristic of the Norfolk countryside, in its succession of habitats and in its layers of colour. In the foreground there is a dense tangle of nettle and rosebay willowherb and tough grasses, with, behind it, a line of willows and maples backed by a dark wall of conifers. In sunlight, after rain, the gradations of colour and texture are exquisite here.

The River Thet is reed-fringed and modest; the Romans are believed to have crossed it using a bailey bridge resting on boats. Where the agger of the Peddars Way runs down to the river, some excavation has taken place. The road was found to be a causeway, sixteen feet/nearly five metres wide, and made up of tightly packed flints with a top-dressing of gravel that was over two feet/sixty centimetres thick at the centre. A cleared extension four feet/over a metre wide was found on the east side of the road, and this is thought to have been an additional pathway. Today, the squat agger of the road can still be seen, under grass, where it runs north from the River Thet to skirt the Brettenham Heath National Nature Reserve. The reserve is one of the largest areas of surviving heathland in Norfolk, a savannah-like sweep of country with scattered clumps of hawthorn and birch and bracken. It was in such countryside that the Iceni would have farmed and hunted around their kraal-like stockades with their tall watchtower entrances. The reserve is a key wildlife site and public access is justifiably restricted.

Ahead lies the A11, the very busy main trunk road between Norwich and London, and, beyond it, a stretch of surfaced road leading to the railway crossing on the Ely to Norwich line. To the east, the land is under military occupation, but non-Roman this time, a theme for the next few miles. The railway can be crossed by going through the gate, or by an underpass so low that it is capable of knocking you unconscious.

The track continues across Roudham Heath by tall trees where the agger is visible, thirty feet/nine metres wide in places, though only a foot/thirty centimetres or so in height. Some stark-looking gas installations are passed, and then the path crosses the Illington Road, and narrows between green walls finally to reach the village of Wretham, known also as Stonebridge for its pains. There is an old windmill here, its wings clipped and its trunk converted into a private home. Beyond the village, the Peddars Way follows a surfaced military road for just over a mile/about two kilometres, then parts company with it at Galley Hill. Here the Roman surveyors realigned the road to the north-west, and maintained that alignment for thirty-four miles/fifty-four kilometres to the shores of The Wash – an astonishing continuity.

From Galley Hill, the track follows a strangely one-sided course between military ocupation to the left and open country to the right. But inside the MoD fences, a marvellous wilderness survives, protected from the inquisitive by the Official Secrets Act and by conspicuous warning notices.

This is the heart of Breckland, where acidic sand covered the basic chalk to produce a mix of heath and open grasslands. The Breckland, the 'breached' land, was cleared extensively from the Neolithic period onwards, and suffered wind erosion because of it. But the Iceni prospered here, and as late as the last century the land was still being engineered. The River Issey was dammed during Victorian enclosures, and the sheet of reed-fringed Thompson Water was formed. Just past Thompson Water, the Norfolk Naturalists' Trust cares for a fascinating area noted for its pools, which are known delightfully as 'pingos'. These are dimpled craters formed during the last Ice Age, when blisters of subterranean ice thrust the soil upwards into hillocks. When the ice finally melted the hillocks collapsed into the void, and formed craters that are now waterlogged and crammed with plants.

The pingos are a delight in early summer, their surfaces veiled with emerald pondweed and a riot of early flowering bogbean, with its pink and white blooms fringed with white hairs. The lovely water violet is also prolific, its feathery leaves submerged, but its tall stem rising above the surface and carrying a fine show of lilac-coloured, yellow-eyed flowers. Handsome oaks trail their leafy branches across the ponds, and in the heat of summer the air hums with insect life and the chimes of birdsong.

The track continues past Shakers Furze, with the low agger of the Roman road always on its eastern side. Paths are followed through Merton Park to where an elbow of muddy track leads us to the ugly shuttle of the Brandon Road and thence to Little Cressingham. From here, the line of the Roman road is lost and a surfaced road is followed uphill to where field paths cross the shallow valley of the River Wissey to North Pickenham.

From North Pickenham a green track known as Procession Way follows the line of the Roman road to the north. It makes for a pleasant interlude, the well-worn track fringed with conifers and beech trees at first, and then by fields, the accompanying hedgerows a froth of may blossom in spring. But the peace is short-lived, and crossing the busy A47 Norwich to King's Lynn road demands care. Beyond here, a surfaced lane leads past Grange Farm, and then by indifferent lanes and a roadside path to the approach to Castle Acre by a lovely ford on the River Nar.

From the river bank, the ruins of Castle Acre Priory can be seen across a broad field. This was a Cluniac foundation of 1090. The Cluniac brotherhood was officially Benedictine but acted independently of the order, and was under the control of the Abbot

Castle Acre Priory.

of Cluny in Burgundy. Such independence, linked to close contacts with France, led to official English persecution, and financial oppression of the order during the fourteenth century. The persecution continued, but ceased after the monks were officially recognized as being 'non-alien'. Today, the ruined buildings have a rare dignity and style, and the west front and prior's lodging are especially fine. The remains of the inner walls of the main building are detached, and have had their flint stonework eroded. They loom through the early morning mist like miniature sea-stacks.

Castle Acre is entered through its thirteenth-century bailey gate. The heart of this wonderful village is Stocks Green, with its surrounding brick and flint houses. Flint is ubiquitous as building material in chalk country, and the combination of brick and flint is very pleasing. Building with flint requires time and patience because it is non-absorbent. Flint walls are built in short courses, and the mortar allowed to take; a course that was too high and heavy would soon collapse. The River Nar was once navigable, and the Castle Acre area was settled long before the Normans established their characteristic motte and bailey castle, whose outer defences still surround the modern village.

North of Castle Acre, the line of the Peddars Way runs uninterrupted towards the sea, through a broad landscape of vast fields and shelter-belt trees. This is a countryside that has been farmed intensively for generations. Cash crops now dominate, and the startling canary yellow of oilseed rape, the faded blue of flax, and the pale buff of maize, colour code the landscape. Fields are ploughed deeply. In wet weather the clay sucks at your feet and overflows onto lanes and trackways where small knuckles of flint crunch underfoot. The skeletal gantries of mobile irrigation systems straddle the fields like giant praying mantises. The land seems drained of its relish; in winter, the vast wrung-out fields match the pallid skies. Yet, at the field edges and along the endless miles of tracks and lanes, dense hedgerows and woodland shelter belts glow with colour in spring and summer, their undisciplined chaos still offering a refuge for birds and insects and mammals.

Here, the old road makes for excellent walking where it strikes ahead with Roman certainty. In fine weather, vast booming skies overpower the landscape; the sun pours from the blue with a heat that is exquisite, and that is made bearable by the chequered shade of the lanes. To either side, the villages and hamlets stand back from the old Roman Way. There is a tedious uphill slog from Castle Acre along the road to Great Massingham, although once again useful field paths break the monotony until the road is escaped to where field tracks lead west of the pretty villages of Massingham, Great and Little.

The Way crosses the A148 Fakenham road, then climbs quite steeply past a row of handsome flint and brick cottages and over Harpley Common, with its vast fields furred with the green of root crops. Where the track reaches the road at Anmer Minque, intact tumuli are islanded in the midst of the fields, but swathed in field weeds and grassy camouflage. The agger of the Roman road is impressive in this open countryside. It is generally about thirty-six feet/nine and a half metres wide, but near Fring, where it runs alongside bronze fields of corn, it is much wider and conspicuously raised. Far to the east, the huge windmill at Great Bircham is prominent on the horizon, arms akimbo.

There is a widening of view now as the land begins its final rise before the coast. The Peddars Way skirts the village of Fring, and strides on across a strangely wizened little 'ford' at Fring Cross, where the Heacham River is more substantial in name than in nature. The Way leads past Dovehill Wood, then detours at Littleport, where it crosses the road to the west of Sedgeford. Here, it follows a driveway past the striking Sedgeford Magazine House, built of honey-coloured carstone, and boasting long-and-short-work corners, globe finials and round-arched apertures. The building dates from the Civil War period of the seventeenth century, and was used as a magazine and powder store.

The Way leads past Magazine Farm, where there is a nice use of mixed carstone and flint in the end wall of one of the buildings. A slog through dull fields leads to Ringstead, from where the official path diverts from the surfaced line of a road that is marked as the Peddars Way. The diversion is more likely to be the true line of the old road, and it leads down a lovely section of hedged pathway that coincides with a parish boundary on a raised agger. Ahead, lies the great broad sweep of The Wash. Across the Hunstanton road, a surfaced lane called Seagate charts the last mile of the Peddars Way to the linear world of the seashore and Holme dunes, and the great shingle banks of the offshore ground.

THE PEDDARS WAY
Information

Distance 46.5 miles/74.4 kms

Maps OS Landranger 144 (Thetford & Breckland); OS Landranger 132 (North-West Norfolk)

Nature of Walk A long-distance walk through undemanding countryside, using field tracks, country lanes and footpaths. It is best walked in two or three days. The route is a National Trail and is well signposted throughout. Sections of the route may be wet and quite muddy at times. Clothing and equipment should be for country walking.

Accommodation At Thetford, Castle Acre, and Holme next the Sea, and at some villages adjoining the route. Camp sites, with short-stay facilities for walkers, at Knettishall and Thorpe Woodlands.

Transport Rail and bus connections from main centres to Thetford and King's Lynn. Connecting buses to Knettishall, Holme next the Sea, and Castle Acre.

Further Information Tourist Information Centre, Thetford, tel. (0842) 752 599.

Start Car park at Blackwater Carr, Knettishall OS 944806

1 Follow the signposted path north through woods to cross a footbridge over the Little Ouse River. Continue, crossing two roads and then the River Thet. Cross another road and continue to the A11 (*cross with care*). Continue over the Ely–Norwich railway line. (*Alternatively, a low tunnel down to the right can be used.*) Keep ahead on a broad track between conifers. Cross a road at OS 928899, then continue to the A1075 at Wretham (Stonebridge). (6¼ miles/10 kms)

2 At Wretham, cross the road *with care*, go up past the post office, then bear off left along a surfaced road. Where the road bends left at OS 922929, keep ahead along a forestry track. (*The land to the west is MoD property and is out of*

bounds.) Pass Thompson Water and continue, crossing two road ends with their accompanying rash of MoD notices. Follow the waymarked route through Merton estate to reach a track crossing at OS 902992. Go left along a track, then right to reach the B1108. Cross the busy road *with care*, then go left along paths that weave to either side of field hedges and sections of woodland. Bear right down a slip road into Little Cressingham. (8¼ miles/13.2 kms)

3 Turn right at the crossroads in Little Cressingham, by the White Horse Inn. Follow the surfaced road north, to cross the B1077 at Hall Farm. Continue past Home Farm, then, on a slight bend, at OS 861051, bear off left and continue inside the field hedge. Cross a field track, then go left at the next hedge. Follow the path on a zigzag course across the River Wissey valley, using several stiles, and emerge at a road to the right of a school. Go right along the road, to another T-junction. (North Pickenham village is to the right.) Turn left and follow the road to another T-junction with the road to Swaffham. (5¼ miles/8.4 kms)

4 Cross the road at this T-junction, and follow the rough track of Procession Way. Reach the A47 King's Lynn–Norwich road, and cross, *with care*. Continue ahead along a surfaced lane past Grange Farm. Follow the lane round left, then go sharp right, then left along a lane to Palgrave Hall. Where the lane bends left, keep ahead along a muddy track to reach a road at Great Palgrave. Turn left along a road, using a signposted path inside the hedgerows on the left. Cross the A1065 *with care*, then follow the lane opposite steeply uphill to a crossroads. Keep ahead down a narrow lane marked 'Ford – unsuitable for motors'. Cross the River Nar by a bridge at a ford. Continue right, along the lane, then turn right at a junction, then left at the next junction, and climb steeply to enter Castle Acre through the bailey gate. (6¼ miles/10 kms)

5 From the bailey gate, turn right, then follow the road round left, and continue along the

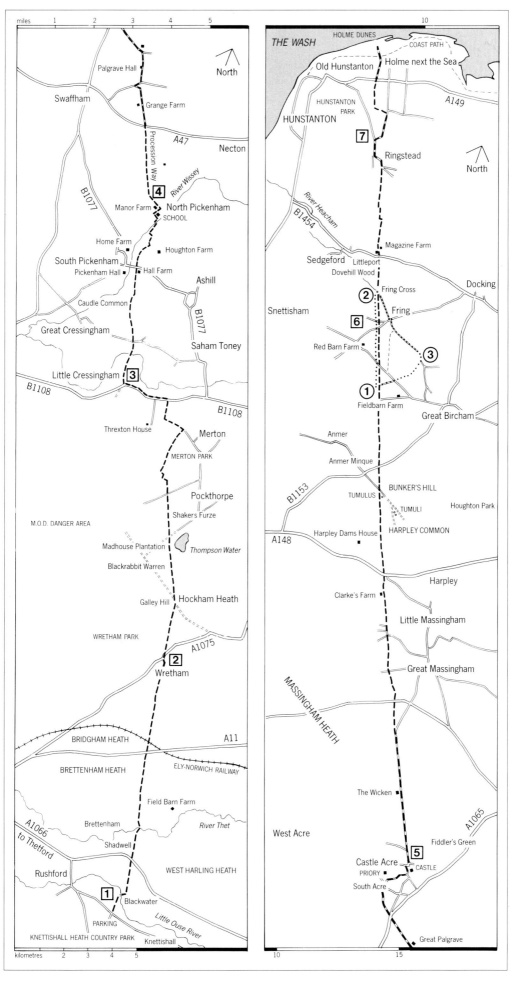

miles
North
Palgrave Hall
Swaffham
Grange Farm
A47
Necton
Procession Way
B1077
River Wissey
4
Manor Farm
North Pickenham
SCHOOL
Home Farm
Houghton Farm
South Pickenham
Pickenham Hall
Hall Farm
Ashill
Caudle Common
B1077
Great Cressingham
Saham Toney
Little Cressingham
3
B1108
B1108
Threxton House
Merton
MERTON PARK
Pockthorpe
Shakers Furze
M.O.D. DANGER AREA
Madhouse Plantation
Thompson Water
Blackrabbit Warren
Galley Hill
Hockham Heath
WRETHAM PARK
A1075
2
Wretham
BRIDGHAM HEATH
A11
BRETTENHAM HEATH
ELY-NORWICH RAILWAY
Field Barn Farm
River Thet
A1066
to Thetford
Brettenham
Shadwell
Rushford
WEST HARLING HEATH
1
Blackwater
PARKING
KNETTISHALL HEATH COUNTRY PARK
Knettishall
Little Ouse River
kilometres
2 3 4 5

THE WASH
HOLME DUNES
COAST PATH
Old Hunstanton
Holme next the Sea
A149
HUNSTANTON PARK
HUNSTANTON
7
North
Ringstead
River Heacham
B1454
Magazine Farm
Sedgeford
Littleport
Dovehill Wood
Fring Cross
Docking
2
Fring
Snettisham
6
Red Barn Farm
3
1
Fieldbarn Farm
Great Bircham
Anmer
Anmer Minque
B1153
BUNKER'S HILL
TUMULUS
TUMULI
Houghton Park
A148
HARPLEY COMMON
Harpley Dams House
Harpley
Clarke's Farm
Little Massingham
MASSINGHAM HEATH
Great Massingham
The Wicken
A1065
West Acre
Fiddler's Green
5
Castle Acre
CASTLE
PRIORY
South Acre
Great Palgrave
10 15

133

Procession Way, a quiet stretch of the Peddars Way near Swaffham.

Great Massingham Road. At a junction, signposted West Acre and Gayton, join a footpath on the left, where it runs behind the field hedge. Rejoin the road by a house and continue uphill. Just past some trees, where the road bends right by a trig point, keep ahead and follow a field track downhill. Continue on lanes and tracks, crossing three roads, to reach the A148. Cross *with care*, continue steeply past Harpley Dams, and follow a field track to another road at Anmer Minque, OS 758285. Continue on a broad track, crossing two more roads to reach another road at OS 734343, just west of Fring. (13½ miles/21.6 kms)

6 A short distance beyond this road, cross another road and follow a short section of surfaced lane down into a dip, then go steeply uphill past a house, and continue on a green lane to Fring Cross. Cross the road and continue alongside hedges, passing a wood on the left. At a field corner at OS 724366, turn left, then right past some cottages, to reach the B1454 at Littleport. (The village of Sedgeford is just under 1 mile/1.5 kms to the left.) Turn right along the road for a short distance, then go left at the Magazine House. Follow a surfaced drive, then continue on a field track beyond Magazine Farm. At a farm lane at OS 719382, turn left then right, and continue past a belt of trees, and on to reach a road. Follow the road round left, then go right at a junction, and walk through Ringstead village. (4¾ miles/7.6 kms)

7 Beyond the village, keep right at a junction on a bend, then go left, signposted Peddars Way North. Pass an old windmill and after ½ mile/0.8 kms, turn off left opposite Wash Cottage. Follow a hedge to the tree-line, then turn right and follow a path between hedges, finally bearing left to avoid the entrance drive to a bungalow, to reach the A149 Hunstanton road. Cross the road *with care*, and follow Seagate lane to reach Holme beach and dunes. (2¼ miles/3.6 kms)

It is possible to follow the coast path west to Hunstanton by going off left at a footbridge over the River Hun at OS 698436. (2½ miles/4 kms)

CIRCULAR WALK 5½ miles/8.8 kms or 4 miles/6.4 kms

A walk along one of the more remote sections of the Peddars Way and then by lanes and field tracks, passing through the village of Fring. Allow two and a half hours.

Start About 3 miles/4.8 kms east of Snettisham at OS 739330, where there is limited parking. Parking is difficult in this area of the Peddars Way, other than informally on road verges. *Access to farms, fields or installations must never be obstructed.*

1 Walk north along the Peddars Way as for the main walk (5), to reach Fring Cross at OS 727356.

2 Go right along the road for ¾ mile/1.2 kms to pass All Saints church. At a T-junction, go left, then bear right at a junction signposted Bircham. Continue along the road for just over 1 mile/1.6 kms.

3 At OS 754337, by an installation, turn right along a wide lane. Continue to a junction with a road at OS 747327. Cross the road and go up a broad track to join the Peddars Way. Turn right, and reach the starting point.

For a shorter alternative, go down the road signposted Bircham as for (2), then turn off right and follow a broad track up past a house. Continue to a road, turn left, and reach OS 747327, from where directions for (3) are followed.

THE PILGRIMS' WAY
Kent

Charing to Canterbury 18½ miles/28.8 kms

One of the most famous of medieval pilgrimages led to Canterbury and the shrine of the martyred St Thomas à Becket. There were many 'pilgrims' ways' to Canterbury, and this walk follows the latter part of a suggested route from Winchester, though an archetypal Kent countryside of tree-shaded tracks and footpaths, orchards and hop gardens and lovely villages.

_____

Thomas à Becket sought fame as much as holiness. He was one of the more theatrical of the mere players on the early medieval stage, a remarkable character who merged the temporal with the divine, and who may have courted martyrdom in the hope of securing immortality. If so, the gambit worked; it earned Thomas sainthood and a posthumous fame that has survived into our own cynical times.

England's most famous martyr was recognizably a 'great' man. He was over 6 feet/1.8 metres tall, and had the impressive personality and handsome looks to match. Thomas was born to Norman parents in London's Cheapside on St Thomas's Day 1118. He rarely used his father's name of à Becket, but remained always Thomas 'of London' and finally 'of Canterbury'. There was immortality enough in such titles.

Thomas was politician rather than priest. He was ordained hurriedly as a priest when elevated to the archbishopric, and though he spent his formative years in the ecclesiastical service of his predecessor, Archbishop Theobald, his political and diplomatic experience was gained as Chancellor to Henry II. The two were

*The Pilgrims' Way: 'In
autumn the hollowed way is
ankle-deep in crisp leaves.'*

soulmates for seven years, during which time Thomas advised and revered his king companion. It was one of the great power pacts of history, this bond between the tall elegant cleric and the tough volatile Angevin king, whose stocky frame was matched by a muscular intellect and a shrewd wit. Thomas rode with Henry amidst the smoke and clamour of the battlefields of Normandy, of Nantes and of Brittany, and he backed the king in disputes with the Church.

Henry believed that Thomas would give him unstinting loyalty for life, regardless of circumstances. But when Henry insisted that Thomas become Archbishop of Canterbury, and thus head of the English Church, Thomas exchanged king for God. He made it clear that he would be his own master − or rather that God, through the Pope, would be his master − and he predicted, with sadness, that he and the king would soon be at odds.

The quarrels between Henry and Thomas were complex and self-perpetuating. They revolved initially round the independence of Church courts and the king's insistence that churchmen accused of crimes should be subject to lay courts. It was a matter of principle, but one which symbolized the wider tensions between Church and Crown. In demanding that the Church acquiesce, Henry precipitated a bitter confrontation with Thomas. The dispute raged for months, and finally Thomas fled to France, where he remained in exile for six years.

The climax to all of this is famous. Apparent reconciliation between king and archbishop at last seemed possible. Thomas returned to Canterbury in December 1170, his position as England's chief prelate reaffirmed. But Thomas offered few concessions. He excommunicated his rivals, scorned his enemies, and dangled over England a threat of papal interdict, which, if applied, would have made the country the pariah of Europe.

It was inevitable that violence should follow. Thomas's refusal to bend the Church to the Crown, together with many slights, real and imagined, produced marvellous Angevin tantrums from Henry; a gnashing of teeth, a beating of the ground, and all the histrionics of an extrovert king. The performance climaxed with Henry's famous rhetorical question to his assembled courtiers: 'Of the caitiffs who eat my bread, are there none to rid me of this turbulent priest?'

It may have been that Henry was simply posturing. But his words were taken in heat by the infamous quartet of knightly assassins: de Tracy, Fitzurse, le Brito and de Morville − names to conjure with indeed. All four detested Thomas of Canterbury, and saw him as a barrier to their own ambitions. They left hurriedly for Canterbury, where they conspired with the de Broc family,

Thomas's hostile neighbours who had openly terrorized the archbishop's supporters and purloined his property. Once the hunt was up, the pack gathered round.

The subsequent murder of Thomas is relished by historians as much as it seems to have been relished by the man himself. Thomas had hinted at his own possible 'martyrdom'. As Archbishop of Canterbury and head of the English Church, he was next in importance to the king, and proxy of the Pope. Only God had the better of him. It seems likely that Thomas had become the victim of his own aggrandisement, and that martyrdom appealed to the vanity of a man who dreamed of becoming a saint.

The murder of Thomas was gloriously theatrical. The venue guaranteed it. The Canterbury cathedral of the time was very different from today's elegant gothic building – it had the greater solidity of Norman architecture, of the Romanesque, of powerful rounded arches, of massive columns, and dense stonework. It was awe-inspiring, cavernous and full of life; it exuded sanctity and holy power, and the echoing cloisters were filled with the mist of incense and the waxy smoke of burning tapers. Candles guttered on altar and bracket, and their weak flames flickered through the gloom. There was no better stage for Thomas's last act – on earth at least.

Thomas's monks and clerks are said to have dragged him forcibly towards the sanctuary of the high altar after an initial aggressive exchange with Henry's knights. There is a suggestion that Thomas resisted pleas to seek the sanctuary of the high altar, in case sanctuary might *deter* the knights from killing him. Instead, the first blow was finally struck in the pooled darkness and light of the north-west transept, after de Tracy and Fitzurse had tried to remove Thomas by force. The physically powerful 'saint' sent Fitzurse flying with the cry, 'Black pander! Touch me not, you owe me fealty.'

That broke the swaying tension of the moment. A wild confusion of shadows on the cloister walls mimicked the terrible deed. Fitzurse lashed out with his sword. It was a messy, brutal blow. It sliced halfway through the protective arm of Thomas's faithful clerk, Edward Grim, and wounded Thomas in the head and shoulder. A second blow by de Tracy felled the archbishop. A third from le Brito, this time poised and with terrible force, sliced off the top of Thomas's skull. The sword shattered in pieces on the stone floor. De Broc's treacherous chaplain, who had led the killers into the cathedral, scattered Thomas's brains with a last contemptuous thrust of his sword. The mortal man was dead; within days, the 'saint' lived.

Many churchmen disapproved of Thomas for his temporality.

He had been sumptuous in his dress and in the table he kept, and had spent great sums on an almost regal entourage. But when, after his death, his monks and clerks stripped the body to prepare it for burial, they discovered beneath the layers of Thomas's robes a hair suit. It was close-fitting but open at the back to allow for daily secretive scourging. The inside of the hair suit seethed with lice and fleas. Such grim evidence of Thomas's self-abasement convinced the monks of Canterbury on the spot. Thomas had been proved to be one of them at last.

Thomas of Canterbury was a prime candidate for sainthood in an age when superstition still gripped Norman overlord and Anglo-Saxon serf alike. Reports of cures and of miraculous events linked to his name proliferated. The more scheming of his enemies tried to play down any suggestion of sanctity. But Henry II was engulfed with remorse and wanted desperately to convince the Pope, and powerful European opponents, that he had neither wished for nor commanded Thomas's murder. Within two years of the deed, Henry prostrated himself before Thomas's tomb and submitted himself to two hundred and fifty lashes, more symbolic than severe. It was an emphatic royal imprimatur for Thomas's sainthood.

In February 1173, Pope Alexander II declared Thomas a saint and martyr. The day of the murder, 29 December, became the saint's feast day, as close to Christmas as any ambitous saint might have wished it to be. Soon after canonization, reports of miraculous cures in Thomas's name grew apace – and grew fantastic. Thomas's shrine at Canterbury became the focus of pilgrimages, and although the initial impulse waned, pilgrimage to Canterbury remained a major element of medieval Christianity for the next two hundred years. Ordinary people and crowned heads alike paid tribute to Thomas, whose cult extended throughout Europe until Canterbury rivalled in popularity the great pilgrim destinations of Rome, Jerusalem, and Santiago de Compostela in Northern Spain. Even Henry VIII paid his dues as Defender of the Faith in 1520, although he later ordered the despoiling of the shrine in 1538.

It seems an anti-climax stepping from the drama of history and from the fevered gloom of the medieval cathedral onto the breezy openness of the 'Pilgrims' Way'. But it was through the North Downs countryside that the players in the piece travelled to and fro, and through which generations of pilgrims passed towards Canterbury. Chaucer has famously portrayed the vigour and humanity of the medieval pilgrims who flocked to Canterbury from London along Watling Street, the present A2. Meanwhile pilgrims from the West Country, and those from Europe who made landfall at Southampton, followed variants of an ancient trackway along the slopes of the North Downs, a notional route labelled 'the Pilgrims' Way' by Hilaire Belloc in his description in 1910 of a walking tour from Winchester to Canterbury.

The modern Pilgrim's Way passes through a countryside, which, though greatly changed, retains its rural peace. This is chalk country, the northern rim of the great anticline of The Weald. It is a well-dressed and well-cultivated landscape, upon which England's human history has left an imprint from the earliest times. It has no dramatic landscape features but in some quarters is satisfyingly remote and distinctively English.

Our 'pilgrimage' begins at the village of Charing, before the surviving fourteenth-century gateway of one of the rural palaces of the archbishops of Canterbury. Today, Charing lacks only the letter 'm' to underwrite its appeal. The village is unaffected by the torrent of vehicles on the nearby A20. The quiet road in front of the palace gates was once part of a busy link between Canterbury and Lewes.

Our way leads east past the church, a handsome building though greatly changed from its original form. It has a late sixteenth-century roof to the nave, with subtly painted timbers that can easily fool an eye expecting carved work. Richard II gave Charing Church an executioner's block, said to be the one on which John the Baptist was executed. It no doubt diverted a fair stream of pilgrims on their way to Canterbury. Most churches along the

Eastwell Lake near Boughton Lees.

pilgrim road maximized their earning potential in some way or another.

A field path leads onto the road by the old manor of Pett Place. Soon a stolid lane is reached beyond Burnt House Farm. This is a green shade in summer, breezy and sweet beneath the great beeches and the pollarded ash and sycamore. In autumn, the hollowed way is ankle-deep in crisp leaves. The line of the track is certainly ancient. It leads unerringly along the dry flank of the downs. To the south are views towards Ashford through the shimmering haze on summer fields; the flicker of distant traffic on the A20 is still at arms' length, and there is even a pleasant memorial seat midway.

Beyond Dunn Street and above Westwell with its lovely thirteenth-century church, this sense of isolation intensifies as the way leads into Eastwell Park and bends to the will of the valley of the River Great Stour. At Eastwell, any pretence of 'ancient way' is bent to the will of land use: the path through the estate has been carefully regulated across the open countryside. To the north lies the pine-wooded swell of the downs. Neat stands of trees are passed, and pheasants scarper into the woods and the dense crops. At the fields' end, the ruined tower of the Church of St Mary's is reached amidst its sheltering trees on the shores of Eastwell Lake.

This ancient church declined through neglect. It was damaged further because of the effect of vibrations from World War II gun batteries that stood nearby. The ruin is now cared for by the Friends of Friendless Churches, and remedial work is being carried out; the churchyard is lovingly tended. There was a church here during the great period of pilgrimage, and there are some very old gravestones in the shady churchyard.

From the church, the original Pilgrims' Way seems to have led more precisely north-east, but is no longer extant as a right of way. Instead, our route leads past the wonderful cottage-loaf building of Lake House, the walls of which seem randomly, though pleasingly pitched. A short distance ahead, where the Way crosses the drive of Eastwell Park, there is a small memorial garden to two young women who died tragically when the car in which they were passengers crashed near the spot.

Boughton Lees has a great wedge of village green, reflecting the meaning of Lees as 'pasture'. The road east from the village leads to a division of the North Downs Way. Here the Pilgrims' Way makes for the Church of St Botulph All Saints, a big gaunt-faced building with broken flints, like bottle-ends, embedded in the gnarled walls. The church is raw-boned within and without, and is partly of thirteenth-century vintage, certainly in its nave. Here small groups of medieval pilgrims waited until their numbers swelled so that they could travel in a protective group through King's Wood, a place notorious for its unsaintly robbers. The pilgrims, in their muddy clothes and with their bundled belongings, might even have slept inside the church, a lively mix of medieval squatters taking sanctuary, and taking advantage of a religion that was more closely tied to everyday life than ours is today. There was little risk, in those superstitious times, of the vandalism or theft that makes it necessary to lock so many churches now.

King's Wood today is dense with coppiced sweet chestnuts, from which staves were cut to prop the hop gardens of the area. Deeper into the wood, mixed beech and oak dominate. The track can be thick with mud here, but the walking is easy and the path soon delivers us downhill to the edge of Godmersham Park with its Georgian mansion and precise field patterns. To the north is Mountain Street, from where a view of the prominent tower of Chilham Church leads us on to this hilltop showpiece of Tudor half-timbers and red-tiled roofs. Space and solidity are nicely balanced here, to make an attractive whole round the lovely square. Yet Chilham has been chopped off. The walls of the adjoining Chilham estate have stolen some of the central space, and make the square slightly disproportionate. No matter; Chilham is loved to death, and beyond the encroaching walls is the splendid Jacobean mansion of Chilham House, designed by Inigo Jones.

Medieval pilgrims would certainly have thronged through Chilham at a time when the square was a stinking morass of mud and ordure, trampled by squealing animals, and the buildings were wonderfully crooked and without their brick façades, dark and filthy inside. Raucous humanity would have fumbled and grabbed at every passing chance, and the heady reek of old ale would have belched from the tavern doors.

The pilgrims passed by the churchyard's ancient yew tree, which is reputed to be one thousand three hundred years old but is now a twisted stump. It lost its branches in the brutal storm of October 1987, when Chilham bore the brunt of devastating winds that smashed down scores of its splendid trees, and threw up bones from the churchyard earth as if from the sea. The bones of Thomas were spirited here in 1535 for fear of their being destroyed by Henry VIII's zealous dismantlers. Where they went from Chilham is unknown.

Our route dips downhill from St Mary's to cross the busy A252, from where it climbs uphill to Old Wives Lees. Beyond here, it is best to follow the official North Downs Way. The path leads down a splendid avenue of tall trees, green-crowned in summer, and, in winter, mimicking with their arched and interlocking branches the gothic tracery of cathedral architecture. The avenue gives way to a tunnel of hawthorns before the path winds on through hop gardens and then through orchards of pears and apples that foam with bright blossom in spring, and are rosy cheeked with original sin in the autumn.

Roads and bypasses have sliced through the landscape on the approach to Canterbury, and there is a feeling of slipping quietly towards the city between competing race tracks. From Chartham Hatch there is a quiet interlude where the North Downs Way threads more orchards and then passes below the wooded heights of Bigbury Camp, an Iron Age site where disorientated Britons first encountered the implacable might of Rome. It was to Bigbury above the River Great Stour that the British withdrew when Caesar and his troops made their second invasion in 54 BC. The hard-faced legionaries made short work of defences and defenders.

Soon the edge of the city is reached, where a descent down the quiet Mill Lane brings the walker onto Rheims Way with its flood of traffic. Ahead, the great spire of the cathedral dominates the featureless outskirts of the city. Rheims Way is crossed by an underpass that leads to London Road, which itself leads to the junction with St Dunstan's Street at St Dunstan's church. It was here that Henry II changed into penitent's robes and shuffled barefooted to Canterbury's great West Gate and thence to the cathedral, to do penance for his infamous 'turbulence'. And it is from St Dunstan's that the modern pilgrim is drawn towards the enduring splendour of the cathedral and of Thomas's Canterbury.

The lovely village of Chilham.

THE PILGRIMS' WAY Information

Distance 18 miles/28.8 kms

Maps OS Landranger 189 (Ashford & Romney Marsh); OS Landranger 179 (Canterbury & East Kent)

Nature of Walk An undemanding walk through the Kent countryside, along paths, green lanes and quiet roads. The walk can be completed in a day by very fit walkers. There are few inclines. The route directions given here are, in general, those for the North Downs Way, and are easily followed with the help of good waymarkers. The going can be quite muddy underfoot during wet weather. Clothing and equipment should be for country walking.

Accommodation At Charing, Chilham and Canterbury. Bed and breakfast is available at various places along the Way. Youth hostel at Canterbury.

Transport Regular rail service between Charing, Chilham and Canterbury (change at Ashford for Charing connection). No regular bus services along the inland lanes, but connections to main centres can be made from the larger villages.

Further Information Tourist Information Centre, Canterbury, tel. (0227) 66567.

Start Charing Church

1 Pass the church door along a surfaced walkway, then keep ahead along the edge of the recreation ground. Go through a gate and keep ahead to cross a field. Just before a gate, turn off left to reach a road. Go right down the road, then left at a junction for a short distance. Go right over a stile, and bear diagonally left across a field to reach a road. Turn right past Burnt House Farm, and follow the road round left, then right. Just past a quarry entrance, bear left at a fork, and after 200 yards/180 metres keep ahead at another fork. Pass Pilgrim's Cottage where the track merges with a surfaced road, and bear left at a

Trees line the path near Old Wives Lees: 'mimicking the gothic tracery of cathedral architecture in their arched and interlocking branches'.

junction with another road. Pass through Dunn Street, and at a T-junction, cross over and go over a stile. Follow waymarks through Eastwell Park to reach the Eastwell Church ruins. (4½ miles/7.2 kms)

2 Continue on the track east from the church. At a junction, keep ahead through a gate. Continue alongside a fence. After about 500 yards/450 metres bear down left to go through a gate onto a drive. Cross the drive, go through another gate, and cross a field to emerge on the A251 at Boughton Lees. Cross the road and keep to the right of the village green. Where the green ends, bear right, then left along Pilgrims' Way. (1¾ miles/2.8 kms)

3 After ½ mile/0.8 kms turn off left by a North Downs Way signpost, and continue by footpath to Boughton Aluph Church. Beyond the church, cross a lane and continue down a raised path across a large field to cross another lane. Continue past Soakham Farm, and follow a track uphill to enter King's Wood. Continue on the woodland track, bearing left at a signpost. After 1½ miles/2.4 kms, turn right and go downhill. At the foot of the hill go left and emerge through a gate at a road end. Continue along the road through Mountain Street, and where the road bends right, keep left up School Hill and into Chilham square. (4¾ miles/7.6 kms)

4 Go through the churchyard, and just past the church door, bear left down a narrow path to reach a road. Continue down the road, cross the A252 *with care*, and follow the road opposite to Old Wives Lees. At a road junction, take the road diagonally right, and after ½ mile/0.8 kms bear left, then right. Cross the road and go through a gate and down a tree-lined path through an orchard. Continue through a hop garden, turn right and then left, and climb steeply uphill. Follow the field edge, then enter an orchard. Soon, cross a railway line and join a farm road. Pass Nickle Farm and continue on a path uphill to bear left along a track. Follow signs to reach a road through a farm. Turn left, then right down New Town Street to reach Chartham Hatch. (3½ miles/5.6 kms)

5 Where the road bends to the left, keep ahead across the entrance to Nightingale Close and go down a fenced passageway. Cross the road and pass the village shop, then bear right through a gate into a play area, and continue along a path to the right through an orchard. Go left down a path and continue through woodland to reach a road. The busy A2 is down left. Turn left to cross the A2 by a bridge, then go right down a muddy ride alongside the A2. Follow the path round left and down to a footbridge. Go uphill to join Mill Lane and continue down to the busy Rheims Road. Go under Rheims Road by a subway (*Victoria Hotel opposite*) and continue down London Road. At the junction with St Dunstan's Street by St Dunstan's Church, turn right and continue to West Gate and so to the cathedral. (3½ miles/5.6 kms)

CIRCULAR WALK 6½ miles/10.4 kms

This walk crosses the valley of the River Great Stour and passes through pleasant countryside to climb onto the high ground of King's Wood, from where it follows the Pilgrims' Way. Allow two and a half hours.

Start Small parking area at OS 064521 south of Chilham

Westwell, near the Pilgrims' Way, whose church was owned by the monks of Canterbury during the medieval period.

1 Go through a gate by the parking area, and follow a track. Where it bends right, keep ahead over a stile, and follow a field track to another gate. Follow waymarks down a track between railed-off paddocks. At a cross track, go left and then right across an open meadow to join the road at the gates of Godmersham Park. *The Palladian mansion of Godmersham dates from 1732. It was inherited in 1797 by Jane Austen's brother Edward, who changed his name to Knight to secure the inheritance. Jane Austen stayed at Godmersham on several occasions.*

2 Follow the road ahead, through Godmersham village. Pass the Church of St Lawrence the Martyr and continue to the main road. (*There is an interesting bas-relief of St Thomas on the south wall of the chancel of St Lawrence's. It dates from the twelfth century.*) Turn left and cross the river by a footbridge, then turn right to cross the A28 *with care.* Go over stiles and follow a field track to pass under the railway.

3 Turn sharp right and go over a stile. *This section of the path may be thickly overgrown with nettles. Shorts are not advised.* Pass an old shack, then veer left across a field to a stile into a lane by some houses. Cross the lane and go up some wooden steps and over a stile. Follow field edges to reach another lane by houses. Turn left down this lane to reach a road at OS 063496.

4 Go right along the road for about a mile/ 1.6 kms, then go right by a footpath sign and down a field to cross the Great Stour by a metal bridge. Follow a field track to a railway crossing *and cross with care.* Continue up the rough lane and keep ahead at its junction with another lane to reach the main road at Bilting.

5 Cross the A28 *with care,* then follow a rising green lane that may be overgrown in summer. At a junction with the Pilgrims' Way in King's Wood, turn right and follow directions for the main walk in the latter part of direction (3), to reach the car parking area.

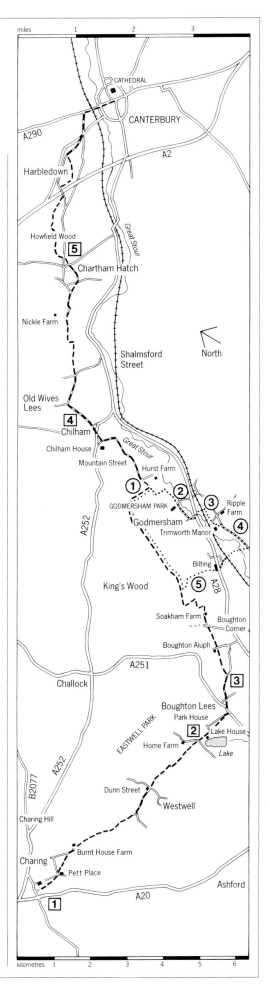

145

THE RIDGEWAY
Oxfordshire and Berkshire

Fox Hill to Streatley 25 miles/40 kms

*'It is not a farm track;
you may walk for
twenty miles along it
over the hills; neither is
it the King's highway
. . . With varying
width, from twenty to
fifty yards, it runs like
a green ribbon . . .'*

Richard Jeffries, *Wild Life in a
Southern County*, 1879

A freewheeling walk along an ancient ridgeway, the high road of England that runs parallel to the low road; the Icknield Way. It traverses the great natural barrier of the Berkshire chalk downs that played their part in British resistance to the Saxon, and in Saxon resistance to the Dane.

The Ridgeway is losing its green ribbon now, as sand and gravel are compacted onto its shredded surface, and as, increasingly, off-road vehicles gouge out the turf. But the Ridgeway is still a splendid walking route along the broad crest of the downs.

It was a route that was trampled out possibly by mammoth and bison, and by the great herds of wild horses and cattle, and the oxen called 'aurochs', that roamed across southern England during the midwinter springs between Ice Ages. The foraging herds followed the easiest ground, the high and dry whalebacks of the downs, less wooded than the valleys, and as they streamed along, grazing and bulldozing their way, they left the broad expanse of the original 'ridgeway' multi-stranded with routes. Behind the beasts came the people of the Old Stone Age, who had ventured across the land bridge between Europe and Britain. They were hunter-gatherers who sought skins and horns, and they followed the herds during the short bearable periods before the resurgence of the ice drove them back to the south.

By the time permanent settlers arrived, during the Neolithic period, the Ridgeway was a well-trampled route. Down this great natural highway these early people travelled into the heart of the island. They sought areas of good grazing for the wild creatures that they were fast domesticating; they cleared forests for this purpose, and spilled down from the Ridgeway to link up with other immigrants from the south coast. The Ridgeway became one of the great spinal roads of southern Britain, ribbed with tributary paths and tracks to either side. To the east, beyond the Thames, it merged with the Icknield Way, and on very old maps it is named as Ickleton Street. It linked the farming culture of East Anglia with the great civilization that flourished on the accommodating downlands of modern Wiltshire and Dorset, and round the great monuments of Stonehenge and Avebury.

Our section of the Ridgeway runs mainly through modern Oxfordshire, but edges into modern Berkshire at its eastern end. To the north lies the Vale of the White Horse, fertile with clay, with, further north, the great basin of the Thames. To the south, the downs fall gently to the valley of the River Kennet and the chalk escarpment of Hampshire. Westward lie the Marlborough Downs and Wiltshire; eastward, the Goring Gap through which the Thames runs below the tree-shrouded slopes of the Chilterns.

This is the heartland of England, the most accessible of its rich lowland country, across which the ebb and flow of conquest and exploitation has shaped the landscape. But on the downs, on the Ridgeway track, the quality of a more primitive country has survived, though the track itself is now pinned down by the asphalt hoops of modern roads that run north to south across it, and though its natural line has been disciplined in places to accommodate the rigidities of Victorian enclosure.

The great script of the Ridgeway is punctuated by some of our most outstanding ancient monuments, including the burial chamber of Wayland's Smithy and the hill forts of Uffington and Segsbury. Above all, there is that eternally fascinating piece of ancient graffito, the Uffington White Horse, its stylized form trapped in mid-flight on the crest of a green hill.

Our walk starts at Fox Hill, to the east of Liddington and within shouting distance of two other great highways. One is the Roman road of Ermin Way – not the great Ermine Street of the north, but an important link between Silchester, Cirencester and Bath, and now a surfaced road. The other is the modern M4. Two thousand years lie between the two, yet both reflect the ascendancy of technology over nature. Their lines are brutally direct; they slice through the lie of the land, whereas the line of the Ridgeway was dictated by its landscape. In its great sweeping arc, between Fox

Looking west from Uffington Castle along the line of the Ridgeway.

Hill and Streatley, it replicates the graceful curvature of the downs themselves.

At Fox Hill, a broad track rises steeply to the generally accommodating flatness of the next twenty miles/thirty-two kilometres. The track emerges from the clasp of overarching beech trees to run bareheaded between hawthorns that are like banks of snow in spring, and are beaded with scarlet berries in the autumn. Where the track levels off, there is a tumulus in the left-hand field, a modest introduction to the Ridgeway's ancient waymarks.

There is little awareness at first of being in high places; the downs are flat-topped and spread out where the track leads across Charlbury Hill, with the gentle swell of Lammy Down to its right. But they fall to the north eventually, to where the settlements of Hinton Parva, Bishopstone, Idstone and Ashbury set the pattern of villages that march along the line of the B4507 at the foot of the downs, where springs encouraged such settlement. Above Idstone, the view back to the south-west emphasizes the seductive softness of this landscape, its fluidity and its purity of line.

Just over a mile/two kilometres south-east from here, is a small hill fort now called Alfred's Castle. The great Saxon Alfred was born at nearby Wantage, and fought a successful battle against the Danes at Ashdown. Below Alfred's Castle is Ashdown Park where the ill-starred Earl of Craven, the unrequited lover of Elizabeth, Queen of Bohemia, built his elegant lachrymose house in the seventeenth century.

The name Ashdown, or Aescendun, was once attached to a large area of the downs and to the low ground on either side of the Ridgeway, and it was in this area that the Saxon leaders Alfred and Aethelred mustered their scattered troops after the Danes had routed them near Reading in the winter of AD 870. At the beginning of January 871 a Danish force, led by the awesomely named Halfdane and Ivar the Boneless, marched west along the frosty turf of the Ridgeway. They met with the English forces somewhere in the area of Uffington Castle at a place called Nachededorne, the place of the 'naked thorn', a fitting name for a sharp encounter. The Danes were routed in their turn.

From the Ridgeway junction with the Ashbury to Lambourn road, a fine stretch of open country sweeps flatly south to the wooded swell of Tower Hill on Kingstone Down. It is a mosaic of green in summer, and in winter, a pale mix of washed-out yellows against the distant inky blackness of the trees. From here, the Ridgeway track leads past the ancient longbarrow of Wayland's Smithy. The name is a romantic allusion to a Scandinavian god mythologized as a ghostly blacksmith who, for a groat, was said to shoe horses that were left tethered overnight.

The name of the site is dramatic enough; the reality even more so. Now well kempt within its stockade of towering beeches, the longbarrow represents a doubling-up of ancient burial chambers. The first was the roof-ridge type of the early Neolithic period, a timber chamber covered by a low mound of earth, faced with stone slabs, called 'sarsens'. The skeletons of fifteen bodies were found inside when the grave was excavated. The bodies were first left in the open air to decompose, perhaps on wooden trestles tufted with horse-hair and draped with the clothing of the deceased. The image is gruesome, yet compelling. There were few trees then, the air was warmer and teeming with insects. In winter, black-winged predators would have had their fill at this reeking charnel house. Later, the bones were separated, the skulls arranged ritualistically within the tomb, the limbs also; pottery and flint implements and offerings of food were added, and the chamber sealed. Much later, a large barrow was built over the existing one. This contained three stone-lined chambers, and held the scattered bones of eight people. The barrow was four times as long as the original, and is still impressive, its entrance pillars are smoothly phallic and striking.

Our route continues east to Uffington between the track's tightly-coiled hedgerows. The rampart of the great hill fort is clearly seen acoss the intervening country. It is soon reached along the white ribbon of track, and it is impressive. Uffington's fort dates from the Iron Age; its single rampart encloses an area of eight acres/over three hectares. Its height at 858 feet/242 metres, and its northern outlook, suggest that it may have guarded a more sophisticated Iron Age society, fearful of barbarian attack from the north. But the purpose of such large 'hill forts' remains unclear. They may have served as civil settlements, herd enclosures, or even as ritual sites.

Impressive though this great enclosure may be, it is outdone by the adjoining Uffington White Horse. Nearly 360 feet/100 metres long by 160 feet/48.5 metres high, the 'horse' is not easily seen except from a distance; the pitch of the hillside is such, that even from the scooped enclosures directly below it, known as The Manger, the carving is barely discernible. Uffington's horse is best seen from above; for UFO enthusiasts the implications are limitless. One theory suggests that the horse was once lower down the slope and thus clearly visible from below, and that movement of surface earth has sent it galloping nearly out of sight.

It is impossible to date the Uffington White Horse. It was recorded first in the twelfth century and has been claimed as being of Iron Age date and contemporaneous with Uffington Castle. The Iron Age Britons were cultish towards horses; they involved them in rituals so bizarre that they verged on the obscene – if the medieval Welsh writer Giraldus Cambrensis is to be believed; but he was a sensationalist. More convincingly, there are horse designs similar to the Uffington model on Iron Age coins. Others say that the horse was a Saxon doodle from Alfred's day. Some say that it is more catlike than equine. The White Horse merely kicks its heels.

For hundreds of years, local people groomed the White Horse every few years, by scouring its features and trimming the turf. The 'obligation' was met well into the nineteenth century, when the horse was taken into official care. The scouring was accompanied by a tumultuous festival, with horse-racing and running, cheese-rolling down the slopes of The Manger, wrestling and dancing and general hilarity. Today, we find human activity of a more suburban kind. At weekends and holidays, Uffington is alive with people. They fly kites through the whirling air – a pastime that would have intrigued and delighted the ancient Britons; they swarm across the cropped grass seeking castles and carvings and 'interpretation'; many seem disappointed and bewildered, victims of our modern craving for diversion, for which there is only a diminishing return.

The love of the Britons for horses might also explain The Manger, that strangely unnatural combe where the voluptuous hills swoop down from the hooves of the White Horse. At the head of the combe is Dragon Hill, a truncated cone on whose flat top all manner of theatricals, or business, might have taken place, never mind the absurdity of St George slaying his dragon, as legend insists. The far entrance to The Manger could be closed easily on milling horses; the lower slopes could be tightly fenced. It is speculative, of course, but we may be looking at an Iron Age corral in this emphatically horsey country, where today racehorses still stretch their limbs on a succession of gallops along the flattened crest of the downs.

From Uffington, the Ridgeway track leads discreetly east over Rams Hill to cross the road at Blowingstone Hill above Kingston Lisle. This is truly ancient ground. The Iron Age fort on Rams Hill was built round a Bronze Age enclosure of about 1,500 BC. The track rises towards Sparsholt Firs, but it is steady rather than steep. The way crosses the B4001 close to the modern artefact of a radio tower, then strikes south-east along the rim of Crowhole Bottom. This is the Devil's Punchbowl, couched between Hackpen Hill and Childrey Warren. It may be a recent confection of a name, because there is no mention of Old Nick on old maps. The Punchbowl is a shallow basin within the protective arm of Hackpen Hill; it is elegant in its curvature and as smooth as a pottery bowl, and only solitary clusters of trees break the flatness of the horizon. Below the rim, there are old flint workings punched into the turf. In summer, a greenness drains to the bottom of the basin; the slopes of the low hills are a rougher texture, and downland flowers speckle the darker ground.

The Ridgeway runs straight-limbed from here, twin-tracked to one side, and with a broad green shoulder to the other. There are grassy gallops to the south. Vast fields swoop down to the north and are absorbed into the immensity of the Vale of the White Horse. There is nothing much to distract the eye, just the vast openness of low country. It is not featureless country, but the features are man-made. The massive cooling towers of the Didcot Power Station are startling enough. Ten miles/sixteen kilometres away to the north-east, they are great nude pagodas of concrete and curvature, in no way absorbed by the landscape but monumental in their own brash way.

On hot summer days, it is exhilarating to be on this high ground. The heat is never too oppressive; the feeling of isolation above a bustling world is complete. In winter, the ground is chequered white and black when there is snow; the pure lines of the downs are even more precise against pearly skies; the air is keen. The moods of the Ridgeway change and they fascinate: but we have lost a great deal. The early travellers along the Ridgeway moved through light and air that was subtly different. They bedded down on the Ridgeway at night, and when it was moonless, would

Near the Devil's Punchbowl: 'it is elegant in its curvature and as smooth as a pottery bowl . . .'

have gazed out into an inky blackness; on clear nights, the stars spilled down to the horizon. Now, in the dark, the northern plain flares with harsh, artificial light, and even the smallest hamlet overflows with it.

But by day, the sun still smiles on the Ridgeway. It filters through the dense hedgerows of hawthorn and blackthorn that grow tall to either side of the track beyond Gramps Hill, and that are stitched with bryony and Traveller's Joy, honeysuckle and bindweed, and strung with black, mauve and blood-red berries in autumn. There is open country all the way to the great earthwork of Letcombe Castle, that is known also as Segsbury Camp. The earthwork encloses a vast area of twenty-six acres/over ten hectares, and the site was of major significance – although the labels of fort and castle may be only part of the story. There are strong traces of Iron Age field systems around Segsbury.

From here the Ridgeway strides on to cross the A338, then follows an irregular route by Whitehouse Farm. Wantage lies two and a half miles/four kilometres to the north. It is a town that is comfortable with its antiquity; its spacious market square and adjoining streets are still centuries old in their undisturbed patterns. From the Ridgeway, on a clear day, the smooth knuckle of Boar's Hill to the west of Oxford is easily identified. On such a flat canvas, the built landscape is emphasized; even the tower of the high-rise flats on the Woodfarm Estate at East Oxford can be clearly seen.

Soon the B4494 is crossed amidst great open spaces that lead onto the pleasant countryside of the Lockinge estate. The Didcot towers lie dead ahead, implacable in their hugeness. By the track stands a rather down-at-heel monument to Robert Loyd Lindsay, Baron Wantage, a well-heeled army man who planted the north-facing slopes of Ardington Down, opposite his monument, with eccentric stands of trees. The Baron was a veteran of Alma and Inkerman and his tree-planting is said to replicate battalions drawn up for war. But they have unwarlike names: Corsica Pine Wood, The Sycamores, Midsummer Wood. No blood spilled here, though there is water enough. A hitching post, and drinking trough with tap, make for a homely touch at the side of the track.

There are deep woods to the south, on Yew Down and The Warren, and there are huge flinty fields to the north, that are dense with barley and winter wheat in season; they seethe like a green ocean in the Ridgeway winds, except where bright yellow islands of oilseed rape intrude. Hidden discreetly off the main track is a charming memorial to Penelope Betjeman who lived at Wantage with her husband for many years; and at Farnborough, two miles/three kilometres south, there is an exquisite memorial window to Sir John Betjeman in the calm little church. The window, by John Piper, glows with the colour and light of the Ridgeway in high hot summer.

The miles roll underfoot, unchallenging as a walk, but delightful when the company is discerning, and the air clear as wine. To the north is Harwell's Atomic Energy Research Establishment: a mouthful of atoms. At Scutchamer Knob, a dense thicket of trees encloses the deep bowl of a plundered barrow. The muddy track is partly obstructed here by another mound, said to have been piled up to discourage long-term parking of vehicles; it is now fenced because off-road drivers were ploughing over it.

Off-road driving on traditional byways like the Ridgeway is controversial. Four-wheels once meant carts and wagons that laboured through the mud on the Ridgeway, drawn by horses or oxen, their drivers and passengers frequently lending a muddy shoulder to the wheel. Now, technology has ambushed tradition; yet there is something unsettling glimpsed in the faces of truck-bound passengers as they trundle along the Ridgeway. It may be boredom.

For the walker, the Ridgeway draws out its engaging course along the swooping downs. Ahead, lie the Chilterns and the Goring Gap. But first, the howling ribbon of the A34 is safely avoided at the fearsomely named Gore Hill, where an underpass makes for a bloodless crossing. The underpass has been engagingly decorated with colourful murals by a local amenity group. Now the track begins its gentle descent towards the Thames along Several Down and through a phalanx of tracks that have been remodelled over the years.

A lonely countryside of soft hills runs off to all sides. The Ridgeway track is packed firmly with chalky earth; there are fast green gallops with jumps here, but soon the track makes a quick turn to the east and runs downhill between clutches of tall hawthorns. Once across a dismantled railway line on Blewbury Down, the track rises quietly, bordered by a linear sweep of fields to the north. To the south, the rolling fields are lined with thick hedges and the green trenches of holloways.

Now the track crosses Roden Downs, and begins a steady descent towards the Thames, along the northern rim of the lovely Streatley Warren, one of those beautiful combes that characterize the downs; not a valley entirely, yet with depth and spaciousness, a green scoop in this seemingly mobile landscape. It merges imperceptibly with the emphatic valley of the Thames, where Streatley and Goring confront each other smilingly across the river, and where thirsty walkers realize that their throats are as dry as the downs.

THE RIDGEWAY
Information

Distance 25 miles/40 kms

Maps OS Landranger 174 (Newbury & Wantage)

Nature of Walk A straightforward and undemanding walk along the broad track of the Berkshire Downs. Very experienced walkers could complete the route described in one day. But the route can be broken off at its midpoint at the B4494 Wantage–Newbury road. The track is generally well drained but may become muddy during wet weather. Clothing and equipment should be for country walking.

Accommodation At most of the larger villages and the towns bordering the Ridgeway.

Transport Rail connections to main centres from Goring. Bus connections to main centres from Streatley. Local bus services from Wantage; a summer service links the Ridgeway between Fox Hill and Goring via the B4494 Wantage–Newbury road that crosses the Ridgeway.

Further Information Ridgeway Officer, Oxford, tel. (0865) 810224.

Start Fox Hill OS 233814

1 Follow the well-defined track of the Ridgeway; cross a number of tracks and roads; pass Wayland's Smithy, and reach Uffington Castle. (5¼ miles/8.4 kms)

2 Continue along the Ridgeway track to cross Blowingstone Hill. Continue to Sparsholt Firs at OS 343851. (3 miles/4.8 kms)

3 Continue past Segsbury Camp OS 385845 and onto the A338. Go right down the road for a short distance, then turn off left to pass Whitehouse Farm, bearing sharp left, then right. Continue to the B4494. (5¼ miles/8.4 kms)

4 Keep ahead past the Loyd Lindsay monument, and continue past Scutchamer Knob at OS 456850. Keep ahead at a crosstrack, and continue to the A34 at Gore Hill. (5 miles/8 kms)

Ridgeway country, where 'only solitary clusters of trees break the flatness . . .'

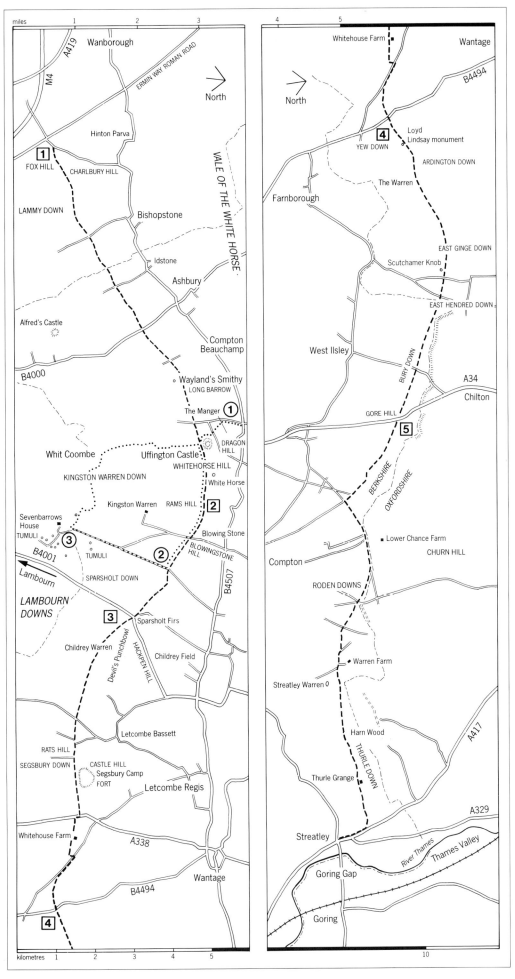

5 Go through an underpass and follow the track across Several Down. Go sharp left at OS 509819, and continue along the track to cross a bridge over a dismantled railway. Follow the track uphill, and at the top of the slope, keep right at a Y-junction. Continue across Roden Downs, and keep left at a Y-junction above Streatley Warren at OS 549812. Reach a surfaced road and continue past Thurle Grange. At the A417, turn right down to Streatley. (6½ miles/10.4 kms)

CIRCULAR WALK 7 miles/11.2 kms

Start At Uffington Castle car park at OS 293866

1 Go up to the earthworks of the castle. From the southern side of the castle at OS 299863, go through a gate onto the broad track of the Ridgeway. Turn left and continue for just over 2 miles/3.5 kms, crossing the road at Blowingstone Hill. *The Blowing Stone of Blowingstone Hill is a large stone block pierced with holes that now lies in the garden of a house ½ mile/0.8 kms down the road towards Kingston Lisle. The stone emits a booming note when one of the holes is blown. It can be viewed by the public by arrangement.*

2 After ¾ mile/1.2 kms at OS 331858, go right and follow the track to join a road at a sharp bend. Continue down the road to the Seven Barrows area. *The name of this remarkable complex of tumuli is typically inaccurate, seven, or nine, being a mythological number pinned to collections of ancient artefacts. There are as many as thirty to forty tumuli here. They date from the Bronze Age.*

3 Turn off right at OS 325834, and follow a track towards some trees. Follow the track on a winding course to reach the crest of Kingston Warren Down at railed-off gallops. Turn sharply right at OS 310836, and, after 100 yards/90 metres, reach a rash of signposts. Keep ahead alongside a row of young trees, and continue to the Ridgeway at Uffington Castle.

The Ridgeway track at Scutchamer Knob.

ACKLING DYKE
Wiltshire and Dorset

Old Sarum (Salisbury) to Badbury Rings 24 miles/38.4 kms

*'For mile after mile,
up hill and down,
practically all the way
to Badbury Rings, the
road is seen . . . as an
enormous agger . . .
One feels that one
must be viewing the
embankment of an
abandoned mainline
railway rather than a
Roman Road!'*

I.D. Margary, *Roman Roads in
Britain*, 1956

An absorbing walk along some of the finest stretches of surviving Roman road in Britain. The route leads from Old Sarum along paths and field tracks, then follows the preserved embankment, or 'agger' of the road along the eastern edge of Cranborne Chase, and past ancient monuments that predate the Roman presence.

Between Cranborne Chase, in Dorset, and the Hampshire border, the landscape is peppered with earthworks. This is chalk country where the soil was easily disturbed and where it lent itself to the building of great embankments and the heaping up of burial mounds. It was a well-populated landscape during the Late Neolithic to Early Bronze Age period, when ancient people raised long barrows and tumuli on every available ridge and eminence. Most spectacularly, they laid out a long barrow, or *cursus*, that ran for six miles/nine and a half kilometres through the heart of what is now modern Dorset. It survives today, blurred by centuries of land use, as parallel banks and ditches one hundred and fifty yards/one hundred and thirty-five metres apart. This strange linear imprint runs from a cluster of tumuli along a north-east alignment, to end at the great fourth-century defensive earthwork of Bokerley Ditch, on a converging angle with the Roman road known as Ackling Dyke.

This was great country for ditches as well as dykes, though there was little to distinguish between the two. There are fragments of a 'Grims Ditch' scattered around Bokerley itself. The many 'Grims Ditches' throughout southern England were long seen as being defensive, but were more likely to have been simple territorial boundaries, like the prehistoric 'reave' embankments of Dartmoor.

Across this extraordinary palimpsest of ancient land use, the Romans built part of their road from London to the south-west. It is probable that the road was originally aligned with Poole harbour, and that it was later extended to Dorchester and to Exeter. Where it crosses modern Wiltshire, Hampshire and Dorset, the road was raised on a magnificent agger, forty to fifty feet/twelve to fifteen metres wide and up to six feet/nearly two metres high. In its mid-section it was known as Ackling Dyke after another more ancient earthwork, and the name is now applied overall to the line of the Roman road from Old Sarum to the Iron Age hill fort of Badbury Rings near Wimborne Minster.

Old Sarum sounds very old indeed. As a fortification it was ancient, and it dates unmistakably from the Iron Age, though the great hill may well have been occupied in some form from the earliest times. The great chalk dome is capped with gravel, in which artefacts of the Mesolithic and Neolithic periods have been found.

The green banks of Old Sarum.

But it was the Iron Age Britons who raised the massive outer earthwork of Sarum, and who gave it the name Sorviadun, 'the fortress by the gentle river'. The Romans are believed to have strengthened the fortifications, though their main encampment was on the banks of the gentle Avon below, at Stratford-sub-Castle.

Later, Old Sarum became a Saxon town, called Searoburh and then Sarisberie. It was formidable as a fortress still. In 1003 Sweyn of Denmark, in vengeful mood, destroyed Exeter and sacked Wilton to the south-west of Old Sarum. But Sarum's mighty defences made him think twice, and he retreated. The site prospered, and minted its own coins. But it was the Normans who took the great hill to heart. They established motte and bailey within the Iron Age ring, built a splendid cathedral and an archbishop's palace, and added fortifications. They also changed the name by a subtle substitution of letters, to produce Salisburia. Latinized to resemble the coveted name of Salzburg, the 'city of salt'. By the thirteenth century, Old Sarum had been supplanted by the town on the plain, new Salisbury. The impressive form of the older settlement remained intact, though the imprint of the Roman roads that radiated from it soon became absorbed into the landscape.

Roman roads in Britain were of great strategic importance. The directness of their alignments, and the supportive structures of forts and supply, were the main elements in Rome's efficient military colonizing of Britain. The roads turned southern England into a fully Romanized province, and for a time subjugated wild Wales and carried legionary force into Scotland. It was an achievement unmatched by Anglo-Saxon expansionists like Offa, who matched Rome's civil engineering ability with his great frontier dyke, but could not subjugate Wales. Even the Normans failed to impose their rule on northern Britain as effectively as the Romans imposed theirs. It was only Rome's failure to supplement its military presence with substantial numbers of civilian colonists that prevented the permanent Romanization of Britain. Once the

Romans left, Roman influence became quickly submerged beneath successive waves of invaders. But Rome's great roads remain as monuments to its remarkable power, and, as with Ackling Dyke, they have often survived in their physical form.

We do not know the exact line of the Roman road immediately to the south-west of Old Sarum, where our walk begins. But we can follow an interesting route from the great hill fort to cross the gentle Avon below Bemerton Heath, where the river widens into quiet pools beneath graceful trees. From here, we know that the Roman road crossed a few hundred yards to the south, and then rose in steep zigzags to the crest of the western escarpment. A suburban street called Roman Road pays tribute to the past, but the busy A36 at Skew Bridge has to be crossed before quieter lanes lead past the old church at Bemerton and then across the wide water meadows of the River Nadder, along a causeway path known as Broken Bridges.

The Roman road struck directly across the Nadder valley from near the site of the old church, then climbed over the ridge of Warren Down, where today a golf course occupies the green slopes. The views back north from the crest of the golf course are remarkable. This is a tended countryside. The course is like a well-trimmed garden dotted with trees and shrubs; it sweeps downhill, park-like, into the broad valley of the Nadder. To the north-east the exquisite spire of Salisbury Cathedral dominates the town; it glitters even in the dullest light. Old Sarum lies due north, blunt-browed and ungainly by comparison, but impressive all the same. To the west is a great sweep of wooded downland, beyond a chequerboard of fat farms and linear fields.

Our route crosses the course of 'The Raceplain', where the famous Salisbury Races are held in season. Soon we descend to the quiet valley of the Ebble and its lovely riverside hamlets of Coombe Bissett, Stratford Tony, Throope, and Bishopstone. These are all ancient settlements, Saxon 'out-farms' that set the pattern of English rural life that Norman influence could not wholly transform. Bishopstone Church is an impressive building; it stands on the site of the old village of Bishopstone. The village was devastated by plague in the seventeenth century, and the survivors did what was necessary: they burned their cottages and moved a mile/a couple of kilometres to the west. Through this countryside the Romans carried their road across three river valleys on the six-mile/nine and a half kilometre stretch between Old Sarum and the downs above Bishopstone. The road was arrow-straight in general, though it flexed here and there to avoid the scooped combes of the high ground ahead.

Above Throope Manor, the way to the downs is lovely. The sides of the combe are well cultivated, the chalk sifted like flour, and dazzling white when newly ploughed. There is a smooth patina to a landscape where no threatening rock grumbles beneath the surface. The fields merge with the grasslands of the high ground, the whole threaded by tree-fringed lanes. Our way leads up the old Faulston Drove past the polished trunks of tall beeches. Here the road deviated slightly to the east, to run above a deep combe. Traces of the agger survive in the adjoining hedgerow of birches and hawthorn. From the top of the slope the tower of Salisbury Cathedral is seen for the last time in its loop of light. In the wide featureless fields on the flat top of Faulston Down an edgy wind cools the skin. The earth of these fields has been turned over for centuries, and in places the misshapen flint pebbles are as thick as hailstones.

Much of the Roman road has been lost to the plough. But in places, the merest ripple of a raised line reveals the agger. The views from this high ground are magnificent. To the west, the downs sweep away into exhilarating distance across a quilted landscape. This is a countryside of cash crops now, such as maize and winter wheat. But it is easy to imagine how it looked in Roman times. Much of its original woodland had been burnt or felled by then, and instead the grassy downs billowed like the sea to all quarters. It was good marching country for the Roman soldiers, and the surface of the road was well drained.

The line of the road edges back to the west once more, then crosses the deeply rutted lane of the ancient Ox Drove. Through Knighton Wood, the Roman agger has survived. In summer, in the bronze light of evening, the shadows lengthen into dark darting folds across the high ground. The wall of trees becomes jet black. At Knighton Wood, the path plunges into a cool woodland where it runs straight-limbed along the top of the agger. Glimpses of great fields are seen through the trees. They run like airstrips into the pale distance where, at dusk, roe deer forage along the edge of the plantations, and pheasants peck quietly beside them.

There is a special pleasure in tramping through these enfolding trees after the openness of the high ground. But soon the way breaks clear along the eastern edge of Vernditch Chase, where the Roman road seems to grow in stature beneath its grassy crest. Where the Chase ends, there is an important change in the direction of the road. So far it has maintained a clear alignment with Old Sarum, but from here the alignment shifts slightly to the south to set the road in line with Badbury Rings twelve miles/nineteen kilometres away. A few hundred yards/metres along this new alignment, the Roman road is submerged beneath the tarmac of the A354 at Woodyates Corner where modern Wiltshire, Dorset and Hampshire meet.

Woodyates was the site of a Roman marching fort, and is where the Roman road was crossed by the great earthwork of Bokerley Ditch. The earthwork runs for three miles/five kilometres along the Hampshire border, and is substantial and well preserved where it crosses Martin Down. It is called Bokerley from the Old English name for 'buck'; but its original name, if it had one, is not known. It was raised during the early part of the fourth century, possibly as a territorial boundary to a collective farming estate where a large and submissive Romano-British population raised cattle and produced grain and other commodities for the imperial exchequer. The dyke may have been strengthened and extended to block the old road in AD 367, when Roman Britain fragmented for a time under the pressure of internal revolt and savage incursions by bands of Saxons, Picts, and Scots from Ireland. The dyke was again strengthened by the Romano-British in the fifth century, after Rome had abandoned them to the Saxon invaders.

Only the modern road intrudes on this ancient landscape. From Woodyates, the walker is faced with an unpleasant tramp along a busy highway, before the Roman road is regained. But a diverting walk on paths and lanes can be made alongside Bokerley Ditch and through the hamlet of Pentridge, to regain the Roman agger at Oakley Down. If the main road is followed, Ackling Dyke is reached by following a path from the garage at Oakley Down. It is a strange way to rediscover ancient Rome, but the reward is splendid. From here, the finest remnant of the road survives, 'the magnificence which now lies ahead', in Margary's words.

At Oakley, the great agger of the road runs past one of the finest series of Bronze Age tumuli in England. It is an intriguing area of grassed-over mounds that are smooth as felt in their uniformity. As so often happened, the Romans left the great burial mounds intact, though their agger sliced across the perimeter of one of them. Here, the road runs alongside a dark wall of trees that leads up onto Bottlebush Down. On winter mornings the grass is laden with glittering frost, and in the shade of the trees the air is as sharp as blades. The line of the road strikes unerringly ahead, etched by frost, the sweep of fields to either side ribbed and furrowed by winter ploughing.

In summer, the broad ribbon of Ackling Dyke merges with those same green fields. But the line of the road is still distinctive. It is easy to imagine a dark column of Roman soldiers in the distance, moving as one, with a haze of white dust billowing round their thudding feet, the clashing of chain mail and the creak of leather growing louder. To the native population, gazing across the open downs, such cohorts would have been a formidable sight, a constant reminder of Rome's military dominance.

On the crest of Bottlebush Down, the agger crosses the Handley to Ringwood road, and continues south, passing unseen its junction with the famous Dorset *cursus*, which runs at an oblique angle here. The land is often wooded to the east. To the west of the agger, the vast fields are dotted with tumuli. Beyond the next road crossing, a broad pebbly track runs steadily uphill, enclosed by tall beeches and sycamores. Owls screech in the night-time wood, and in high winds the trees roar with a sound like the sea. At a crossing of tracks there is a modern memorial stone, touching, but slightly out of keeping on this ancient highway.

The road now levels off. It is well defined as a broad high mound, unquestionably like Margary's abandoned railway, yet much more absorbing. Fast progress can be made along a flanking track, but there is also a path along the top of the agger. It threads its way through the deep grass and tangled hawthorns, and is a damp wade in wet weather. This is a peaceful section of Ackling Dyke, languid on hot summer afternoons when the air is heavy with the sweet scent of sun-warmed grass and wild flowers. The banks and hedgerows are aglow with pink campions and knapweed, the red of valerian, the white lace of cow parsley and the yellow of cat's ear and hawkweed. Stonechats and linnets, the modest dunnock and chattering yellowhammers flit through the tangled shrubs, and the air hums with insect life.

Soon, the road makes another slight change of alignment towards Badbury Rings. Roman roads were planned by surveyors who worked out their plans using poles, flags and beacons, aligning them by use of a crude but ingenious form of theodolite. When Ackling Dyke was first constructed, it would have sliced across the disturbed landscape as a white linear scar, the piled embankment of flint pebbles and crumbly chalk rising fom wide scoop-ditches of scraped and trampled ground. Local labour was recruited for the work, and there would have been many hands available in this densely populated and subservient countryside.

From now on the line of Ackling Dyke diverges steadily from the A354, and runs deeply into the peaceful countryside round Gussage St Michael, Gussage All Saints and Moor Crichel. The route crosses the stream and road that link the two Gussages, then cuts across the sharp little height of Sovell Down where the surveyors pitched it through an ascending line of zigzags. Beyond Sovell, it is difficult to identify the agger, and our route diverges to follow rights of way. Once across the road from Sovell Down, a field track leads down to a quiet twist of road west of Moor Crichel. Here a small stream is crossed by a nicely drunken

footbridge, and a broad muddy track is followed uphill.

This is the Cock Road, an old farm way in its own right. It runs, shrouded by trees, to the lane between Cockroad Farm and Moor Crichel, where a quick sidestep west regains the line of the Roman road, and a path leads across a field and through woodland to Manswood. Again the lost line of the road across adjoining fields is shadowed by a track that runs past the handsome building of the Old School House. Then, at a public road junction, a signpost reassures with its message 'Roman Road – Witchampton'.

From here, we must take the public road, but it follows a straight southerly line towards the high ground of Badbury Rings, and is soon left for a final section of path and field track that runs along the crest of the agger towards King Down Farm. Beyond the farm the mighty earthwork is reached. Like Old Sarum, this immense structure was mainly the work of Iron Age Britons. Badbury was called Vindocladia initially, 'the town with white ditches', when the great banks were of fresh chalk gleaming like snow. It was a native stronghold from the sixth century BC to the first century AD, mightily impregnable until the Roman troops under Vespasian shattered its defences with ballista in AD 43.

The Romans dismantled the fort's stonework and its laced timber, and left the earthen core that remains today. But Badbury was temporarily re-fortified by the Britons in their struggle to limit the thrust of Anglo-Saxon invasion after Rome's withdrawal. Its surviving name is a composite of the Old English personal name, 'Badda', and 'burh', a fortified place. Some say that Badbury was where the legendary King Arthur fought his great battle of Mount Badon against the Saxon, but the truth is clouded with legend.

As with Old Sarum, the Roman road bypassed the fort, the Romans being content to site their marching camps and enclosures outside the walls. From Badbury, the road is believed to have struck south-east to Kingston Lacy and on to Poole harbour. Later, the great arterial extension to Dorchester and thence to Exeter was added. Today, Badbury Rings seems desolate, though it is well cared for by the National Trust, and draws large numbers of visitors. Much regenerative work has been done. The central area of the site is reached as if through a maze, but it is strangely empty of substance, or inspiration, as if the Romans in their efficiency had robbed it not only of its fortifications but also of its past.

It is difficult to judge which is most impressive, the mighty earthworks of Old Sarum and Badbury Rings, or the linear agger of the Roman road. Hill forts have a pleasing completeness and great presence. But the long lonely ribbon of Ackling Dyke, as with all Roman roads, seems to set its imprint more emphatically on the landscape through which it is so pleasurably followed.

ACKLING DYKE
Information

Distance 24 miles/38.4 kms

Maps OS Landranger 184 (Salisbury & The Plain); OS Landranger 195 (Bournemouth & Purbeck)

Nature of Walk A varied and intriguing walk that is not too strenuous, though there are some steepish inclines in the first few miles. Field sections can be very muddy. The walk may be completed in a day by experienced walkers, but can be broken off midway at Woodyates Corner.

Accommodation At Salisbury and Blandford Forum. Some accommodation along the way at villages just off the route. Youth hostel at Salisbury.

Transport Railway and bus stations at Salisbury. Bus connections to main centres from Blandford Forum and Wimborne Minster. Daily bus service between Salisbury and Blandford Forum and between Blandford Forum and Wimborne Minster.

Further Information Tourist Information Centre, Salisbury, tel. (0722) 334956

Start Old Sarum OS 138327

1 Descend a track down the south-west flank of Old Sarum, and follow a path between fields to reach a road by some thatched cottages. Go right for 200 yards/180 metres, then go left down Mill Lane, signposted Devizes Road. At the lane end, bear left along a surfaced path, then cross a bridge and continue steeply to the Devizes Road. Turn left for ¼ mile/0.4 kms, then turn right by a cemetery down 'Roman Road'. At a main road, turn right, then left down Church Lane to Old Bemerton Church. Go left along Lower Road, then after a double bend, go right, signposted West Harnham. Follow a surfaced path over several bridges. Beyond a narrow bridge at a Y-junction, go right, and over a stile to follow a path along field edges, finally bearing left down a farm track to reach the busy A3094 at OS 114295. (4 miles/6.4 kms)

2 Cross the road *with care*, and go up the approach road to the golf course. Just before the club house, bear off left up a tree-lined lane, and, at its top, follow black arrows right, then left to cross a race course. Go left along a muddy track for a few yards, then bear right at a junction onto a surfaced road. After 50 yards/45 metres, go right through a gate, and follow field edges and then a field track to emerge by a lane junction at OS 093270. (2 miles/3.2 kms)

3 Follow the right-hand lane, then go right at a junction for about ½ mile/0.8 kms. At OS 084265, go left down the lane past Bishopstone Church, then turn left at a T-junction. By Throope Manor House turn right, signposted 'bridleway', and continue up the combe to some isolated barns where a right turn leads uphill to a T-junction with a green lane at OS 080253. Go left up the lane. (2¼ miles/3.6 kms)

4 Go through a gate at the top of the lane, and keep ahead and uphill. At the top of the rise, go through a field gate on the right, then bear left to the broken mound of a tumulus. Continue to a gate. Beyond the gate, cross a field diagonally left to go through another gate, then continue to a grassy mound. Bear diagonally right from the mound, go through a fence gap, then bear right round the rim of a combe at OS 070234 to cross a grassy track. Continue to the apex of a wood, then go right along a muddy lane, the Ox Drove, to a T-junction with a farm lane. Go left for 100 yards/90 metres, then bear off right into the woods. (1½ miles/2.4 kms).

5 Follow the agger of the Roman road along a good track through Knighton Wood, to reach a junction with a public road at OS 047215. Cross the road to an open space by the start of a forestry road. Bear left down a shady track, and continue along the edge of Vernditch Chase. Go through a gate at OS 035202, turn right for a short distance, then go left along a track to reach the A354 at Woodyates Corner. (2½ miles/4 kms)

The line of the Roman road now merges with the A354 for 1½ miles/2.4 kms as far as Oakley Down. The road-walking is unpleasant, and a detour can be made by breaking off left at OS 035202 to cross the A354 to reach the car park of Martin Down Nature Reserve. From here, follow Bokerley Ditch to go right through a gap at OS 043190. Follow a track for ¼ mile/0.4 kms, then go left down another track to reach the road leading to Pentridge. Go through Pentridge, and at OS 031172 go right for just under 1 mile/1.5 kms, to reach Ackling Dyke just south of Oakley Down filling station, at OS 021175. (3 miles/4.8 kms)

6 If the A354 has been followed, Ackling Dyke is regained by going left along the left edge of the forecourt of Oakley Down filling station, to go through a gate. Follow a path down right to join Ackling Dyke at OS 021175. Follow the obvious line of Ackling Dyke, at times along the top of the dyke, or on tracks alongside it, crossing several roads before reaching a road at OS 990098 just west of Moor Crichel. (6¾ miles/10.8 kms)

Bokerley Ditch on Martin Down.

7 Go down the road for a few yards, then keep ahead across a footbridge signposted Cock Road, to follow a green lane. Emerge from trees at a road opposite a cottage. Go right for 50 yards/45 metres, then go left through a gap in the hedge, signposted Manswood. Join a short section of lane that leads past houses to a road. Cross the road and follow a green lane past the Old School House to emerge at another road at OS 982071. (2 miles/3.2 kms)

8 Turn right along the road to reach a T-junction signposted 'Roman Road – Witchampton'. Turn left, and follow the road to a crossroads. Keep straight ahead, signposted 'Bradford – No Through Road'. After ¼ mile/0.4 kms, go off right at OS 977058 along a bridleway, signposted Badbury Rings. Keep ahead along paths and farm lanes, passing King Down Farm, to reach Badbury Rings. (3 miles/4.8 kms)

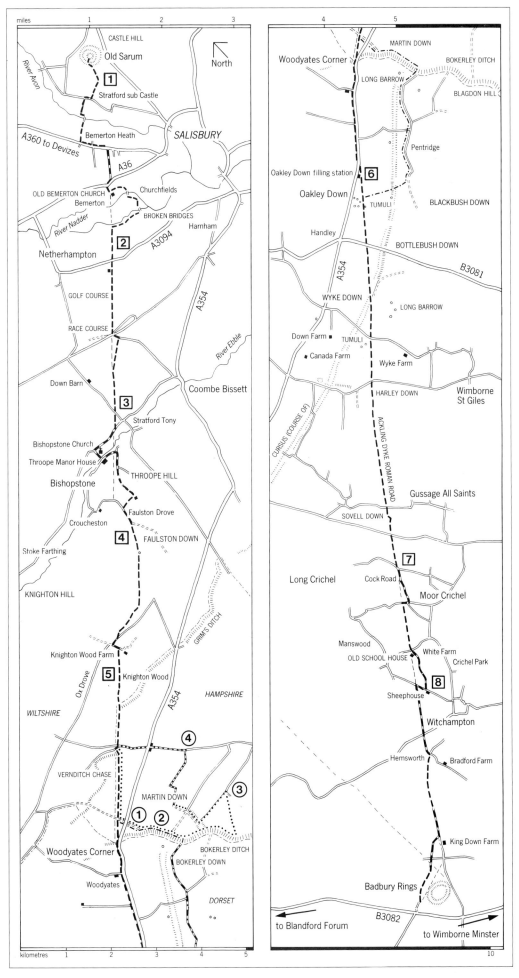

CIRCULAR WALK 6 miles/9.6 kms

A level walk that takes in the earthworks of Bokerley Ditch and Grims Ditch and then follows Ackling Dyke across Vernditch Chase. Part of the walk passes through the Martin Down National Nature Reserve. Allow two and a half hours.

Start Martin Down Reserve car park OS 036201

1 From the car park, follow a broad track leading onto the down. *Martin Down National Nature Reserve is managed by the Nature Conservancy Council. It comprises 620 acres/249 ha of chalk downland rich in plant life and insect fauna.*

2 Reach a series of parallel embankments. Go right by the largest of these, to reach the distinctive embankment of Bokerley Ditch. Turn left and follow the embankment to reach a dip by woodland where the embankment bears right and uphill. Turn left along a grassy track. *The parallel embankments first encountered were raised as rifle ranges during World War II.*

3 After ¼ mile/0.4 kms, reach a track junction just past a clump of thorn trees. Bear sharp left, then at the next junction go right alongside a hedge. *The hedge is on the line of Grims Ditch, a territorial earthwork, probably of the Bronze Age.* Keep ahead over a crossing of tracks, then, where the hedgerow bends right, go right and follow a green lane through several sharp bends to reach a surfaced lane at OS 056204.

4 Go left along the lane, cross the A354 *with care*, then continue along the road opposite for just under ½ mile/0.8 kms until abreast of an open space at the entrance to a forestry road. Go along a shady track to the left of the forestry road, and continue along the south-east edge of Vernditch Chase. At OS 035203 turn left, then cross the A354 *with care*, to reach the car park at Martin Down.

Badbury Rings.

THE EXMOOR RIDGEWAY
Somerset and Devon

Dunkery Gate to Parracombe 21 miles/33.6 kms

'. . . on some desolate English moorland it is even easier to feel this identity with the dead of the Bronze Age, who lie near by under a piled-up cairn or under the heathery blanket of a burial mound . . .'

W.G. Hoskins, *The Making of the English Landscape*, 1955

This is an exhilarating walk across the high ground of wildest Exmoor. There is some evidence that the route was part of a prehistoric ridgeway that ran from modern Avebury in Wiltshire to the North Devon coast, from where sea routes led to Wales. Bronze Age burial mounds stand at intervals along the way.

High Exmoor is a wilderness of rolling hills and deeply incised valleys, unrelieved by rocky summit or sudden escarpment. Some people call Exmoor featureless. But it is the vast emptiness of the moor that is spectacular, rather than its individual parts. The horizon draws you ever onwards across the forlorn beauty of those empty hills.

The first Exmoor settlers made their way along smooth-browed ridges where wild animals had tramped out broad 'ways' soon after the end of the last Ice Age. Much later, small bands of hunter-gatherers of the Mesolithic and Neolithic periods (*c.* 6000 to 2300 BC) foraged above the densely wooded and dangerous valleys. The Neolithic people were less nomadic; they practised primitive farming. But both groups had a light touch with the landscape, and left only meagre traces of their existence in the form of chert and flint weapons and crude tools.

During the Early Bronze Age (*c.* 2300 to 1300 BC), when the climate was warmer and drier than it is today, people from the Iberian peninsula colonized the high ground of Exmoor. These immigrants were known as Beaker people after the type of pottery that they made. They led a settled life, clearing the primeval forest and grazing livestock on moorland grass that was far more nutritious than the rank vegetation of today's wilderness.

The Beaker people had a strong sense of identity and believed in an afterlife. They buried their leaders in high places and above ground, initially in the foetal position beneath the mounds of turf, clay and stone, known as 'tumuli' or 'barrows', that are the theme of this high moorland walk. Later generations cremated their dead, the ash being placed in urns beneath the barrows. On Exmoor, three hundred such burial sites have been recorded.

The Beaker people travelled along the routes established by their predecessors. The modern road from Porlock to Lynmouth is probably on the line of a coastal ridgeway. Another ridgeway ran to the south, along the distinctive line of the road that now leads from Dulverton across West Anstey Common. It is characterized also by substantial burial mounds such as those at The Wambarrows and Five Barrows. But the ridgeway that concerns us here followed the southern edge of the central moor to Blackmoor Gate, then continued west to the coast along the line of the present B3343 past numerous surviving tumuli.

This central ridgeway route entered Exmoor from the east, along the crest of the Brendon Hills, where a minor road now runs. It is a road which is fun to drive along but not to walk. It is level and direct and says everything about ancient tracks as being lines of least resistance. The Brendon road leads on to Wheddon Cross, and passes the remains of burial mounds at Huish Champflower, Wivelscombe, Leather Barrow and Cutcombe Barrow, until the wild moorland and the looming height of Dunkery Beacon command the airy distance.

From its start at Dunkery Gate, the ridgeway follows a broad track to the west, across the southern flank of Dunkery Beacon. A detour can take in the Beacon, though its accessibility has made it something of a Piccadilly Circus-on-the-Moor. A Bronze Age barrow lies beneath the modern cairn, and the rocky piles of the Rowbarrows lie to the west along a path from Dunkery's summit.

Dunkery translates blandly as 'rocky hill', but its rock has been plundered for usable stone over the years, and the scattered tumuli and barrows have been badly damaged. Yet, in winter or in sombre autumn, there is a brooding loveliness about this broad-backed hill under its grey ghostly skies. And from the rising ridgeway track in the early light of a summer's day, the eastern Quantocks, the Brendons, and the blurred hills to the south, loom through a blue haze, while the sun bathes Dunkery's slopes of heather and crowberry in the clear morning light.

The way ahead soon leaves Dunkery behind, then contours above Ember Combe on a good broad track. Left of the track is Exford Common. On the flat summit of the common lies Bendels Barrow, a low mound marooned amidst nightmare drifts of heather, sedge and sphagnum moss, that are best avoided on foot. Right of the track is Ember Combe, a scooped-out hollow that often harbours deer.

The red deer is a handsome but contentious symbol of modern Exmoor, where hunting with hounds has been long established. Opponents see such 'sport' as nothing less than barbaric, while apologists claim a right to cull for conservation's sake and through honoured tradition. Certainly a close sight of these elegant animals is always exhilarating. They move with a fluency that diminishes our best efforts, and even the Mesolithic hunters needed artifice to bring them down amidst the sweet grasslands of the ancient moor.

The way continues across Almsworthy Common. To the right of the rising track is a scattered setting of small standing stones that was discovered earlier this century. The pattern of these gnomic stones is hard to make out amidst the dense heather, but they are not accidental, and others probably lie fallen and smothered

Opposite: The Chains: 'the most desolate yet enduring part of Exmoor'.

by the peat. Such stone settings may have been used by Bronze Age people for ritualistic purposes. Almsworthy has traces of a pre-historic field system, and Alderman's Barrow to the north-west suggests that the area was an important Bronze Age site.

South-west from Alderman's Barrow is Larkbarrow Common. Ahead lie four miles/six and a half kilometres of testing country that lead to the next road at Blackpits Gate. Larkbarrow sets the scene, with its vastness of scale. Westward, the heathland runs into unnerving distance, and there is a nice sense of anxiety about which direction to take.

Larkbarrow is a junction of ancient ways. The central ridgeway contours south and then west from here. Other routes run west over Great Tom's Hill to Badgworthy Water and north-west to Robber's Bridge at Oareford. It is all Lorna Doone country to the north, an exquisite landscape smothered in the romance of the robber barons of R.D. Blackmore's rich imagination. Today, the lovely Lorna and the book's hero (that epitome of Exmoor Man, John Ridd) dominate Exmoor's tourist image. They are enduring characters, but fictitious nonetheless. The real romance lies along the lonely ridgeways where the ancient people, in their deerskins and furs and gleaming bronze amulets, moved in harmony with their sacred landscape.

The descendants of those anonymous people have had scant respect for monuments, sacred or otherwise. Larkbarrow itself is a poor remnant, its mound broken and scratched out. It lies north-west of the Larkbarrow Corner gate, near a wide gap.

The way goes through this gap, then follows a lovely sunken track for two miles/over three kilometres as it contours to the south of Elsworthy Hill and then sweeps leftwards round Ware Ball. To the south, lies the River Exe clasped between the steep sides of Exe Cleave, where beech and willow thickets hug the slopes, and the red-berried mountain ash marks a transition between bare upland and sheltered valley. Buzzards glide lazily in the skies, and in summer the air is sweet with the smell of bruised grass and meadow flowers, and spiced by the freshness of moorland wind. And though the winter moor can be gloomy, glittering frost or the long drifts of Exmoor snow can sparkle in the sharp sunlight.

In prehistoric times, the track here would have edged its way above valley slopes that were clothed in hazel scrub. Oakwood grew on sheltered banks, and dense alder and birch woods on the valley floors. Today, the valleys are green and well farmed. This is the country of Victorian entrepreneur John Knight, Midlands ironmaster and man of iron who, early in the last century, cultivated 2,500 acres/1,000 hectares of wild Exmoor. Knight bought the Royal Forest in 1825. (The name 'Forest' is a historical reference to the hunting preserve of Norman kings.) Knight set out to bend the wilderness to Victorian enterprise, and his hand is seen on the moor all the way along the ridgeway as far as Pinkworthy Pond. In Knight's day, Exmoor was still considered to be the 'filthy, barren ground', as described rather dismissively by William Camden in the sixteenth century. But the Midlands ironmaster dreamed of turning the high moorland into fields of golden wheat and barley.

He was over two thousand years too late. The relatively temperate climate of the Bronze Age had changed to a cooler and wetter one, with the result that the barrow builders retreated valleywards, with raw winds at their backs, leaving acid peat and rank deer grass to colonize the abandoned moor. Its curdled acres must have mocked the would-be super farmer.

But Knight tried hard enough to subdue the high moor by enclosing it within twenty-nine miles/forty-five kilometres of boundary wall. Gangs of labourers drove yoked oxen to plough up a vast area of the south-facing lower slopes, then drenched the ground with lime to fertilize it. Knight's son, Sir Frederick, kept up the work – but more cannily. Twenty miles/thirty-two kilometres of road and hollow lane were built along the southern moor, and new farms established – like the square-set house at Warren Farm, that lies below the ridgeway track amidst the loveliness of Exe Cleave. The track we have followed from Larkbarrow Corner was created by the Knights to carry a railway from Warren Farm to Porlock. But the project was abandoned.

The walkers' way to the west runs above Warren Farm. Ahead, lies the featureless moorland of West Pinfold and Great Buscombe. This is rough and bitter ground, where the ancient ridgeway track has long been absorbed into the blanket bog. The low mound of Rexy Barrow lies just under a mile/one and a half kilometres to the west-north-west, amidst a tangled grassland that in windy conditions seethes and flows about your ankles like the sea. When the mist is down, this is an anxious and claustrophobic place, where precise compass work is needed. In clear weather, a hard tramp across the moor leads to the road at Exe Head Bridge, a midway break in the Ridgeway route.

West of Exe Head Bridge lie The Chains, the most desolate yet enduring part of Exmoor. The first part of the route follows the infant River Exe to its modest source at Exe Head. Across the river to the north is the desolate Exe Plain. Deer sometimes graze here in the dusk. They merge slowly with the heathland, while car headlights flicker along the Simonsbath road only a few hundred yards/metres away.

Exe Head is a dull morass, slashed through by grubby moorland tracks where the source of the great river oozes underfoot from

Pinkworthy Pond: 'a glittering sheet under the sun, or gloomy and menacing beneath gunmetal skies'.

sphagnum moss and reedy ditch. Water has always been the dominant force on Exmoor, lest we mock the oozing puddles of Exe Head. The word Exe derives from the Celtic word '*isca*' for 'water'. The Chains are a peat-capped reservoir where a layer of impermeable clay lies beneath the surface, an 'iron pan' that brims like a basin during prolonged heavy rain. It was from The Chains that the moorland water spilled over into the murderous flood that devastated the coastal village of Lynmouth in 1952. It took one final cloudburst after days of rain to send an estimated ninety million gallons/four hundred million litres of water pouring down into the deeply incised northern valleys. The East and West Lyn Rivers carried the full force of a great wall of water and tumbling boulders, that crashed down the gorges in the dark night, crushing and drowning fifty-four people, and tearing the heart out of Lynmouth.

The crossing of The Chains should be a navigational challenge for the modern walker. But the Knights built part of their boundary wall along the brow of the southern slopes, and the route ahead is easily followed along this wall. To the south, the southern ridgeway rises like a green wave, with the mounds of Five Barrows clearly visible on its distant crest.

The vegetation to either side of The Chains wall is strikingly different. South of the wall, grazing and management has left a richer, more varied mix of heather and purple moor grass. To the north, blanket bog dominates, with its dense pelt of tough deer grass, amidst which Chains Barrow, with its incongruous trig point and protective fence, stands out like a green island.

From Chains Barrow, in clear weather, the great shoulder of

Foreland Point above Lynmouth is visible beyond the smooth billows of the northern moor. To the west, the numerous barrows that mark the western culmination of our route are enticingly visible. They can be reached by contouring north-west from Chains Barrow, but this is not advised. It is hard going, and the 'stone compass' of the Chains wall is too convenient a guide to relinquish. Besides, the wall leads directly past the intriguing Pinkworthy Pond, a Victorian imposition on this ancient moorland, but one with some character.

Pinkworthy was another of John Knight's projects. Gangs of Irish labourers dammed the headwaters of the River Barle in its moorland cusp, to create a deep lake of about seven acres/three hectares. Knight's reasons for creating the pond have never been explained, since he left no records of the work. It is likely that Pinkworthy was to be a source of water power, possibly for driving machinery or for irrigation, but was never put to use.

The pond has survived and has absorbed some of the moorland character; a glittering sheet under the sun, or gloomy and menacing beneath gun-metal skies. Round its steep sides the pink and purple of ling, heather and cross-leaved heath defy the coarse moorland grasses, and the orange-yellow bog asphodel grows in rare patches on the marshy ground. The name Pinkworthy is pronounced 'Pinkery', a lightsome word at odds with the mood of the place. The fern-draped drainage cleft at the pond's eastern end has a nice aura of menace, and the pond surely deserves even a little resident monster. There is a ghost, of course: the desolate spirit of a young farmer who drowned himself in the bleak waters in 1889.

Beyond Pinkworthy, the way leads to Wood Barrow, where a gaunt and wind-driven beech tree stands sentinel on the moor wall at the boundary between Somerset and Devon. It is on this western edge of The Chains that the greatest number of barrows and monuments lies. These are so placed above the western end of the central ridgeway as to be visible from the lower slopes and from the valleys, and the area seems to have been of great significance to Bronze Age people. The substantial Chapman Barrows are the most westerly of a series of burial mounds, punctuated midway by the nine-foot/three metres high standing stone known as the Long Stone.

Vandals were early at work here. Their plundering of Wood Barrow in 1865 was famously attended by an apocalyptic thunderstorm. According to the terrified diggers, a bolt of lightning sizzled into the top of the disturbed mound, leaving only a corroded metal pan with a shining hole where alleged 'treasure' had lain. The diggers took off with their hair on end, and probably as white as the surrounding deer grass. There is now a sunken pit on top of

Wood Barrow, and the remains of a stone circle that ringed the barrow are still visible.

There is no definitive right of way for walkers across the moorland west of Wood Barrow, although the ancient ridgeway route evidently carried on to Chapman Barrows and the area is rich in ancient artefacts. The Long Stone lies a short distance west of Wood Barrow. It is impressive enough, grand in height but remarkably slim, being a mere six inches/fifteen centimetres in breadth. It stands like a crooked knife-blade in its bowl of peaty water. Further west are Chapman Barrows. They have been opened twice, once in 1885, and again in 1905. There were stone chambers at the heart of the plundered mounds, and they contained human bones. The spell of two thousand years was broken. But there was proof at least that the Bronze Age people lived and died on these high places.

There are no remains of buildings. The ancient people lived in temporary wooden huts because of a lack of moor stone. Their burial cists beneath high mounds of earth emphasize that they believed in an afterlife. They were also practical. The positioning of the barrows on exposed heights may have been intended as a signal to incomers that the surrounding land was 'occupied', and that grazing rights had been established.

The linear group of nine mounds at Chapman Barrows has marked the boundary between Challacombe and Lynton and Lynmouth parishes for generations. The barrows have been unceremoniously clipped by a boundary wall for the privilege. The name of the group is puzzling. One suggestion is that, as landmarks on the ridgeway, the barrows acquired the name from travelling pedlars, or chapmen, who used them to navigate by. But there is no hard evidence of this, and the name may be a distortion of some older word.

West of Chapman Barrows there is one other burial mound. This is Holwell Barrow and it lies within private land. This is the descending line of the ridgeway, and the countryside is bland with farmed fields, although there are still tumuli on Challacombe Common. To the north, below the brow of the ridgeway, lies the lovely village of Parracombe and the adjoining Holwell Castle, a fine example of a Norman motte and bailey fortification. Parracombe has two churches that are worth visiting. One is a rather formal Victorian building. The other is the original church, which has had its eighteenth-century interior imaginatively preserved, complete with musicians' gallery and box pews. Both are 'modern' sacred sites, but they are more than a religious world apart from those of the mysterious Bronze Age people, along whose ancient moorland ridgeway this walk has led us.

The Exmoor Ridgeway Information

Distance 21 miles/33.6 kms

Maps OS Landranger 181 (Minehead & Brendon Hills); OS Landranger 180 (Barnstaple & Ilfracombe)

Nature of Walk The Exmoor Ridgeway follows good tracks and paths, but there are a few indistinct sections where the going can be quite hard. Compass work may be necessary in thick mist. The route can be completed in a day by fit walkers, but makes a pleasant two-day walk if split at Exe Head Bridge. There are no pubs or other facilities along the way. Clothing should be for hill conditions. *The weather during late autumn and winter can be severe.*

Accommodation At Wheddon Cross and Parracombe. Seasonal camp site at Parracombe.

Transport Wheddon Cross, Dunkery Gate and Parracombe have service bus connections to main centres. The summer service through Exe Head Bridge is greatly reduced in winter. Timetables from TICs or the National Park Office at Dulverton.

Further Information Exmoor National Park Information Centre, Dulverton, tel. (0398) 23841.

Start Dunkery Gate (car park) OS 896404

1 Follow the broad track that runs west below Dunkery Beacon. After 2 miles/3.2 kms, a track veers off right at OS 864412, just before the road at Porlock Post. Cross two roads and follow the track round the rim of Ember Combe to cross another road at OS 850415. (3 miles/4.8 kms)

2 Continue down a track to a junction by the curve of a beech hedge. Keep ahead on the left-hand track that leads uphill past the setting of small stones on Almsworthy Common, to reach a road just south of Alderman's Barrow. Go left down the road for about 1 mile/ 1.6 kms, then go right through a gate marked

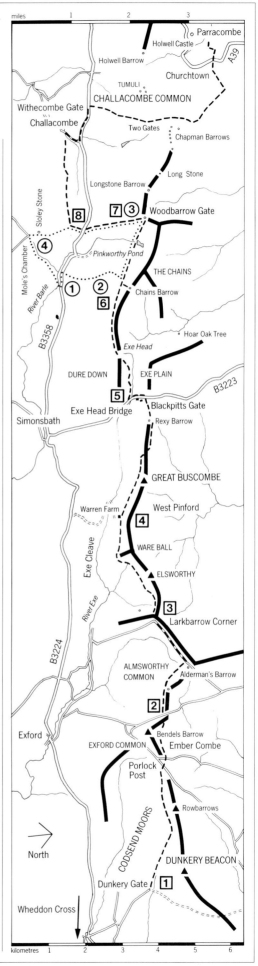

Larkbarrow Corner. Bear down left to pick up a faint track that leads to a wide gap at OS 823416, signposted Simonsbath via Warren Farm. (2 miles/3.2 kms)

3 Beyond the gate, continue along the right-hand fence for about 50 yards/45 metres, then bear left along a wide grassy track. Follow this track for 1 mile/1.6 kms round Elsworthy and Ware Ball, then go through a gate. Turn left and follow a raised bank, and after 1 mile/ 1.6 kms reach the moor gate above Warren Farm at OS 799408. (2¼ miles/3.6 kms)

4 Keep ahead past the gate. *The first reedy section can be very wet and marshy.* Continue along the left-hand wall for 1½ miles/2.4 kms to where a wall leads north across the moor. Go through a gate in this wall, and, a short distance ahead, turn sharp right to follow a vestigial track north for about 300 yards/270 metres. From here, the low mound of Rexy Barrow at OS 770419 lies west-north-west. Head for the barrow across difficult and pathless ground. From Rexy Barrow, go

west to reach an area of rough reedy pasture. Continue to where a gate leads onto the B3223 at Blackpitts Gate, and then turn left to reach Exe Head Bridge (2½ miles/4 kms)

5 Go through the gate by Exe Head Bridge. Go steeply left to another signpost, then bear right along a path. Continue to Exe Head, and on through gates. Follow the Chains wall to where Chains Barrow is seen 250 yards/ 225 metres to the right. (2 miles/3.2 kms)

6 Keep alongside the Chains wall past Pinkworthy Pond to reach Woodbarrow Gate. (1¼ miles/2 kms) *There is no definitive right of way from Woodbarrow Gate to Chapman Barrows.*

7 From Woodbarrow Gate, follow the track south to reach the B3358. (1 mile/1.6 kms) *If walkers do not wish to make this point the end of the walk, it is possible to reach Parracombe by rights of way.*

8 Cross the road, *with care*, and go through the gate opposite. Follow a track as it bears down

High Exmoor. *'The horizon draws you ever onwards across the forlorn beauty of those empty hills.'*

right, then continue uphill. A short distance uphill go right along a path signposted to Challacombe. From Challacombe walk north to reach the B3358. Go left along the road, *with care*, for about ½ mile/0.8 kms to reach Withecombe Gate at OS 684414. Turn right up a concrete farm road and continue north to reach a gate at Two Gates, just west of Chapman Barrows. Beyond the gate keep along a rough track that becomes a surfaced road. At a junction at OS 684451 go left then turn right by a house, then left, to reach the A39. Cross the road *with care* and continue into Parracombe. (7 miles/11.2 kms)

CIRCULAR WALK 7 miles/11.2 kms

This walk offers a bonus of ancient tracks. It leads onto the moor by Chains Barrow, then goes west to Woodbarrow. The route then follows the line of a Bronze Age connecting track to reach Exmoor's southern ridgeway route at Mole's Chamber, from where a return is made along part of the Saxon military route known as the Herepath.

Start The large lay-by on the B3358 Blackmoor Gate to Simonsbath road at OS 729401

1 At the east end of the lay-by, a gate opens onto a field. *The route from here north to the moor is along a path which the public may use at its own risk.* Keep by the hedge on the right, go through a gate, and then cross rougher ground to a gate onto open grassland.

2 Follow wooden posts to reach a gate in the Chains wall. Turn west, and follow the Chains wall past Pinkworthy Pond to reach Woodbarrow Gate. *Longstone Barrow, the Long Stone and Chapman Barrows lie to the west of here. There is no definitive right of way from Woodbarrow Gate to Chapman Barrows.*

3 From Wood Barrow, follow the track south to the B3358. Cross the road *with care*, and go through the gate opposite. Follow a track as it bears down right, then continue uphill. Keep

The Long Stone near Woodbarrow Gate.

ahead over the brow of the hill and through rough grassland. Descend gently, and go through the right-hand of two gates and then through another gate to follow a track between high hedges, to reach the Sloley Stone and Mole's Chamber. *Mole's Chamber is said to be named after a farmer who drowned in a notorious bog. The distinctive, but misspelt, 'Sloley Stone', set in the hedge on the right, was an eighteenth-century marker between two estates.*

4 Just before the Sloley Stone there is a gate. Go through this gate and follow a path north-west and downhill to cross a stream at a very wet area. Continue by a wall crowned with a beech hedge. Cross another stream, and follow a muddy and rutted track over the hill to come down to a surfaced track that leads up to the B3358. Turn left to the lay-by. *This last section is on a prehistoric route adapted by Saxon invaders as their 'Herepath' or military track.*

THE CROSS ROAD
Dartmoor

Buckfast Abbey to Tavistock 21 miles/33.6 kms

. . . the cross, though bearing no inscription, spoke with a yet louder voice, was even eloquent, and delivered a message clear as the sun at noon.'

William Crossing, *The Ancient Stone Crosses of Dartmoor and Its Borderland*, 1902

This splendid walk follows a sequence of granite crosses that served as occasional waymarks on a route across Dartmoor between the medieval abbeys of Buckfast and Tavistock. The route passes through the quiet landscape of rural Devon at either end of a vast stretch of magnificent moorland.

To follow a sequence of stone crosses over Dartmoor's rolling hills is something of a pilgrimage, even for pagans. You do not need religion to feel uplifted when spotting the next cross on the horizon, or to feel relieved when bumping into it in the mist.

Whether the route described here was a monastic route between Buckfast and Tavistock Abbeys, with a branch to Buckland Abbey, is not certain. Another transmoorland route followed a course to the south of the Cross Road. This route is known as the 'Abbot's Way', and although the name was invented in the late eighteenth century, the route's monastic association has some credence historically. It was known for centuries as the 'Jobbers' Path', along which packhorses carried woollen yarn from the sheep-rearing monasteries. But the modern Abbot's Way has only a few stone crosses, compared with the Cross Road's eighteen survivors. The crosses of the Cross Road chart a logical route across the moor, and circumstantial evidence is a great comfort to wishful thinking.

There were certainly rough ways across Dartmoor in prehistory, when the heart of the moor was the busy centre of Bronze Age communities. These early people lived, worked and travelled within the moorland area, and evidence shows that the eastern and western sections of the Cross Road lay within populated areas. But the Cross Road does not have the ridgeway element of a prehistoric route. Nor does it use hill passes or river valleys as natural lines of communication. Only the solid presence and the continuity of the stone crosses suggest that here might have been a medieval way at least.

The medievalism of most of the crosses is patent in their Latin design. They reflect the Christianity of the Anglo-Saxon and Norman conquests, rather than the older Christianity that produced the more elaborate Cornish crosses of the far west. Establishing stone crosses as waymarks was a common practice in medieval England. The stylized cross may even have supplanted the simple standing stone or guidepost of pre-Christian times, being less phallic and coarse, and more fulfilling of a dual purpose, temporal and divine.

The monks of Devon's monastic houses were as industrious as their counterparts elsewhere in England. They owned numerous manor farms, and grazed large numbers of sheep on moorland pasture. Tavistock Abbey was a Saxon foundation of the late tenth century. It was completed in 981 but was sacked by Danish raiders in 997 and the monks slaughtered. The abbey was quickly rebuilt, the tide of Danish anarchy receded, and Tavistock enjoyed a fruitful life until the Dissolution of 1539. The abbey buildings were then again dismantled – as brutally as they had been by the marauding Danes, but without bloodshed this time. Scant evidence of the magnificent complex survives, other than fragments now merged with the modern townscape.

Buckfast was a Benedictine community founded by Cnut soon after 1020, at a time when that clever monarch had begun his programme of reconciliation between Saxon and Dane and between his own natural savagery and a later Christian enlightenment. The abbot of Tavistock was Livingus, a close friend of Cnut, and it is probable that he helped to establish Buckfast. Tavistock and Buckfast were Benedictine foundations initially, and monks would have travelled between the two on monastic and commercial business. It may have been that the route of the crosses was established at this time. Buckfast later became Cistercian, a shared brotherhood with the smaller Buckland Abbey, which was founded in 1278 and lay to the south of Tavistock. The Cistercians were great wool producers, and a transmoorland route would have been essential to both houses.

The heart of modern Buckfast is the ideal starting point for our walk. The abbey is an impressive building, monumental and enduring in its certainties. The original abbey was dismantled at the time of the Dissolution and the site lay abandoned for centuries. It was purchased by French Benedictines in 1872 and an abbey church subsequently rebuilt, using local limestone and Somerset sandstone. This remarkable expression of faith ensured that the reconstruction remained true to the style of the medieval original. But even monumental replicas lack the rough patina of age and decay, and Buckfast's necessary commercialism detracts from the building's aesthetic. The grounds are too neatly designed and well kempt; the trappings of tourism are too overt. But the merging of shadow and light within the great cathedral-like space of the church is convincingly medieval.

The two crosses at the centre of the abbey forecourt are a pleasant introduction to the theme, as is the exit fom the forecourt through its rough-hewn medieval archway. From here, the way lies along typical Devon lanes and through junctions that seem to lock doors behind you. This is the kind of pleasantly confusing countryside where a bewildered motorist can end up passing the same signpost twice. The first cross we meet is at Hawson. It stands

Buckfast Abbey: 'an impressive building, monumental and enduring in its certainties'.

beside an ancient quasimodo of a tree known as 'Stumpy Oak', whose pollarded trunk squats by the side of the road sprouting gnarled and twisted branches. Hawson Cross has been restored and has an impressive cross head. Beyond Hawson the Holy Brook is crossed by Langaford bridge, and an ancient lane, Langaford Steep, is then followed uphill to the charming village of Holne.

From Holne, it is a short distance by road onto the open moor at Holne Moorgate. Behind us lie three miles/five kilometres of pastoral countryside that centuries of land use have neatly parcelled and patterned. As with so many ancient tracks that still cross wild country, the first and last stretches of the Cross Road thread a surviving way through a tamed landscape. At Holne Moorgate, the trapped fields and sunken lanes wash up against a stubborn wilderness. Yet, even here people have been at work. The moorland track now followed is a tinners' road to the tin mines on Holne Lee. It follows the line of the ancient track, but its purpose was industrial; its slabby 'clapper' bridges were crowded roughly into position by the broad-backed moormen who hacked out the rough tracks and the artificial waterways called leats during mining development in the nineteenth century.

At one such clapper bridge we leave the main track and bear off west alongside a leat. From this point, it is fairly certain that the route follows the line of a very ancient track. The ground has been scoured by mining use and is scrubland because of it. But further west, distinctive grass-covered banks rise from the gorse and heather. The most symmetrical of these are ancient boundaries known as 'reaves'. The Middle Bronze Age on Dartmoor saw the development of the reave system, by which low banks of earth and stone enclosed river valley territories and their adjoining moorland. Dartmoor was virtually cleared of native forest by about 1500 BC, and quite intensive farming patterns established. The reave system may have been planned through collective agreement between tribal chiefs. The low banks of surviving reaves run for miles in places, and shorter cross-reaves lead off at right angles, subdividing the enclosed ground into long strips.

Venford Reservoir lies in the sump of Venford Bottom, in what was once open country. It came into service in 1909 and was known initially as the Paignton Reservoir. The reservoir has fitted well into the landscape, though its surrounding conifers rest uneasily in a moorland setting where scattered thorn trees are the norm. Our route leads across the head of water where the old road crossed Venford Brook at a point known as Workman's Ford. Stiles breach the boundary fence of the reservoir. By the western exit, the land running inland is a chaos of grass and ferns and trees. The scattered stones of a medieval longhouse lie hidden beneath the tangled undergrowth, and further inland, barely detectable below the greenery, there are stone and earth banks that may be reaves. Once clear of the fence, our route leads uphill towards a reave that strikes unerringly to the west. In late summer the path is lost amidst tall ferns, but its line is marked by thorn trees and follows a sunken holloway to pass a small clapper bridge over a dried-up leat. The bridge looks very old but was built in the 1850s.

From here, the open moorland draws us in. It is a welcome escape from Venford Bottom, where the tangled undergrowth is claustrophobic and irritating in hot sunshine. Ahead, lies Horn's Cross, a splendid monument boldly emphasized by its moorland setting, its rough granite stained with ochrous lichen. To the south, the ground rises to Holne Ridge and Ryder's Hill. Northwards is Combestone Tor beside the busy moorland road. Beyond lies a magnificent sweep of moorland that runs from the great heights of the northern moor to the foreground summits of Sharp Tor above Dartmeet, and the dome of Corndon and Yar Tor beyond. Just north of the road are the rough lines of Mel Tor and Bench Tor, while to the north, the granite 'alps' of Haytor and Low Man, and the great sweep of Rippon Tor, dominate the horizon.

West of Horn's Cross the dwarfish outline of Horse Ford Cross is seen on the crest of the farthest hill. The way continues into the valley of the O Brook, past a cluster of stones that may have been part of a burial cist. The O Brook marks the boundary between

Horn's Cross, just west of Venford Reservoir.

Holne parish and the ancient Forest of Dartmoor, the bounds of which were delineated in 'Perambulations' of 1240 and 1609. The name O or Wo Brook derives from the Saxon for 'crooked', a word which sums up the stream's meandering course.

Where we first meet it, the O Brook bustles down its rocky bed. There is a confusion of leats and marshy pools to be crossed, then a rocky track leads upstream to a stony crossing place known as Horse Ford, where the old route once crossed the O Brook. The ford was altered greatly after floods of 1965 tumbled the stream bed with boulders. On the opposite bank the ground rises steeply along a line of thorn trees and through rough grass and ferns towards Horse Ford Cross, but it is better to continue upstream to cross below the restored wheelpit of the old Hexworthy tin mine, and to gain the cross from the track above. Horse Ford Cross is held together with an iron clamp, and has a boulder for its base. It is streaked with bird droppings, crosses being ideal perches for buzzards.

West from here, another cross is soon located amidst a featureless stretch of moorland. This is Skir Ford Cross, between which and the next cross on Ter Hill there is a desolate wilderness of boggy ground. The best route is to cross Skir Ford and follow the long hollow of Skir Gut through old mining country. Skir Gut was excavated by early miners as opencast, and today it still has the uneasy look of a man-made feature. But our route follows good firm ground and may well have been waymarked by crosses that were lost during tinning work.

But Ter Hill makes up for things with its cross cluster. This is high Dartmoor at 1,575 feet/471 metres, and the views in clear weather embrace Princetown to the west, although the menacing fortress walls of the famous prison are insignificant at this distance. The view is expansive. In the foreground is the sweep of brindled heathland; in the middle distance the lighter tones of green fields and blue-green plantations along the low hills of the western moor. Above is a broad vault of sky, sketched in on fine days with breezy clouds, where buzzards drift lazily on the thermals.

At Fox Tor Newtake a large section of moorland was enclosed during the speculative farming activity of the early nineteenth century. The wall of this 'newtake', as such enclosures were known, runs for a great distance to either side. The cross here is a fine specimen; it stands just inside an old gateway gap which itself is flanked by a curious arrow-headed pillar. From here, reedy ground sweeps down to Foxtor Mires, a vast basin of quaking ground. This quarter is known as Mount Misery, an epithet applied in the last century by a disgruntled Scottish shepherd who must have spent too much time weighed down by Dartmoor mist. Such mist is certainly oppressive. It smokes across the sodden ground and blinds you. When it is very dense, the newtake wall is a handy stone compass, like Knight's wall on Exmoor. It leads south, then west, all the way to the Devonport Leat.

Downhill from the Mount Misery cross lies the ruin of the nineteenth-century Fox Tor Farm. From here we cross an area of ground that has been devastated by tin workings. The scattered channels of the Swincombe Brook are awkward to negotiate, and then a rough way leads through a sequence of old reaves to the cross of Childe's Tomb, a monument that is linked to the apocryphal tale of Amyas Childe.

Childe was 'a man of fair possessions', according to the seventeenth-century commentator Tristram Risdon; he was hunting on the moor and became benighted in a bitter snowstorm. In a drastic act Childe killed his horse, disembowelled it, and crawled inside the steaming carcass in hopes of staying warm. Lacking the horse sense to appreciate that a live horse is warmer in the long run than a dead one, Childe froze to death. He had previously willed that the church where he was buried should inherit all his lands at Plymstock. Legend says that Tavistock men found Childe's body, and although Plymstock sent an angry mob to block the bridge over the River Tavy, the body was spirited across a makeshift bridge elsewhere, and buried at Tavistock Abbey. A cross was erected where Childe died.

Thereby hangs the tale. William Crossing doubted its authenticity; he suggests that its source lies in far older folk tales, and that some form of prehistoric burial chamber may have existed on the site. Crossing was more gracious about the next cross to the west, which is reached along sketchy paths through the green sweep of newtake ground. This was claimed to have been dis-covered by a naval Lieutenant, M. Lennon Goldsmith, in 1903. Goldsmith restored the artefact with Crossing's blessing, and the cross became self-fulfilling as part of the suggested monastic route.

From Goldsmith's Cross, the way leads across the Devonport Leat and on to the substantial Nun's Cross, one of Dartmoor's most famous monuments. The cross is over seven feet/two metres high. It was recorded as 'Crucem Siwardi' during the territorial 'Perambulation' of the Forest boundary in 1240, and 'Syward' is inscribed on the east face. Siward was a Norman Earl of Northumberland who owned Dartmoor land. On the west face is an incised cross and the inscription 'Boc Lond', for Buckland. Crossing suggests that the title 'Nun's Cross' derives either from the Celtic word '*nans*', meaning 'valley', or from some later corruption of an old name. In the seventeenth century the cross was known as Nannecross.

There is a flatness to the landscape here. Broad tracks meet at the nearby Nun's Cross Farm, itself a replacement of an earlier thatched building. The Abbot's Way comes in from the south here, and merges with the Cross Road, as well as sending a branch through Princetown to Tavistock. Our way leads west into more interesting ground where a hollow in the moor shelters the ruins of a building and its attendant beech and hawthorn trees. Beyond here, the Devonport Leat, on its wandering traverse of the moor, emerges from a dark tunnel. This remarkable waterway was constructed in the 1790s to carry water to Devonport at Plymouth. It survives today, and still makes its quietly flowing way across, and under, the moor. The leat is followed downstream past a rather grand cross, a modern memorial that has little apparent connection to the suggested monastic route, but contributes pleasantly to the continuity of the crosses.

The landscape ahead is more complex and broken than that of the long lazy swell of the moorland behind us. The granite has intruded more freely here, and has formed shapely hills with knuckly tors and frost-splintered screes. Due west is the rocky fist of Leather Tor above Burrator Reservoir. Beyond is the bulkier summit of Sharpitor, overlooking the green swathe of conifers that fills the valley of the River Meavy. South-west is Sheeps Tor, with its small curtain wall of crags, and, in the foreground, the broad summit of Combshead Tor rounds off the picture. Our route crosses the Devonport Leat by a clapper bridge, drops into the steep-sided Newleycombe Bottom through a chaos of old tin workings, and then climbs steeply to a handsome cross that was restored by William Crossing.

A broad track is soon joined, and a quarter of a mile/half a kilometre ahead, yet another cross is seen on the slope of the hill. This is Crazy Well, or Clazeywell Cross, nicely restored on a new shaft. Just west of the cross is the gloomy Crazy Well Pool, a deep quarry pit that is now flooded. To the south-west the more substantial Burrator Reservoir gleams in the light. In the shallow valleys that lead down to the reservoir are the chequered patterns of ancient fields. This was farmed country for generations, but when Burrator was built at the end of the nineteenth century, the people were evacuated and the farms abandoned in order to protect water sources from possible pollution. The human landscape was submerged in its turn.

The original line taken by the Cross Road is not certain from here, but the present track through the woods leads down to the handsome Leather Tor Bridge, and continues to a surfaced road beside the hammer-headed cross at Cross Gate. From here, narrow roads lead west out of the high moor to cross the Yelverton to

Princetown road at the battered little cross of Dousland, half hidden by the roadside, and bearing the undignified marks of its former use as a gate post.

Ahead lies Walkhampton Church with its saracen pinnacles and its background of tall cypresses and pines. The way to the church leads up a dark holloway. There is a cross stump by the church house, another monastic waymark. Beyond here the route leads down another holloway, arched over with trees and thorns and known as Jimmie Pickles's Lane. Fields and roads have fragmented the countryside ahead, and the true line of the Cross Road is again lost. But roads and tracks lead from the lovely Huckworthy bridge past the one-armed Huckworthy Cross to reach the great green expanse of Whitchurch Down.

At the apex of the down stands Pixie's Cross within its island of gorse bushes. Whitchurch Down was once common land but is now an uncommon golf course. The line of the Cross Road ran across the down to a final cross at the roadside. But there is no defined right of way now, and the road is best followed from Pixie's Cross on down to Tavistock. Here the handsome Church of St Eustachius gives a flavour of the magnificent abbey that once graced the town, and was the arrival and departure point for the travellers of the Cross Road.

The handsome Leather Tor Bridge above Burrator Reservoir.

THE CROSS ROAD
Information

Distance 21 miles/33.6 kms

Maps OS Outdoor Leisure 28 (Dartmoor)

Nature of Walk An intriguing walk across some of South Dartmoor's loveliest countryside. Most of the route is across open moorland where paths are not always well defined, and where the going can be very wet underfoot. Navigation skills may be required in misty weather. Experienced walkers should be able to complete the route in a day. Clothing and equipment should be for hill conditions. *The weather can be wet and windy at any time and may be severe outside the summer season.*

Accommodation At Buckfastleigh, Holne, Princetown and Tavistock.

Transport Seasonal rail links to Buckfastleigh from Totnes mainline station. Bus connections to Buckfast and Tavistock from main centres.

Further Information Dartmoor National Park Information Centre, Bovey Tracey, tel. (0626) 832093.

The directions are especially detailed for the moorland section of the walk where paths are not continuous.

Start Buckfast Abbey

1 From the door of the abbey church, walk past the two stone crosses in the central flowerbed, and go through the old stone archway beyond. Follow the lane round left, and keep ahead at a junction. Go right at Fritz's Green junction, then left, signposted to Scorriton and Holne. At next junction go first right, signposted to Scorriton and Holne, and continue past Stumpy Oak and Hawson Cross. Just past the cross, at a junction, keep straight ahead. Keep right at the bottom of the hill, then, where the road bends right at OS 707687, bear off left up a steep track. Turn right at a road and keep ahead at a T-junction. *Holne village is to the right.* At next junction keep ahead, pass a quarry on the left, and a short distance ahead, at OS 697700, bear off left along a rough track onto the moor. (4 miles/6.4 kms)

2 After about ½ mile/0.8 kms, at a slab bridge over a narrow leat, bear off the track and follow the leat north-west along a narrow path through scrubby ground. *The route is not well defined here.* Continue alongside the leat, then just before a cluster of thorn trees bear up left. Keep ahead to reach the perimeter fence of Venford Reservoir. Turn right for a few yards, then go left over a stile in the fence. Turn left on a good track alongside the reservoir. At the head of the reservoir, cross a footbridge, then go left off the perimeter path to reach a stile in a fence beside a notice board. *The next section is overgrown with tall ferns in summer.* Beyond the stile, go right for a few yards, then bear up diagonally left to follow a path past a solitary thorn tree. Continue alongside a line of thorn trees on a reave. Pass a small clapper bridge on the right, and continue to clearer ground. Keep ahead alongside a low reave to reach the distinctive Horn's Cross at OS 669711. (1¾ miles/2.8 kms)

3 Continue west and descend to the O Brook. Follow a path upstream to cross the stream just before a restored wheelpit at some old mine workings. Follow a holloway uphill to a junction with a stony track. Turn right for a short distance until abreast of a cross on the right. Go left off the track and follow a faint path through the heather to reach Skir Ford Cross at OS 655714. From the cross, bear sharp left along a very faint path. After about 20 yards/18 metres, join a better path and follow it to the right to reach Skir Ford at OS 650714. Across the stream keep ahead up a stony track that becomes a good path. Where the path branches, go down right to cross a stream at some very wet ground. Continue along Skir Gut with a steep bank on the left. Just past a pile of stones follow a path up right to pass a pointed stone. Continue to reach Ter Hill Cross at OS 642707. (2¼ miles/3.6 kms)

4 Keep ahead past a second cross. *This cross*

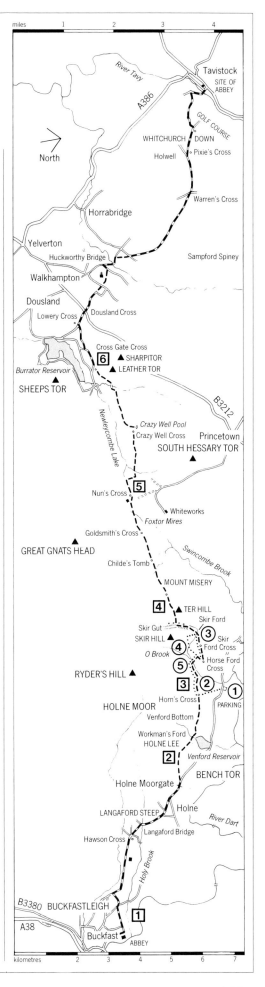

was due to be replaced in 1994 after restoration.
Continue for about 600 yards/540 metres,
then keep right at a Y-junction to reach a
cross beyond a gap in a wall. Keep ahead and
downhill, equidistant between the enclosure
walls. Cross a stream amidst very broken
ground to reach Childe's Tomb. Keep ahead
for about ½ mile/0.8 kms across open ground,
with the newtake wall up to your left (south).
Reach Goldsmith's Cross at OS 616703. Bear
up left to the newtake wall. Follow it west and
cross over at the next convenient step-stile.
Turn right along the wall, and where it bends
right, go up to the bank of the Devonport
Leat. Turn left, then cross the leat at a clapper
bridge and keep ahead to reach Nun's Cross.
(2½ miles/4 kms)

5 Go west from Nun's Cross, and pass
through a dip by a ruined house to where the
Devonport Leat emerges from a tunnel.
Follow the leat past a memorial cross, then, at
a clapper bridge, cross it. Go down into a dip,
and continue uphill to pass a cross at OS
592703. Join a good track and follow it west.
*Crazy Well Cross can be reached by keeping ahead
off the track at OS 586704. Keep ahead from the
cross to reach Crazy Well Pool, then go due south
from the pool to regain the main track.* Follow the
track, and at OS 569699, go right to cross
Leather Tor bridge. Continue along the main
track to join a surfaced road by Cross Gate
Cross at OS 563695. (3¼ miles/5.2 kms)

6 Continue to Lowery Cross. Turn right, and
at the B3212, cross over *with care*, and go down
a lane. At a right-hand bend, go left and follow
a holloway up to Walkhampton Church. Keep
ahead past the church, and go down a
gravelled drive. Cross a stile and keep ahead
down a field, and then down a lane, to a road.
Turn left, then right, cross Huckworthy
bridge, and a short distance up a steep hill,
go right along a rough track. Continue to
Huckworthy Cross at OS 530711. Keep ahead
along a lane to reach Warren's Cross at OS
514734. Keep ahead, and at a road junction by
Pixie's Cross, at the edge of a golf course, bear
right. Continue along the road, and just past

another cross, turn sharp left, then sharp right. Go downhill to a T-junction, turn right, then left over the River Tavy into Tavistock. (7¼ miles/11.6 kms)

CIRCULAR WALK 4 miles/6.4 kms

This airy walk takes in some of the stone crosses of the Cross Road and passes old tin mines and workings on the moor. Good navigational skills may be required in misty conditions. Allow about two hours.

Start Car park at Combestone Tor OS 670719

1 Cross the road from the car park. Bear left towards two thorn trees, then follow a green track uphill to Horn's Cross.

2 Follow directions as for (3) on main walk to reach Skir Ford at OS 650714.

Nun's Cross. 'There is a flatness to the landscape here.'

3 Cross the ford and, after a few yards, turn off left and follow a path through scrubby ground to reach the mouth of a deep ravine. *This is the old Hensroost tin mine working.* Keep ahead across the mouth of the ravine, and follow a wider track downhill to a clapper bridge over the O Brook. *The mine workings and spoil heaps on the right are those of the Hexworthy Mine that was worked from the late nineteenth century into the early years of the twentieth century.*

4 Follow the track across the bridge and reach ruined buildings. *These were the mine captain's (manager's) house, the mine office, and the barracks for mine workers.* Just beyond the ruin, go left down a track and reach a restored wheelpit. *The massive wheel that once stood here was worked by water power and operated machine stamps that crushed the ore.*

5 Cross the O Brook just below the wheelpit, and follow a path downstream to an open area. Cross some leats and retrace the route back to Horn's Cross and back to the car park.

THE SAINTS' WAY
Cornwall

Padstow to Fowey 28½ miles/45.6 kms

'. . . we need not doubt
the historicity of these
missionaries who lived
and worked in
Cornwall, or passed
through on their way
from Wales or Ireland
to Brittany, in that
time of wandering . . .'

A.L. Rowse, *Tudor Cornwall*,
1941

The Saints' Way follows the suggested line of an ancient 'isthmus' route that spanned the waist of Cornwall between Padstow and Fowey. Cornwall is famous for its spectacular coastline, but this walk goes against the grain of the county, and leads from coast to coast through delightful countryside.

Cornwall's dwindling peninsula strikes west to Land's End, hard-faced against the ocean, and buttressed by great cliffs and bare-knuckled promontories. Early seafarers were reluctant to make passage round Land's End, which had a fearsome reputation as 'Belerion', the 'Seat of Storms'. It was safer to combine sea and land travel by using 'isthmus roads' along which pack animals could transport goods from a vessel off-loaded on one coast, to a second vessel on the opposite coast. The Greeks had used such roads across the Isthmus of Corinth in the Peloponnese; travellers between Ireland, Wales and Brittany found it convenient to land on one or other Cornish coast and cross the peninsula to the other side.

It is not clear how these Cornish routes evolved, but the part played by tin seems to be the key. The earliest voyagers from Europe landed on the south coast of England and dispersed throughout the countryside as settlers rather than traders. But during the Late Bronze Age, 1500 to 500 BC, a regular traffic in tin developed out of Cornwall, and the county soon became a major source of the metal. The sea route from the Mediterranean through the Straits of Gibraltar was often obstructed, as a result of regional disputes and the vagaries of Atlantic weather, so Greek and Roman traders developed land routes through Southern Gaul to the Breton shore, and on across the sea to Britain's south coast.

The Cornish peninsula also attracted travellers and traders from Wales and Ireland, who used the transpeninsular routes, the southern sections of which were already the main conduits of tin export. There were river inlets on Cornwall's coasts that allowed ships to penetrate quite far inland. At Hayle on the north coast, in the far west of the county, 'good talle ships' once sailed two miles/over three kilometres upriver, and from there a cross-country route of only three miles/four kilometres led to St Michael's Mount on the south coast, one of the main exporting centres of tin to Europe. On the north coast, the great estuary at Padstow was used by shipping, although its dangerous shoals meant that early seafarers often preferred to land at Harlyn Bay, a short distance to the west.

Thirty miles/forty-eight kilometres away on the south coast lies the port of Fowey and the sheltered anchorage of St Austell Bay, from where France is only a short voyage away. It is likely that an isthmus route between Padstow and Fowey was used from very early times. Gold lunulae and other artefacts from Ireland and Wales have been found dispersed throughout mid Cornwall. The route declined in use during the Roman period, but the Dark Ages saw a fresh impetus as religious and cultural exchange between Ireland, Wales and Brittany was channelled across Cornwall. The agents of this exchange were the fifth- and sixth-century 'saints' who laid the foundations of the so-called 'Celtic' inheritance that distinguishes Cornwall to this day.

Saints were real people. It is their sanctity that is suspect. Often they were handed sainthood on a plate, and were blindly revered by later generations if not by their contemporaries, who knew them warts and all. Cornwall jostles with saints' names from end to end. One hundred and seventy-four of the county's two hundred or so parishes are dedicated to saints.

Saints gathered myths like moss. St Ives is named after St Ia, the daughter of an Irish chief. She is said to have crossed the Irish Sea floating on an oak leaf. St Piran bettered this marvellous absurdity by paddling across on a millstone; St Illick sailed on a harrow; St Petroc in a silver bowl. Scholars have justified these fantastic tales by suggesting that initial reports were mythologized and that Ia, for instance, arrived on a 'leaf-like' coracle.

Most saints, being sensible as well as saintly, arrived aboard sturdy boats. They brought with them a Christianity steeped in the rich traditions of native culture, and still hot with pagan elements. It was a liberal Christianity, less formal and political than that of Rome. The Cornwall of the Dark Ages was ripe for a resurgence of the old faith, and while Anglo-Saxon England soon embraced Pauline Christianity, the Irish, Welsh and Breton saints stitched Cornwall firmly into the Celtic fringe.

The great saint of South Cornwall was St Samson, patron of Dol-de-Bretagne in Brittany, from where his most important monastic work was carried out. A life of St Samson, the *Vita Samsonis*, was written during the early seventh century. It records that Samson was born in Wales and that he reached Cornwall via Ireland. He is said to have travelled, with a small 'chariot' and numerous retainers, across country to Golant on the River Fowey. Samson converted pagans, raised the dead, and slew a serpent as he went. This was standard fare for saints. More probably, Samson inspired Christian piety and enterprise as he passed by. He remained closely involved with life in Cornwall for many years.

Petroc of Padstow was another of Cornwall's great saints. He is said to have arrived during the early years of the fifth century at Trebetherick on the east shore of Padstow Bay. Petroc founded a monastery at Lanwethinoc, as Padstow was then known. He travelled throughout mid Cornwall and Europe and had great influence in the Padstow area. Numerous other 'saints' and their associates moved into and through Cornwall during the fifth and sixth centuries, and it is likely that their activities encouraged others to use the seaways and the land route between Padstow and Fowey.

The Saints' Way of today is an imaginative reconstruction of that notional route. The concept was inspired by two residents of Luxulyan, a small village lying six miles/nine and a half kilometres north-west of Fowey. In 1984, the pair uncovered a section of abandoned pathway close to the village; they found magnificent granite stiles and a cobbled causeway beneath brambles and tangled grass. Imaginations were fired by the discovery, and by speculation that the path might be part of the ancient route followed by Cornish saints and others. A project to establish a walking route known as 'Forth an Syns', the 'Saints' Way', was started by the Co-operative Retail Services Community Programme, and hard work and dedication saw the official opening of the route in 1986. It begins, ideally, from Padstow's Church of St Petroc.

Padstow, on the River Camel, is tied irrevocably to the sea by its sandy estuary. The entire coast in this part of North Cornwall is besieged by wind-blown sand, and in places the landscape has been overwhelmed by it. On the eastern side of the estuary is Daymer Bay, where the dunes are almost two hundred feet/sixty metres high. Padstow's ties are of death also. It is a town that has seen more sea-going tragedy than most. Where the sand lies in broad-backed ridges across the mouth of the estuary, it causes the sea to overwhelm. This is the notorious Doom Bar, which shifts but never eases. At its worst, in a brutal chaos of strong winds and hard tide, the sea is a maelstrom here. Doom Bar has wrecked countless ships and has taken a bitter toll of Padstow's fishermen and seafarers since Petroc's day. Yet the town remains spirited, not least in its life-affirming May Day ceremony of the 'Obby Oss', a colourful and boisterous festival with its roots in fertility rites and its mood one of great good humour.

The Church of St Petroc is a fitting place to start a walk that for a time escapes from the sea. The church is impressively dark amidst its setting of tall trees within the sheltering crook of the hillside; it seems land-locked but is a seagoing church all the same. The original monastery of St Petroc stood on this sheltered site, but was not safe from seaborne attack. In AD 981, the Danes, in their storming progress round Britain's coast, razed the church and monastery to the ground, and left only shattered fragments of Celtic stonework. A Saxon church was built on the Padstow site in the early twelfth century, but it decayed, and the present building was founded during the fifteenth century in typical castle-keep Norman style.

The first stretch of the Saints' Way leads by a narrow walkway from the handsome lychgate of St Petroc's, and then across the upper town by road to Dennis Cove. From here it climbs a grassy path over Dennis Hill, passes the Victoria Jubilee memorial, and then strikes south along the wooded banks of Little Petherick Creek. At the mouth of the creek are the banked walls of Sea Mills lagoon, a seventeenth-century millpond created within the muddy gut of the creek. Here water was impounded at high tide, then released through sluices to power the wheel of a gristmill.

At low tide the River Camel is ripe with mud. Above Padstow, the honey-coloured sand of the estuary shades into the greyness of tidal lees, still heavy with salt but enriched with organisms, a feeding ground for numerous birds, and supportive of salt-resistant plants. The shoreline is dense with trees, and there is a lushness here that contrasts strikingly with the barrenness of the great sand dunes and the raw sea that lie such a short distance to the north.

The path winds high and low towards Little Petherick. It crosses wooden footbridges at the creeks of Trerethern and Credis, where banks of sea purslane are exposed at low water, their silvery leaves and greenish-yellow flowers entangled with the shells of dead crabs, lank seaweed, and the detritus of the tideline. High above the main creek the way runs through the coppiced beeches and sycamores of St Mary's Wood, then drops steeply to the head of the creek and to a junction with the busy main road at Little Petherick.

Modern traffic has robbed Little Petherick of its peace but not of its style. This is Betjeman country; the poet is buried not far away at the sand-blown church of St Enodoc above Daymer Bay. Little Petherick has Betjemanesque style. The village hall stands beside the busy road where the Saints' Way emerges. It is a surprisingly serene little corner where cream teas are occasionally served by genteel parishioners, and where crumpled linen jackets and straw hats inspire homely couplets wreathed in blue exhaust fumes.

The Church of St Petroc Minor at Little Petherick is a delight. It was founded as the cell of Petroc at Nansfounteyn, the 'fountain in the valley'. Genteel eccentricity seems to have been the prevailing text for local churchmen. St Petroc is said to have spent damp hours reciting the psalms while sitting up to his neck in the muddy waters of Little Petherick Creek. How he dealt with the vagaries of tide is not recorded. The church's nineteenth-century incumbents were no less eccentric. One vicar, George William Manning, slept in a coffin made from ship's timbers.

From Little Petherick the Saints' Way plunges cross-country

Opposite: The Saints' Way passes through the flower-filled woods of mid-Cornwall.

through the parish of St Issey, another of those saints' names that may record a genuine Dark Age presence or a patron later adopted by the parish. The Way crosses small meadows and follows lanes that are sunk between high hedges. To the west are the remains of an Iron Age settlement, suggesting that the ground here was trodden long before the saintly imprint. Beyond the spider's web of lane junctions at Trenance, the Saints' Way merges with a farm track, then leads across fields and along lanes to cross the A39 at West Park Farm. Ahead lies St Breock Downs, where tumuli punctuate a descending ridge to the west and where the stark turbines of a recently installed wind farm now dominate the highest ground, their wind vanes flailing hypnotically through the air.

From West Park, the Saints' Way rises through featureless fields to the roof of Cornwall. The view back to the north is of a shining sea. It is a strangely linear view. The coast is clean-cut against the skyline, and is seen for great distances to north and south; the sky fills with long ribbons of cloud, and, at dusk, sunsets of heart-stopping beauty flood the western horizon with torrents of colour. As with so many places on the edge of great oceans, Cornwall overpowers with its light and the vastness of its skies.

Such spaciousness is seen in the view to the south and west of St Breock Downs. The land slopes widely towards St Columb and towards the famous spoil heap 'alps' of the china clay country above St Austell Bay. Much of this high ground has been broken in for farming, but on the surviving moorland to the west of Pawton-springs, the rough pelt of the moorland survives, dimpled with ruined tumuli and hauntingly remote.

Modern wind farms apart, this is still an ancient landscape beneath its matrix of fields and lanes. By the roadside leading from Pawtonsprings stands the *Men Gurta*, the 'stone of waiting', a traditional meeting place of those associated with St Petroc. The stone lies now within a flat and uninspiring countryside, out of which the Saints' Way leads us south across the dark and muddy Ruthven River, and on to the church town of Withiel.

Cornwall's peninsular nature has encouraged ribbon development at its most soulless, and the country's remarkable coastline has drawn most of the glory. Yet, buried within the heartland through which the Saints' Way passes, are quiet villages and hamlets of enduring loveliness. Withiel is one such place. Its Church of St Clement is a handsome building with a distinctive tower, and its houses are nicely spaced in a typical medieval form, unstructured and natural.

One is reluctant to leave such places. But the Saint's Way draws us on across the green countryside by quiet lanes and past a fine Cornish cross that marks a road that was old in medieval times, when it was the main route between St Columb and the old county town of Bodmin. Beyond is Lanivet, a village pinned down at the heart of Cornwall by the main road into Bodmin. But the village is delightfully peaceful to either side of the streaming traffic.

Lanivet marks the midpoint of the Saint's Way. From here our route leads up the steepening incline of Rectory Road, then dips and twists under the busy A30 through an echoing tunnel, and on past Reperry Cross. From the high ground above St Ingunger, Bodmin town is clearly seen. To the east is the magnificent Lanhydrock house, in the care of the National Trust. Ahead lies Helman Tor, a natural magnificence of granite bosses and boulders couched in heather and gorse and deep grass, and overlooking the wetland nature reserve of Breney Common.

From the road turning that leads to Helman Tor, the eastern leg of the Saints' Way leads at first along twisting lanes. But it soon follows pathways from Tredinnick Farm into the green leafy valley of Luxulyan. Beneath this green skin is bare-boned granite. Huge rounded boulders litter the ground and swell up from the grass of surrounding fields like silver-grey whalebacks. To the south-east of Luxulyan village is the reputed 'Largest Block in Europe', an individual monolith of granite fifty feet/fifteen metres long, with a girth of seventy-five feet/twenty-two and a half metres and a weight of 1,700 tons/1,727 tonnes. To the east of the path is the huge Luxulyan Quarry, hidden behind trees and intervening ground.

It was here that the discovery of massive stiles and a cobbled footway inspired the idea for the Saints' Way. Even though the stiles and cobbling are typical of quarrying country, and are probably of a much later date than that of the Dark Age saints, the association of the footpath with an ancient track has borne fine fruit in the form of a 'Saints' Way' walk.

At Luxulyan, the Church of SS Ciricius and Julitta reflects the granite theme of the parish as much as the 'saintly' theme of our journey. The building is of handsome granite blocks and has an unbuttressed tower with a tall stair turret. The arcaded piers of the interior are of fine silvery granite, and the ceiling of the porch is stone-vaulted and has tracery panelling.

From Luxulyan, the Saints' Way continues south through the peaceful countryside of Trevanney and Prideaux, before plunging suddenly into a tangle of road and rail at the busy village of St Blazey. From here there is an escape into peaceful countryside on the approach to Tywardreath, the 'house on the strand' of Daphne du Maurier's novel of the same name. This is du Maurier country, as atmospheric inland as it is along the glorious coast round Fowey. Tywardreath is reached across a dark causeway flanked by tangled

undergrowth and gloomy marsh pools where yellow flag iris shine like tapers in spring.

Beyond Tywardreath, a switchback route takes us across a complex of field paths, busy roads and lanes towards the bulky promontory of The Gribbin. For many years Daphne du Maurier lived at the nearby Menabilly House, the inspiration for the beloved 'Manderley' of her novel *Rebecca*. The coast here is exquisite and varied in its beauty, from the green shoulder of Gribbin Head with its tall candy-striped navigational tower, to the loveliness of Polridmouth Cove, where a wild shoreline is matched by an ornamental landscape. Much of this coast is in the care of the National Trust.

The last stretch of the Saint's Way leads to the charmingly named Readymoney Cove down a very old holloway called Love Lane. This lane was used by farmers to collect goods from beached ships, and to collect seaweed and sand for use as fertilizers. The name of the cove should really commemorate a shipwreck of glinting doubloons, but instead, it translates prosaically from the Cornish word for 'stony ford'.

From the cove a short walk leads to Fowey, that 'fair and commodious haven', as described by the Elizabethan chronicler, Richard Carew. There is a commodious seaway, certainly, but the handsome town rather steals the waterfront with its interlocked buildings. Fowey has a proud sea-going history, and has that particular loveliness that comes from the sea's intrusion on lush countryside. The Church of St Finbar is the symbolic end of the Saints' Way. Finbar was an Irish saint who made a pilgrimage to Rome, and it is tempting to imagine him travelling by Cornwall's isthmus road, as did Samson and the many other saints – and sinners – in whose footsteps the modern Saints' Way has led us.

The Saints' Way
Information

Distance Via Luxulyan 28½ miles/45.6 kms;
Via Lanlivery 29 miles/46.6 kms

Maps OS Landranger 200 (Newquay, Bodmin
& surrounding area)

Nature of Walk The Saints' Way passes
through the heart of Cornwall along paths,
green lanes and country roads. The route is
best walked in two days. It is easily followed
and is waymarked with a Celtic cross motif.
Sections of the route may be quite muddy
during wet weather. Clothing and equipment
should be for country walking.

Accommodation At Padstow and Fowey.
Bed and breakfast available at several places
along the Way, and in nearby villages. Camp
sites at Padstow and near Fowey; youth hostel
near Golant (Fowey).

Transport Bus to Padstow and Fowey from
main centres; rail and bus connections from
main centres to Bodmin. No regular bus
services along the inland lanes. Bodmin is near
the midpoint of the walk at Lanivet; there are
bus connections between the two.

The quiet green shade of Padstow churchyard.

Further Information Tourist Information
Centre, Padstow, tel. (0841) 533449; Cornwall
Tourist Board, Truro, tel. (0872) 74057.

Start Padstow Church OS 915754

1 Leave the churchyard by the lych gate and
follow a surfaced walkway round to the left to
reach a busy junction. Go straight across, and
continue down Dennis Road and Dennis
Lane, then turn up left just past a boating lake.
Bear up right, through a farm and caravan
complex, then follow a field edge until abreast
of the Victoria Jubilee monument. (1 mile/
1.6 kms)

2 Go right and over a stile, then left down a
field edge and over another stile. Bear down
right to join a path that leads to a footbridge
over Trerethern Creek. Follow a good path
along Little Petherick Creek to Little
Petherick. (1½ miles/2.4 kms)

3 Walk left up the busy A389 for about 200
yards/180 metres, then go over a stile on the
right. Go down towards a stream, then uphill
across two fields to join a lane. Turn right
through Mellingey hamlet. Continue to
Trenance and follow a track and field path to

Blable Farm. Turn left, then right, along lanes to the A39. (2¾ miles/4.4 kms)

4 Cross the A39 *with care*, go left for 50 yards/ 45 metres, then turn off right at West Park Farm. Follow broad tracks across St Breock Downs to Pawtonsprings at OS 960686, then on down the lane past St Breock Longstone to a T-junction. (2½ miles/4 kms)

5 Turn left at the T-junction, continue to the second turning on the right, and go down the road, bearing right at a house. Where the road swings left at OS 988673, keep ahead down a green lane to reach Tregustick. Turn right along the road, and about 100 yards/90 metres after the road bends to the right, go left down a lane, cross two footbridges, and pass Blackhay Farm to reach Withiel village. (2¾ miles/4.4 kms)

6 Go right past Withiel Church, then after 70 yards/63 metres, go left through fields and downhill to a stile and footbridge. Continue diagonally right and uphill to go through a gate. Bear diagonally left to reach a lane. Turn right, and go left at a junction, keeping left at the next junction. Continue to the Celtic cross at Tremore crossroads at OS 020650. (2½ miles/4 kms)

7 Turn right to Higher Woodley. Follow the road left, then at a right-hand bend keep ahead off the road and cross three fields. Go down a short section of lane, then turn right down a road, go over a crossroads, and continue down Clann Lane and into Lanivet. (1¼ miles/2 kms)

8 Cross the busy A391, *with care*, go up Rectory Road and continue to an underpass beneath the A30. At Reperry Cross, turn left for 1 mile/1.6 kms to St Ingunger Cross. Turn right through Fenton Pits and Trebell Green to reach a junction at OS 057619 below Helman Tor. (2¾ miles/4.4 kms)

There are alternative routes from this point. The western route via Luxulyan is described here. The eastern route goes past Helman Tor to Lanlivery, then on by paths and lanes to Golant and Fowey. It is generally well signposted and waymarked.

9 For Luxulyan, keep ahead and follow lanes to Tredinnick at OS 048597, where the Way turns left down a track. After 200 yards/ 180 metres, cross a stile on the right and descend to the valley to follow a stream. Cross fine granite stiles, then go up a field to a road. Cross a triangle of grass and go down right to Luxulyan village. (3 miles/4.8 kms)

10 Cross the road by the church at Luxulyan, and continue past the post office to cross a stile and then a railway bridge. Go downhill across three fields, and continue to Trevanney Farm at OS 055566. Go right from the farmyard down a lane, bear slightly right through woods, then go up a field to cross a road. Go down the drive to Prideaux Farm, turning up right through the farmyard. About 50 yards/ 45 metres beyond the last building, go left over a stile and on alongside the left-hand hedge to a stile leading left. *The next section of path is rather confined here and may be overgrown.* Go along the top edge of steep fields, then follow the woodland path steeply downhill to a road. Turn right to a T-junction, then go left to reach the A390. (2½ miles/4 kms)

11 Turn left, and about 150 yards/135 metres beyond a filling station, at OS 074553, go right along a path and then along a stony track to reach a road. Turn left, then after ½ mile/ 0.8 kms, go right on a downhill path and through a marshy wood across a causeway. Go under a railway and along a holloway to follow Marsh Lane into Tywardreath. Go over the crossroads and follow Church Street, bearing left past the church. Turn right down Well Lane to reach a junction with the A3082. Cross this busy road *with care*, and go beneath an underpass. Follow a path that starts between the Ship Inn and the old Almshouses. After 200 yards/180 metres keep left at a branch and go diagonally left and uphill through two fields to reach the A3082. (3 miles/4.8 kms)

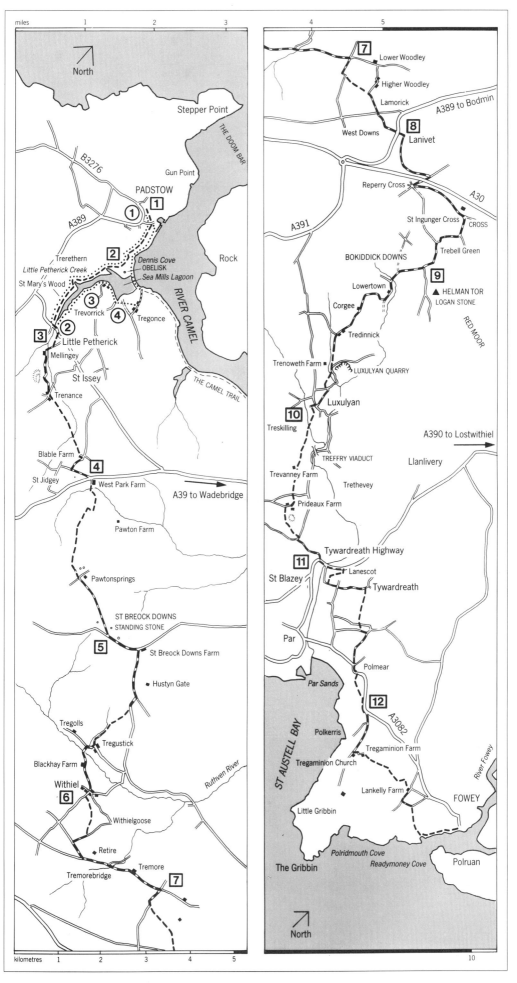

miles

North

Stepper Point

THE DOOM BAR

B3276

Gun Point

PADSTOW 1

1

A389

Trerethern

Little Petherick Creek

St Mary's Wood

2

Dennis Cove
OBELISK
Sea Mills Lagoon

Rock

RIVER CAMEL

3

Trevorrick

4

Tregonce

3

Little Petherick

Mellingey

THE CAMEL TRAIL

St Issey

2

Trenance

Blable Farm

4

St Jidgey

West Park Farm

A39 to Wadebridge

Pawton Farm

Pawtonsprings

ST BREOCK DOWNS
STANDING STONE

5

St Breock Downs Farm

Hustyn Gate

Tregolls

Tregustick

Ruthven River

Blackhay Farm

Withiel

6

Withielgoose

Retire

Tremore

Tremorebridge

7

kilometres   1   2   3   4   5

Lower Woodley

7

Higher Woodley

Lamorick

A389 to Bodmin

West Downs

8

Lanivet

A391

Reperry Cross

A30

St Ingunger Cross

CROSS

BOKIDDICK DOWNS

Trebell Green

Lowertown

9

HELMAN TOR
LOGAN STONE

Corgee

RED MOOR

Tredinnick

Trenoweth Farm

LUXULYAN QUARRY

Luxulyan

10

A390 to Lostwithiel

Treskilling

TREFFRY VIADUCT

Llanlivery

Trevanney Farm

Trethevey

Prideaux Farm

Tywardreath Highway

11

Lanescot

St Blazey

Tywardreath

Par

Polmear

Par Sands

12

A3082

Polkerris

ST AUSTELL BAY

Tregaminion Farm

Tregaminion Church

River Fowey

Lankelly Farm

FOWEY

Little Gribbin

The Gribbin

Polridmouth Cove
Readymoney Cove

Polruan

North

10

12 Go right along the road for 200 yards/ 180 metres, then go right down a road signposted Polkerris. At Tregaminion Church at OS 096519 go left to Tregaminion Farm, then follow signs through fields to Lankelly Woods at OS 106518. Follow the path down through the woods and up to Lankelly Farm. Turn right down the road for 400 yards/ 360 metres, then turn left for 250 yards/ 195 metres. Turn right down a shaded holloway to reach Readymoney Cove, from where a road leads left to the heart of Fowey. (3 miles/4.8 kms)

CIRCULAR WALK 5 miles/8 kms

A lovely walk along the start of the Saints' Way from Padstow to Little Petherick, then by the northern side of Little Petherick Creek and so back to Padstow. Allow two hours. *The section alongside Sea Mills is impassable at high tide during spring tides, when the walk should be attempted only during the period from three hours before low water to three hours after low water. Current tide tables should be checked for details. The creekside section to Sea Mills can be wet underfoot. Waterproof footwear is advised.*

Start Padstow Church OS 915754

1 Follow directions (1) and (2) on the main walk to reach Little Petherick.

2 Go left along the A389, cross the bridge, then turn left up a surfaced drive. Go over a stile and follow a path across a muddy creek. Continue along field edges and over stiles. After two stiles in quick succession, go through a metal gate (signposted to Sea Mills). Continue along the creekside and past slaty banks. *Many wading birds feed on the mud banks of the creek. During spring and autumn, rare birds of passage, such as little egrets, can sometimes be seen here.*

3 Just past the Sea Mills lagoon, follow a track to a narrow lane by some houses. Continue along the lane and go sharp right at a footpath sign and down a narrow path. Go over a stile and keep left past uprooted trees. Continue over stiles. After a slate stile with a metal top, continue round the field edge, then go over a stile onto the driveway of a house. Go right to reach a lane, and turn left to reach the creek shore. Turn right over a muddy area, then climb two steps and cross a footbridge. *If the tide has covered this last section, a right of way leads over a slate stile a short distance back up the road, then over a grassy area in front of a house to reach the footbridge as above.*

4 From the footbridge continue straight up a field to cross a lane, then continue over the brow of another field. Go over a stile and cross a field, keeping right, to a stile into a lane opposite Tregonce Farmhouse. Turn left and join a path open to the public. Pass a duck pond and keep to the track, passing to the left of some buildings. Continue on, to join the Camel Trail. Turn left, cross the bridge over the mouth of the creek, and continue to Padstow.

Left: Luxulyan Church. 'The arcade piers of the interior are of fine silvery granite . . .'
Right: The Saints' Way at the green heart of Cornwall.

BIBLIOGRAPHY

Allan, R. and Candlish, I. (joint editors), *The Scottish Borderland – The Place and the People*, Border Country Life Association, 1988.

Anderson, J. R. L. and Godwin, Fay, *The Oldest Road, an Exploration of The Ridgeway*, Wildwood House, London, 1975.

Barber, Chris and Godfrey Williams, John, *The Ancient Stones of Wales*, Blorenge Books, Abergavenny, 1989.

Bowen, E. G., *Saints, Seaways and Settlements*, University of Wales Press, 1969.

Breakell, Bill, *Tracks*, North York Moors National Park Department (first published as *Stone Causeways of the North York Moors*, Footsteps Books, Hebden Bridge, 1982).

Bryant, Arthur, *The Medieval Foundation*, Collins, London, 1966.

Burton, S. H., *Exmoor*, Robert Hale, London, 1969.

Chapman, Malcolm, *The Celts. The Construction of a Myth*, Macmillan, London, 1992.

Charlton, John, *Brougham Castle*, English Heritage, 1985.

Coad, J. G., *Castle Acre Castle*, English Heritage, 1984.

Colyer, Richard, *Roads and Trackways of Wales*, Moorland Publishing, 1984.

Condry, William, *Snowdonia*, David & Charles, Newton Abbot, 1987.

Coppack, Glyn, *Gisborough Priory*, English Heritage, 1993.

Court, Glyn, *Exmoor National Park*, Webb & Bower, Exeter, 1987.

Crossing, William, *The Ancient Stone Crosses of Dartmoor and Its Borderland*, J. G. Commin, Exeter (first published 1902).

Crossing, William, *Crossing's Guide to Dartmoor*, Peninsula Press, Newton Abbot, 1990 (first published 1912).

Cunliffe, Barry, *Iron Age Communities in Britain*, Routledge & Kegan Paul, London, 1974.

Dillon, Myles and Chadwick, Nora, *The Celtic Realms*, Weidenfeld & Nicolson, London, 1967.

Dixon, J. H., *Gairloch, and Guide to Loch Maree*, Truexpress, Oxford, 1975 (first published Edinburgh Co-operative Printing Company Limited, 1886).

Dodd, A. E. and Dodd, E. M., *Packhorse Ways in Derbyshire*, Moorland Publishing, 1974.

Dyer, James, *Ancient Britain*, Batsford, London, 1990.

Fox, Sir Cyril, *Offa's Dyke*, Oxford University Press, 1955.

Fraser, D., *Glen of the Rowan Trees*, Standard Press, Montrose, 1973.

Garlick, Tom, *The Romans in the Lake District*, Dalesman Books, 1982.

Gill, Michael and Colwill, Stephen, *The Saints' Way*, Quintrell & Company Ltd, Crown Copyright, 1986.

Haldane, A. R. B., *Drove Roads of Scotland*, Thomas Nelson & Sons, 1952.

Haldane, A. R. B., *New Ways through the Glens*, Thomas Nelson & Sons, 1962.

Hall, D. J., *English Mediaeval Pilgrimage*, Routledge & Kegan Paul, London, 1966.

Hayes, Raymond H., *Old Roads & Pannierways in North-East Yorkshire*, North York Moors National Park, 1988.

Hindle, Brian Paul, *Know the Landscape. Roads, Tracks, and their Interpretation*, Batsford, London, 1993.

Hawkes, Jacquetta, *A Guide to the Prehistoric and Roman Monuments in England and Wales*, Chatto & Windus, London, 1951.

Hemery, Eric, *Walking Dartmoor's Ancient Tracks*, Robert Hale, London, 1986.

Hogg, James, *Highland Tours*, Byway Books, Hawick, new edition 1981.

Hoskins, W. G., *The Making of the English Landscape*, Hodder & Stoughton, 1955.

Jeffries, Richard, *Wild Life in a Southern County*, 1879.

Jennett, S., *The Pilgrim's Way from Winchester to Canterbury*, Cassell, London, 1971.

John, C. R., *The Saints of Cornwall*, Lodenek Press and Dyllansow Truran, Cornwall, 1981.

Jones, Jonah, *The Lakes of North Wales*, Wildwood House, London, 1983.

Jones, R. Merfyn, *The North Wales Quarrymen 1874-1922*, University of Wales Press, 1982.

Laing, L., *Celtic Britain*, Routledge & Kegan Paul, London, 1979.

Laing, L. and J., *The Origins of Britain*, Routledge & Kegan Paul, London, 1980.

Lewis, M. J. T. and Denton, J. H., *The Rhosydd Slate Quarry*, The Cottage Press, Shrewsbury, 1974.

Mackenzie, Osgood Hanbury, *A Hundred Years in the Highlands*, Edward Arnold, 1921.

Margary, I. D., *Roman Roads in Britain*, Vols I and II, Phoenix House, London, 1956.

Moir, D. G., *Scottish Hill Tracks. Old Highways & Drove Roads*, Vol. I, *Southern Scotland*, Vol. II, *Northern Scotland*, Bartholomew, Edinburgh, revised editions 1975 (first published 1947).

Murray, W. H., *Rob Roy MacGregor. His Life and Times*, Richard Drew, Glasgow, 1982.

Pearson, Michael Parker, *English Heritage Book of Bronze Age Britain*, Batsford, London, 1993.

Pochin Mould, D. D. C., *The Roads from the Isles. A Study of the North West Highland Tracks*, Oliver & Boyd, Edinburgh, 1950.

Purcell, William, *Pilgrims' England*, Longman, London, 1981.

Raby, F. J. E. and Bailie Reynolds, P. K., *Castle Acre Priory*, English Heritage, 1952.

Robertson, Rev. A. E., *Old Tracks, Cross Country Routes and Coffin Roads in the North West Highlands*, Darien Press, Edinburgh, 1941.

Rowse, A. L., *Tudor Cornwall*, Macmillan, London, 1969 (first published by Jonathan Cape, 1941).

Salway, Peter, *Roman Britain. The Oxford History of Britain*, Clarendon Press, Oxford, 1981.

Shortt, H. de S., *Old Sarum*, English Heritage, 1988 (first published 1965).

Simpson, W. Douglas, *The Highlands of Scotland*, Robert Hale, London, 1976.

Smith, Roland, *The Peak National Park*, Webb & Bower, Exeter, 1987.

Southworth, James, *Walking the Roman Roads of Cumbria*, Robert Hale, London, 1985.

Stanford, S. C., *The Archaeology of the Welsh Marches*, Collins, London, 1980.

Street, Pamela, *Illustrated Portrait of Wiltshire*, Robert Hale, London, 1971.

Taylor, Christopher, *Roads and Tracks of Britain*, Dent, London, 1979.

Vaughn Thomas, Wynford, *The New Shell Guide to South and Mid Wales*, Michael Joseph, London, 1987.

Ward, H. Snowden, *The Canterbury Pilgrimages*, Adam and Charles Black, 1904.

Watson, F., *The Braes of Balquhidder*, William Hodge, 1914.

Webster, Graham, *The Roman Conquest. Boudica of Britain*, Batsford, London, 1978.

Williams, M., *The Slate Industry*, Shire Publications, 1991.

Wood, Michael, *In Search of the Dark Ages*, BBC, London, 1981.

Documents and Records

Glen Doll Right of Way Case, Anton, Prof. A. E. (pamphlet), Scottish Rights of Way Society, n.d.

Court Records, Court of Session, Edinburgh, 1887.

Geographical Journal, Crawford, Dr O. G. S., 1912.

Lords' Journals, 1888.

Pitcairn's Criminal Trials, 1591.

Plan of Intended Road from Poolewe to Achnasheen, 1793.

Report of Rural Transport (Scotland), 1919.

Report on Roads in Derbyshire, John Farey, 1807.

Report to Commissioners for Highland Roads and Bridges, 1803.

Transactions of the Cumberland and Westmorland Antiquarian and Archeological Society, 1867, 1898, 1962, 1976, 1983, 1984.

INDEX

Page references in *italics* refer to illustrations.